SONET AND T1:

Architectures for Digital Transport Systems
Second Edition

ISBN 0-13-065416-7

Prentice Hall Series in
Advanced Communications Technologies

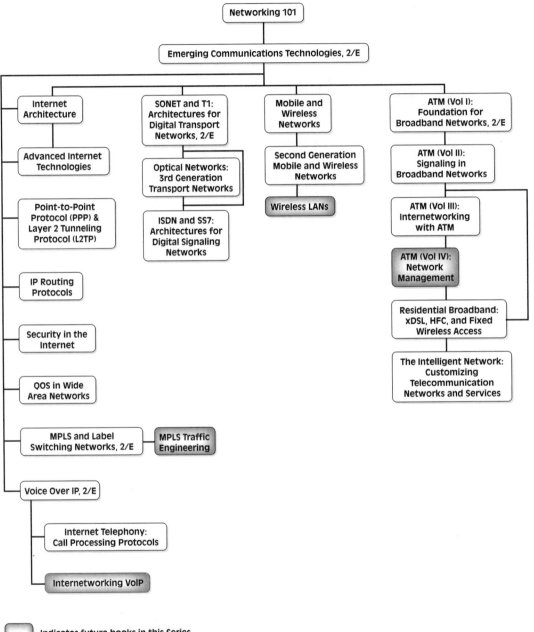

Networking 101

Emerging Communications Technologies, 2/E

Internet Architecture

Advanced Internet Technologies

Point-to-Point Protocol (PPP) & Layer 2 Tunneling Protocol (L2TP)

IP Routing Protocols

Security in the Internet

QOS in Wide Area Networks

MPLS and Label Switching Networks, 2/E — MPLS Traffic Engineering

Voice Over IP, 2/E

Internet Telephony: Call Processing Protocols

Internetworking VoIP

SONET and T1: Architectures for Digital Transport Networks, 2/E

Optical Networks: 3rd Generation Transport Networks

ISDN and SS7: Architectures for Digital Signaling Networks

Mobile and Wireless Networks

Second Generation Mobile and Wireless Networks

Wireless LANs

ATM (Vol I): Foundation for Broadband Networks, 2/E

ATM (Vol II): Signaling in Broadband Networks

ATM (Vol III): Internetworking with ATM

ATM (Vol IV): Network Management

Residential Broadband: xDSL, HFC, and Fixed Wireless Access

The Intelligent Network: Customizing Telecommunication Networks and Services

Indicates future books in this Series

SONET AND T1

ARCHITECTURES FOR DIGITAL TRANSPORT NETWORKS

SECOND EDITION

UYLESS BLACK AND SHARLEEN WATERS

PRENTICE HALL SERIES IN ADVANCED
COMMUNICATIONS TECHNOLOGIES

To join a Prentice Hall PTR internet mailing list, point to:
www.prenhall.com/register

Prentice Hall PTR
Upper Saddle River, New Jersey 07458
www.phptr.com

Library of Congress Cataloging-in-Publication Data

Black, Uyless D.
    SONET & T1 : architectures for digital transport networks / Uyless Black and Sharleen Waters.
      p. cm. -- (Prentice Hall series in advanced communications technologies)
    Rev. ed. of: SONET and T1. c1997.
    Includes bibliographical references and index.
    ISBN 0-13-065416-7
      1. SONET (Data transmission) 2. T1 (Telecommunication line) 3. Digital
communications--Standards. 4. Computer network architectures. I. Waters, Sharleen. II.
Black, Uyless D. SONET and T1. III. Title. IV. Series.

TK5105.415.B58 2001
621.382'75--dc21

2001052366

Editorial/Production supervision: Laura Burgess
Acquisitions editor: Mary Franz
Cover designer: Anthony Gemmellaro
Cover design director: Jerry Votta
Manufacturing manager: Maura Zaldivar
Marketing manager: Dan DePasquale
Compositor/Production services: Pine Tree Composition, Inc.

© 2002, 1997 by
Uyless Black
Published by Prentice Hall PTR
Prentice-Hall, Inc.
Upper Saddle River, New Jersey 07458

Prentice Hall books are widely used by corporations and government agencies for training, market-ing, and resale.

The publisher offers discounts on this book when ordered in
bulk quantities. For more information contact:
    Corporate Sales Department
    Prentice Hall PTR
    One Lake Street
    Upper Saddle River, New Jersey 07458

    Phone: 800-382-3419
    Fax: 201-236-7141
    email: corpsales@prenhall.com

Printed in the United States of America
10 9 8 7 6 5 4 3 2 1

ISBN: 0-13-065416-7

Pearson Education LTD.
Pearson Education Australia PTY, Limited
Pearson Education Singapore, Pte. Ltd.
Pearson Education North Asia Ltd.
Pearson Education Canada Ltd.
Pearson Educación de Mexico, S.A. de C.V.
Pearson Education — Japan
Pearson Education Malaysia, Pte. Ltd.
Pearson Education, Upper Saddle River, New Jersey

In Loving Memory:
Mary Gleason and Eleanor Brenner

I also dedicate this book to Donna Inglima, whose sense of integrity and desire to be the best she can be, as well as her passion and dedication, make her an exemplary role model.

Sharleen Waters

"The secret to success is timing."
— *from a company Chief Executive Officer (CEO)*

"The secret to success is timing."
— *from a T1 / SONET engineer*

The focus of much of this second edition is the subject of modern telecommunications systems that convey information with synchronized digital signals. These signals are coded into pulses of electrical or light energy and transmitted on a copper wire, through the air or through optical fibers.

During our research for this book, we became interested in older light-based systems that use the same methods as the modern techniques. We found that light semaphores with fire (and later, mirrors) have been used for centuries in both commercial activities and warfare, and we learned that the earliest digital light-signaling machine in existence is probably the firefly (or lightning bug).

We are told by the experts that fireflies use their lights to signal to each other to find mates (the subject matter of this book is not quite that interesting). Some tropical species congregate in groups and flash their lights in unison. Perhaps they are having a party, but the experts don't know the reason for this type of behavior. Several authorities believe the flashing is a protective mechanism to warn predators of the firefly's bitter taste. Some predators don't care; certain frogs eat such large number of fireflies that they themselves glow.

The firefly's signals are much more complex than those we describe in this book. There are over 2,000 known species of fireflies, and each species produces different signaling patterns. For example, when a female detects a male flying by that is flashing a correct signal, she answers with her own signal, but these signals differ within each species, if only by a small degree.

While the signals may be complex, the firefly's signaling rate is not very impressive. Most species emit only two or three pulses every few seconds. The upper end systems described in this book are capable of rates well over 10 billion signals per second.

Nonetheless, as we have done in the other books in this series, it is instructive to note that the technical marvels of the modern world (and the immense resources used to create them) are once again preempted by nature, and in this case, an insect.

Contents

CHAPTER 2   **Digital Transmission Carrier Systems**   **22**

CHAPTER 3   Timing and Synchronization in Digital Networks   57

CHAPTER 5   **SONET Operations**   **146**

CHAPTER 6   **Payload Mapping and Management**   **165**

CHAPTER 7   **Topologies and Configurations**   **195**

Preface

This book is part of a series titled *Advanced Communications Technologies*. This particular book also has a close "companion" in this series, titled *ISDN and SS7: Architectures for Digital Signaling Networks*.

When we were planning this book, our initial intent was for it to be a SONET book, with little discussion of the T1 technology. However, we decided that the book should also include T1 because many of the SONET operations are centered around T1. In addition, as we surveyed the literature on T1, we were surprised to discover that the existing books on T1 did not cover several important aspects of the subject—omissions that we have corrected in this book.

Also, we have included material on some of the original T1 channel banks. To our knowledge, this material has not appeared in any text, and the information is essential to understanding how T1 is the way it is.

In setting out to write this book, we established two goals. First, we wish to complement the overall series, and avoid undue overlapping of the subject matter of the other books. Second, we wish to explain aspects of the subject matter that have not been provided in other reference books. We found that not much tutorial literature exists on synchronization and timing, on the Building Integrated Timing Supply (BITS), on SONET configuration (crafting) operations, and some other important subjects. This information is provided in this book.

Acknowledgments

Thanks to the following educators, with whom I share the passion for teaching: Alice Hunter, Connie Bayer, Barbara G. Bennett, G. Jeanie Martinez, Kay C. Dowd, Dan Harrell, Charlie Holomon, Steve Hodges, Drew Ritchie, Albert Stewart, Thomas A. McFall, Richard Chavez, Larry Gerber, Spence Tada, Al Gross, Jay Wilson, Dan McIntyre, Linda Guillen, Pat Sperry, and Arthetta Robinson.

Thanks to Barbara G. Bennett and G. Jeanie Martinez—you both have been great friends over the years. Many thanks for the contributions you've made toward the research for this book.

A very special thanks to the following family members for their support and encouragement: my mother, Jeanne E. Malin; my foster parents, Connie and Bob Bayer; my siblings, Holly Waters, Katherine S. Evans, Bradford and Tahnee Waters, Elizabeth G. Pojar Waters, and Brett Miner. Thanks to my nieces and nephews for reminding me just how important it is to support our youth and their dreams through education: Bond Pojar, Jason Waters, Jared Waters, Verity Pojar, Hollis Pojar, Travis Evans, Alexandria Evans, and Britnee Waters.

Last but not least, thanks to my faithful companions Buggsie T. Bear and Lucy, who helped me sift through reams of paper well into the wee hours of the morning.

Sharleen Waters

Notes for the Reader

T1/DS1 and T3/DS3 clarifications:

The term T1 is used in this book in two contexts. First, it is used as a generic term to identity a family of digital transport technologies, which includes DS0, DS1, DS3, and other systems. Second, it is used to identify a specific carrier standard, originally published by AT&T/Bell Labs. This convention follows the industry practice.

The DS3 signals operate at 44.736 Mbit/s. It is common industry practice to cite this transfer rate as 45 Mibt/s.

Most people use T2 and D2 synonomously, as well as T3 and DS3. Prior to divestiture in 1989, the terms T1 and T3 were used. After divestiture, ANSI focused on the terms DS2 and OS3. Unless stated otherwise, we use T1/DS1 and T3/DS3 interchangeably in this book, reflecting common industry practice.

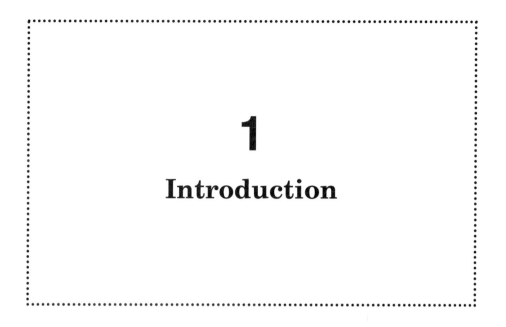

1

Introduction

This chapter introduces the Synchronous Optical Network (SONET) and T1 technology. A brief history of SONET is provided, as well as the reasons that SONET came into existence. We also provide a brief history of the T1 system and make a general comparison of T1 and SONET. As a prelude to later chapters, a general description is provided of the major features of SONET.

WHAT ARE SONET AND T1?

Digital carrier systems, such as the well-known T1 technology, have served the telecommunications industry well for over 40 years, and they shall continue to do so for quite some time. T1 was first installed in 1962 to provide a high-speed (1.544 Mbit/s) digital carrier system for voice traffic. It was modified later to support data and video applications.

In terms of communications technology, 1962 is a very long time ago. Since this date, extraordinary progress has been made in the fields of computers and communications. Many of the technical underpinnings of SONET exploit this new technology.

We have cited T1 in a previous paragraph to help explain the nature of SONET. T1 and associated systems (such as T3 and similar technology in other parts of the world) are first-generation digital transport systems. SONET is a second-generation digital transport system. Like T1, its purpose is to transport, multiplex, and switch digital signals representing voice, video, and data traffic to and from users' applications.

However, T1 and SONET differ significantly in how they accomplish these functions. Many facets of the T1 architecture are based on technology that is over four decades old. In contrast to T1, the SONET architecture is based on the technology of today. With this brief comparison in mind, let us take a look at how SONET came into existence and then examine some of the major features of SONET.

THE DEVELOPMENT OF SONET

Some people view SONET as a new technology, and it is only in the last decade that SONET has been deployed extensively. However, SONET did not just appear suddenly on the scene. Extensive research has been underway for well over a decade on many of the features that are found in SONET. One notable achievement began in 1984. It focused on the efforts of several standards groups and vendors to develop optical transmission standards for what is known as the *mid-span meet* (also known as *transverse compatibility*). The goal was to publish a specification that would allow different vendors' equipment to interoperate with each other at the fiber level.

In addition, due to the breakup of the Bell System in 1984, there were no standards developed beyond T3 technology. Prior to the divestiture, all equipment was built by AT&T's manufacturing arm, Western Electric (WECO), which ensured that there would be no compatibility problems in any network components.

After the breakup, there was little incentive for the other carriers (such as MCI and Sprint) to purchase AT&T-based equipment. Indeed, there was no incentive to purchase AT&T equipment, since AT&T, MCI, and Sprint had begun competing with each other for long distance services. This situation led to the rapid growth of alternate equipment vendors (such as Nortel Networks), who were developing advanced digital switching technologies.

The 1984 divestiture paved the way for alternate long distance carriers through the equal access ruling. The alternate carriers were given equal access to the local exchange carrier (LEC) infrastructure and connections to AT&T for end-to-end long distance service. The LEC could connect to MCI, Sprint, and others through their switching facilities at an interface in the LEC or long distance carrier offices called the point of presence (POP).

During this time, higher capacity schemes beyond T3 became proprietary, creating serious compatibility problems for network operators who purchased equipment from different manufacturers. In addition, the early 1980s witnessed the proliferation of incompatible and competing optical fiber specifications.

Precursors to SONET

We interrupt the discussion on divestiture to explain some of the technology that was being developed during the early 1980s. A landmark project that contributed to SONET was Metrobus, an optical communications system developed at AT&T's Bell Labs in the early 1980s. Its name was derived from its purpose: It was situated in a metropolitan area to serve as a high-speed optical transport network.

Metrobus demonstrated the feasibility of several new techniques that found their way into SONET. (They are explained in this chapter and subsequent chapters.) Among the more notable features were (a) single-step multiplexing, (b) synchronous timing, (c) extensive overhead for network management, (d) accessing low level signals directly, (e) point-to-multipoint multiplexing, and (f) the employment of multimegabit media for achieving high bandwidth network transmission capacity (of approximately 150 Mbit/s).

This latter decision along with the ensuing research and testing was important, because a 150 Mbit/s signal rate can accommodate voice, video, and data signals, as well as compressed high definition television (HDTV). Moreover, these techniques permitted the use of relatively inexpensive graded-index multimode fibers instead of the more expensive single mode fibers, although single mode fiber is now the preferred media for SONET.

The various standards groups began the work on SONET after MCI send a request to them to establish standards for the mid-span meet. The SONET specifications were developed in the early 1980s, and Bellcore submitted its proposals to the American National Standards Institute (ANSI) T1X1 Committee in early 1985,[1] based on a 50.688 Mbit/s transfer rate. The initial SONET work did not arouse much interest until the Metrobus activity became recognized.

---

[1] The initial proposal stipulated a transfer rate of 50.688 Mbit/s, a 125 microsecond (μsec) signal, and a frame format of three rows by 265 columns (264 octets × 3 rows × 8 bits per octet × 8000 = 50,688,000). Later chapters explain the concepts of rows and columns.

Later, using the innovative features of Metrobus, the SONET designers made modifications to the original SONET proposal, principally in the size of the frame and the manner in which T1 signals were mapped into the SONET frame.

From 1984 to 1986, various alternatives were considered by the ANSI T1 Committee, who settled on what became known as the synchronous transport signal number one (STS-1) rate as a base standard. Finally, in 1987, the ANSI T1X1 committee published a draft document on SONET.

Participation by ITU-T

During this time, the international standards body now known as the International Telecommunication Union-Telecommunication Standardization Sector (ITU-T) had rejected the STS-1 rate as a base rate in favor of a base rate of 155.520 Mbit/s. For a while, it appeared that the North American and European approaches might not converge, but the SONET frame syntax and structure were altered one more time to a rate of 51.84 Mbit/s which permitted this rate to be multiplexed (concatenated) by an integer of three to the European preference of 155.52 Mbit/s. This work has resulted in almost complete compatibility between the North American and ITU-T approaches. The ITU-T Recommendations are now considered the "official" standards and are collectively called the Synchronous Digital Hierarchy (SDH).

Once the major aspects of the standards were in place, vendors and manufacturers began to develop SONET and SDH equipment and software. These efforts came to fruition in the early 1990s and, as of this writing, SONET and SDH have been deployed throughout the United States and other parts of the world.

Key ITU-T Documents

Listed below are some of the most commonly cited SDH standards available from the ITU-T.[2]

- ITU-T G.707: Network Node Interface for the Synchronous Digital Hierarchy (SDH)
- ITU-T G.781: Structure of Recommendations on Equipment for the Synchronous Digital Hierarchy (SDH)

---

[2]Go to the ITU web site at *www.itu.int* for a complete list of SDH standards, along with information on purchasing the documents.

- ITU-T G.782: Types and Characteristics of Synchronous Digital Hierarchy (SDH) Equipment
- ITU-T G.783: Characteristics of Synchronous Digital Hierarchy (SDH) Equipment Functional Blocks
- ITU-T G.803: Architecture of Transport Networks Based on the Synchronous Digital Hierarchy (SDH)

ROLE OF ANSI AND KEY STANDARDS DOCUMENTS

Today, ANSI coordinates and approves the SONET standards. The standards are developed by the T1 committee. T1X1 and T1M1 are the primary T1 Technical Subcommittees responsible for SONET. T1X1 deals with the digital hierarchy (shown in Figure 1–5) and synchronization. T1M1 deals with internetworking operations, administration, maintenance, and provisioning (OAM&P). Listed below are some of the most commonly cited SONET standards available from ANSI.[3]

- ANSI T1.105: SONET—Basic Description including Multiplex Structure, Rates and Formats
- ANSI T1.105.01: SONET—Automatic Protection Switching
- ANSI T1.105.02: SONET—Payload Mappings
- ANSI T1.105.03: SONET—Jitter at Network Interfaces
- ANSI T1.105.03a: SONET—Jitter at Network Interfaces – DS1 Supplement
- ANSI T1.105.03b: SONET—Jitter at Network Interfaces – DS3 Wander Supplement
- ANSI T1.105.04: SONET—Data Communication Channel Protocol and Architectures
- ANSI T1.105.05: SONET—Tandem Connection Maintenance
- ANSI T1.105.06: SONET—Physical Layer Specifications
- ANSI T1.105.07: SONET—Sub-STS-1 Interface Rates and Formats Specification
- ANSI T1.105.09: SONET—Network Element Timing and Synchronization

---

[3]Go to the ANSI web site at *www.ansi.org* for a complete list of SONET standards along with information on purchasing the documents.

- ANSI T1.119: SONET—OAM&P, Communications
- ANSI T1.119.01: SONET: OAM&P, Communications, and Protection Switching Fragment

THE NETWORK AND SERVICES INTEGRATION FORUM (NSIF)

In order to assist in the SONET standards process, the Network and Services Integration Forum (NSIF) was formed to provide an open industry forum for the discussion and resolution of multiple technology integration and SONET interoperability issues.[4] Its goal is to enable the delivery of services across a set of networks from different vendors and different network operators. NSIF coordinates with the appropriate standards groups, such as ANSI and the ITU-T, as required by a specific issue.

NSIF is a nonprofit membership organization comprised of equipment vendors, service providers, and other industry players who cooperatively develop end-to-end multitechnology service delivery capabilities based on industry and international standards.

SONET AND T1

While the primary focus of this book is on SONET, we devote considerable coverage to T1 technology. With this in mind, we will use this section to introduce T1 and compare the T1 and SONET technologies.

Comparison of SONET and T1

Figure 1–1 shows the placement of T1 and SONET in a communications network. Currently, several configurations exist in commercial systems. SONET may operate end-to-end or it may act as the transport system within the network carrying T1 traffic through the network between customer premises equipment (CPEs). Of course, in some networks SONET has not been implemented so T1/T3 may operate within the network. Another widely used placement is the installation of fractional T1 (FT1) at the CPE switch, which then multiplexes user payloads into a T1 or T3 transport frame. As you can see from Figure 1–1, SONET

---

[4]Go to *www.atis.org / atis / sif / sifhom.htm* for more information.

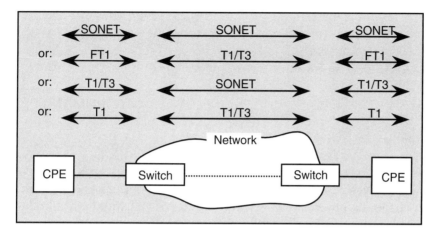

Figure 1–1   T1 and SONET.

can operate end-to-end or can function as a backbone technology, operating within the network.

Figure 1–2 shows the relationship of the Open System Interconnection Model (OSI) layers to the layers of T1 and SONET. The first observation is that T1 and SONET operate at the physical layer of the OSI Model. As such, they are concerned with the physical generation of the signals at a transmitting machine and their correct reception and detection at a receiving machine. While this statement may imply that these technologies are rather simple, we shall see that the opposite is true, especially regarding SONET.

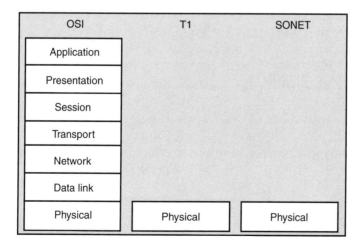

Figure 1–2   Comparison of the layers in regard to OSI.

The layers operating above the physical layer are quite varied. Some products run the Internet protocols in these layers, others run SS7, still others run vendor-specific protocols, such as IBM's Systems Network Architecture (SNA). Later chapters explore the relationships of these layers and SONET.

FEATURES OF SONET AND T1

This section explains why SONET differs from other digital transport systems. First, SONET is an optical-based carrier (transport) network utilizing synchronous operations between the network components/nodes, such as multiplexers, terminals, and switches. SONET's high speeds (some systems operate at the gigabit rate) rely on high-capacity fiber. Much of the T1 technology is geared toward the use of copper (twisted pairs) media and operates at more modest transmission rates.

As just stated, the SONET network nodes are synchronized with each other through very accurate clocking operations, ensuring that traffic is not "damaged," or lost due to clocking inaccuracies. T1 clocking systems are very accurate, but are not as reliable as SONET systems. Later discussions explain how synchronous networks experience fewer errors than the older asynchronous networks and provide much better techniques for managing payloads.

SONET is quite robust and provides high availability with self-healing topologies. In the event a SONET link is lost due to node or fiber failure, SONET can recover by diverting the traffic to back-up facilities. Most T1 systems can be configured for backup, but "robustness" is not an inherent part of the original design of the T1 architecture.

SONET and its ITU-T counterpart SDH are international standards. As such, SONET paves the way for heterogeneous, multivendor systems to operate without conversions between them (with some exceptions).[5]

SONET uses powerful, yet simple, multiplexing and demultiplexing capabilities. Unlike T1, SONET gives the network node a direct access to low-rate multiplexed signals, without the need to demultiplex the signals back to the original form. In other words, the payloads residing inside a SONET signal are directly available to a SONET node.

---

[5]First-generation digital carrier systems (such as T1 and E1 in Europe) are not standardized on a worldwide basis, and different systems exist in various parts of the world.

Because of these capabilities, SONET efficiently combines, consolidates, and segregates traffic from different locations through one machine. This concept, known as *grooming*, eliminates back hauling[6] and other inefficient techniques currently being used in transport networks. In older transport network configurations, grooming can eliminate back hauling, but it requires expensive configurations (such as back-to-back multiplexers that are connected with cables, panels, or electronic cross-connect equipment).

SONET provides extensive operations, administration, maintenance, and provisioning (OAM&P) services to the network user and administrator. Indeed, about 4% of the bandwidth in a SONET network is reserved for OAM&P. A T1 system only allows one bit per 193 bits for OAM&P. With this comparison in mind, it is easy to conclude that SONET has the capability for more extensive and powerful network management operations than T1.

Finally, like T1, SONET employs digital transmission schemes. Thus, the traffic is relatively immune to noise and other impairments on the communications channel. Of course, with the use of optical fibers, random errors on the channel are very rare.

SYNCHRONOUS NETWORKS

One of the most attractive aspects of SONET deals with how network components send and receive traffic to and from each other. The original, first-generation digital transport networks were designed to work as asynchronous (or more accurately, nearly synchronous) systems. With this approach, each device in the network runs with its own clock, or devices may be clocked from more than one source. That is, the clocks are not synchronized from a central source.

The purpose of the terminal clock is to locate precisely the digital 1s and 0s in the incoming data stream on the link attached to the terminal—a very important operation in a digital network. Obviously, if bits are lost in certain user traffic (user traffic is called payload in this book) then the traffic may be unintelligible to the receiver. Equally important,

---

[6]*Back hauling* is a technique in which user payload (say, from user A) is carried past a switch that has a line to user C and sent to another endpoint (say, user B). Then, the traffic for B is dropped, and user C's payload is sent back to the switch and relayed (dropped off) back to C. We explain this concept in more detail later in the chapter.

the loss of bits or the inability to locate them accurately can cause further synchronization problems. When this situation occurs, the receiver usually does not deliver the traffic to the end user because it is simpler to discard the traffic than to initiate retransmission efforts.

To give the reader an idea of how precise the timing must be, consider a T1 system that operates at a modest 1.544 Mbit/s. Obviously, a receiver must be able to detect each bit as it "shows itself" at the link interface at the receiving machine. Each bit is only 648 ns in duration (1 sec/1544000 = .000000648). This means that the receiver's clock must be aligned accurately with the transmitter's clock.

Because a sender's clock may run independently of the receiver's clock in an asynchronous network, large variations can occur between the sender's clock (machine 1) and the rate at which the bits are received and *then transmitted* by the receiver's clock (machine 2). The problem is not at the receiving link at machine 2, since machine 2 can "lock" onto machine 1's incoming signal and accept the traffic. In this regard, machine 2 extracts the clock from machine 1's signal.

The problem occurs when machine 2 then prepares that traffic for transmission onto the next outgoing link. If it is using its own clock, it usually varies from the rate that was received from machine 1. These different timing operations can create a big headache for the network administrator. For example, experience has demonstrated that a T3 signal may experience a variation of up to 1789 bit/s for a 44.736 Mbit/s signal in a network that does not have precise and accurate timing.

The Perils of Bit Stuffing

Moreover, T1 signals such as DS1s are multiplexed in stages up to DS2, DS3, etc., and extra bits are added to the stream of data to account for timing variations in each stream. The process is called *bit stuffing*. The lower level signals, such as DS1, are not accessible nor visible at the higher rates. Consequently, the original stream of traffic must be demultiplexed if these signals are to be accessed. The demultiplexing process is very expensive and adds delay and overhead to the network.

SONET TIMING

SONET is based on synchronous transmission, meaning the average frequency of all the clocks in the network are the same (synchronous) or nearly the same (plesiochronous). As a result of this approach, the clocks are referenced to a stable reference point. Therefore, the need to align the data streams directly is less necessary. As we stated earlier, the user payloads, such as DS1, are directly accessible so demultiplexing is not necessary to access the bit streams. Also, the synchronous signals can be stacked together without bit stuffing.

The Benefits of Byte Alignment

Byte multiplexing (also called octet multiplexing) is more efficient and less error-prone than the bit multiplexing operation explained earlier. Most hardware and software today are designed to process data in chunks of eight bits, often called byte-aligned processing. In addition, bit aligned processing is more error-prone than its byte-aligned counterpart, because of the use of smaller buffers and shorter timing increments. There is less tolerance for errors in the bit aligned operation (and we show examples of bit processing in Chapters 3 and 4).

SONET requires byte alignment operations, and any timing adjustments that are performed in the SONET network are done on a byte basis, not on a bit basis.

Floating Payloads

Another major aspect of synchronous systems (in general), and SONET (specifically), pertains to how payload, such as DS1 or DS3 signals, is inserted into the SONET channel. For those situations in which the reference clocking signal may vary (even if only slightly), SONET uses pointers to allow the payload streams to "float" within the payload *envelope* (the term envelope is used to describe the SONET signal on the channel; the term *frame* is also used). Indeed, synchronous clocking is the key to pointers; it allows a flexible allocation and alignment of the payload within the transmission envelope. Thus, SONET's payload is called a *synchronous payload envelope* (SPE).

The concept of a synchronous system is elegantly simple. By holding specific bits in a silicon memory buffer for a defined and predictable period of time, it is possible to move information from one part of a payload envelope to another part. It also allows a system to know where the bits are located at all times. Of course, this idea is "old hat" to software engineers, but it is a different way of thinking for other designers. As one person has put it, "Since the bits are lined up in time, we now know where they are in both time *and* space. So, in a sense, we can now move information in four dimensions, instead of the usual three."

The U.S. implementation of SONET uses a central clocking source—for example, from a telephone company's end office. This office must use an accurate clocking source known as *stratum 3*. Stratum 3 clocking requires an accuracy of 1.6 parts in 1 billion elements. Chapter 3 provides more detailed information on synchronization and clocking operations as well as the accuracy levels of the stratum 1, 2, 3, and 4 clocks.

PAYLOADS AND ENVELOPES

SONET is designed to support a wide variety of payloads. Table 1–1. summarizes some typical payloads of existing technologies. The SONET node accepts these payloads and multiplexes them into a SONET envelope. These payloads are called *virtual tributaries* (VTs) in North Amer-

Table 1–1   Typical SONET payloads.

Type	Digital Bit Rate	Voice Circuits	T–1	DS3	System Name
North American multiplexing hierarchy					
DS1	1.544 Mbit/s	24	1	—	
DS1C	3.152 Mbit/s	48	2	—	
DS2	6.312 Mbit/s	96	4	—	
DS3	44.736 Mbit/s	672	28	1	
DS4	274.176 Mbit/s	4032	168	6	
European multiplexing hierarchy					
E1	2.048 Mbit/s	30			M1
E2	8.448 Mbit/s	120			M2
E3	34.368 Mbit/s	480			M3
E4	139.264 Mbit/s	1920			M4
E5	565.148 Mbit/s	7680			M5
Japanese multiplexing hierarchy					
1	1.544 Mbit/s	24			F1
2	6.312 Mbit/s	96			F6M
3	34.064 Mbit/s	480			F32M
4	97.728 Mbit/s	1440			F100M
5	397.20 Mbit/s	5760			F400M
6	1588.80 Mbit/s	23040			F4.6G

ica and *virtual containers* (VCs) in SDH. Later chapters will explain how SONET manages these payloads.

As you can see, the first-generation digital carrier systems are not the same across different geographical regions of the world. Shortly after the inception of T1 in North America, the ITU-T published the E1 standards, which were implemented in Europe, and Japan followed with a hierarchy that was similar to the North American specifications at the lower speeds (but not at the higher speeds).

OPTICAL FIBER—THE BEDROCK FOR SONET

It is likely you understand and appreciate the advantages of using optical fiber as the transmission medium for a telecommunications system. This section summarizes the major aspects of optical fiber, and Appendix A explains these aspects in more detail. Optical fiber is widely used as the physical medium in SONET for the following reasons:

- Optical transmission has a very large information capacity. Gigabit/s rates are easily obtainable in today's systems.
- Optical fibers have electrically nonconducting photons instead of the electrons found in metallic cables such as wires or coaxial cables. This characteristic is attractive for applications in which the transmission path traverses hostile environments. For example, optical cables are not subject to electrical sparks or interference from electrical components in a building or computer machine room.
- Optical fibers suffer less loss of signal strength than copper wire or coaxial cables. The strength of a light signal is reduced only slightly after propagation through several miles of the glass cable.
- Optical fibers are more secure than copper cable transmission methods. Transmission of light does not yield residual intelligence that is found in electrical transmission.
- Optical cables are very small (roughly the size of a hair) and weigh very little. For example, 900 copper wire pairs pulled through 1000 feet in a building would weigh approximately 4800 pounds. Two optical fibers, with protective covers pulled the same distance, weigh only 80 pounds and yet yield greater capacity.
- Optical fibers are relatively easy to install and operate in high and low temperatures.

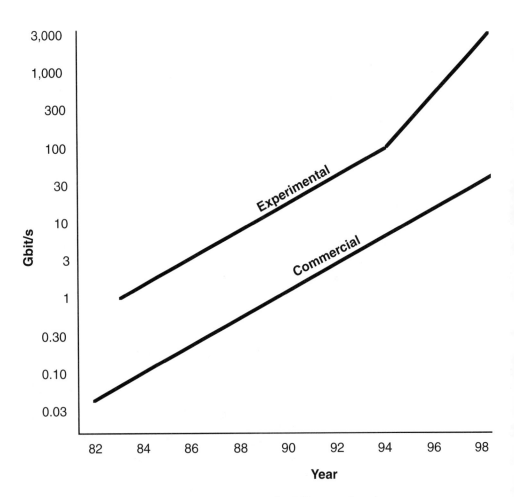

Figure 1–3   Progress in optical fiber technology.

- Due to the low signal loss, the error rate for optical fibers is very low. Some systems operate with a bit error rate (BER) or 10^{-12}, which is several orders of magnitude better than copper media.

Figure 1–3 shows the progress made in transmission capacity of single-mode fibers since 1980 [CHAR99]. The top line represents experimental systems, and the bottom line represents commercial systems. The commercial results have lagged behind experimental results by about six years. The dramatic growth in the experimental capacity was due to improved laboratory techniques and the progress made in optical signal management.

While optical fiber is an excellent medium for the transport of SONET traffic, it is by no means the only alternative. Other cable-based systems, such as twisted pair, and wireless systems, such as microwave, are applicable as well.

TYPICAL SONET TOPOLOGY

Figure 1–4 shows a typical topology for a SONET network. This topology is a dual ring. Each ring is an optical fiber cable. One ring is the *working* facility. The other ring is the *protection* facility, which acts as a standby in the event of fiber or system failure on the working facility.

End-user devices operating on LANs and digital transport systems (such as DS1, E1, etc.) are attached to the network through a SONET service adapter. This service adapter is also called an access node, a terminal, or a terminal multiplexer. This machine is responsible for supporting the end-user interface by sending and receiving traffic from LANs, DS1, DS3, E1, ATM nodes, etc. It is really a concentrator at the sending site because it consolidates multiple user traffic into a *payload envelope* for transport onto the SONET network. It performs a complementary, yet opposite, service at the receiving site.

The user signals (such as T1, E1, and ATM cells) are converted (mapped) into a standard format called the *synchronous transport signal* (*STS*), which is the basic building block of the SONET multiplexing hierarchy. The STS signal is an electrical signal. The notation STS-n means that the service adapter can multiplex the STS signal into higher integer multiples of the base rate. The base rate is 51.84 Mbit/s in North America and 155.520 Mbit/s in Europe. Therefore, from the perspective of a SONET terminal, the SDH base rate in Europe is an STS-3 multiplexed signal ($51.84 \times 3 = 155.520$ Mbit/s).

The terminal/service adapter (access node) shown in Figure 1–4 is implemented as the end-user interface machine, or as an add-drop multiplexer (ADM). The ADM implementation multiplexes various STS input streams onto optical fiber channels. The optical fiber channels are now called the optical carrier signal and designated with the notation OC-n, where *n* represents the multiplexing integer. OC-n streams are demultiplexed as well as multiplexed with the ADM.

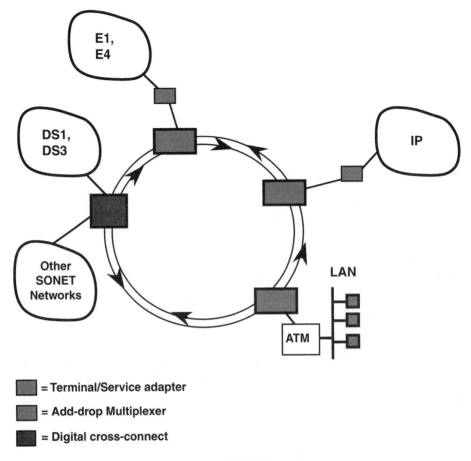

= Terminal/Service adapter

= Add-drop Multiplexer

= Digital cross-connect

Figure 1–4   SONET topology.

The term *add-drop* means that the machine can add or drop payload onto one of the fiber links. Remaining traffic that was not dropped passes straight through the multiplexer without additional processing.

The *digital cross-connect* (*DCS*) machine usually acts as a hub in the SONET network. It can not only add and drop payload, but it can also operate with different carrier rates, such as DS1, OC-n, E1, etc. The DCS can make two-way cross-connections between the payload and can consolidate and separate different types of payloads.

The DCS is designed to eliminate devices called back-to-back multiplexers. As we learned earlier, these devices contain a plethora of cables, jumpers, and intermediate distribution frames. SONET does not need all these physical components because cross-connection operations are performed by hardware and software.

The topology can be set up either as a ring or as a point-to-point system. In most networks, the ring is a dual ring, operating with two or more optical fibers. As noted, the structure of the dual ring topology permits the network to recover automatically from failures on the channels and in the channel/machine interfaces. This is known as a *self-healing ring* and is explained in later chapters.

PRESENT TRANSPORT SYSTEMS AND SONET

The present digital transport carrier system varies in the different geographical regions of the world. The structure is different in Japan than it is in North America, which is itself different than the structure in Eu-

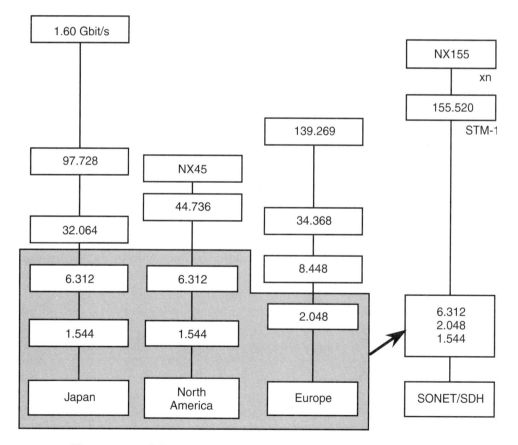

Figure 1–5   SONET support for current technologies. Note: Unless noted otherwise, speeds in Mbit/s.

rope. This disparate approach is complex and makes the interworking of the systems difficult and expensive. Moreover, it means that companies that build hardware and software for carrier systems must implement multiple commercial platforms for what could be one technology.

While SONET does not ensure equipment compatibility, it does provide a basis for vendors to build worldwide standards. Moreover, as shown with the shaded area in Figure 1–5, SONET is backwards compatible, in that it supports the current transport carriers' asynchronous systems in North America, Europe, and Japan. This feature is quite important because it allows different digital signals and hierarchies to operate with a common transport system, SONET. By the way, don't be concerned with all the details shown in Figure 1–5; they are explained later.

CLARIFICATION OF TERMS

Before we proceed into a more detailed discussion of the subject matter, it is appropriate to pause and define some terms that will be used in subsequent chapters. In the early 1980s, AT&T introduced the digital access and cross-connect system (DACS) as a major enhancement to its digital transport system products. It is also called the digital cross-connect system, or DCS. The subject of DCS is introduced here in order to explain several concepts that are central to subsequent chapters.

The original DACSs were considered complex implementations of microelectronics technology. They had a RAM (random access memory) of 256 words! At that time, they were considered very esoteric machines.

Figure 1–6 shows some of the major operations of a DCS, which uses a combination of time-division and space-division switching techniques. The original DACS terminated up to 127 DS1 signals (3048 DS0 channels) and provided up to 1524 cross-connections.

The DCS permits the assignment and redistribution of DS0 channels for drop-and-insert (also known as ADM in today's technology) services. As Figure 1–6(a) shows, the operation provides for the distribution of traffic to nodes reachable by the DCS (the drop operation). It also allows a node to send traffic to the DCS for delivery to another node in the network (the insert operation). Figure 1–6(b) shows how the DCS performs back hauling (sending traffic downstream and returning it back), which does not require back-to-back channel banks (or the conversion of the digital signals to analog and back to digital again). A DCS also performs groom-and-fill operations (Figure 1–6(c)), a technique in which the

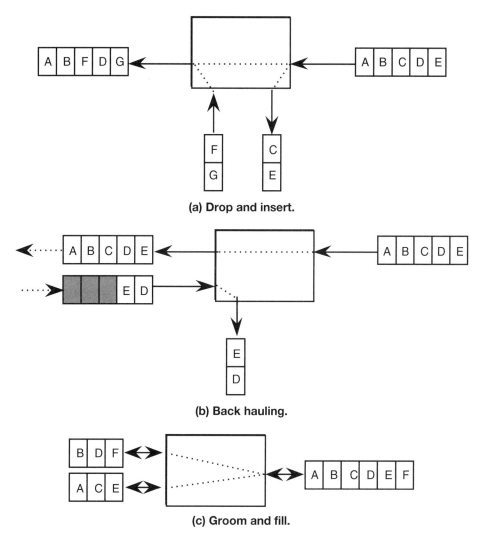

(a) Drop and insert.

(b) Back hauling.

(c) Groom and fill.

Figure 1–6   Terms and concepts.

machine accepts input from two or more low-speed lines and multiplexes these signals into a higher speed line.

Figure 1–7 shows some examples of equipment and configurations that exist at the customer premises equipment and the telephone central office. Be aware that a wide variety of options are available and these examples are only a sampling of possible services and arrangements.

Figure 1–7(a) shows a voice interface into a channel bank, which converts the analog signal into a digital signal with a CODEC (a

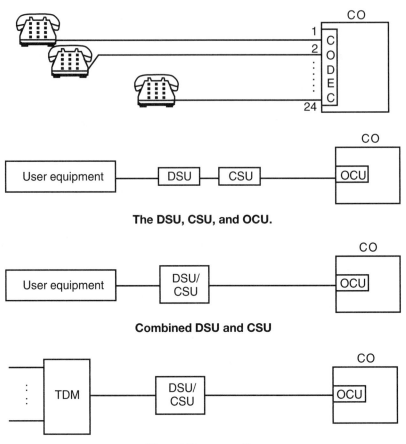

The DSU, CSU, and OCU.

Combined DSU and CSU

Mux at the user site.

Figure 1–7   Examples of configurations.

coder/decoder). The CO then multiplexes multiple digital signals together for transmission into the network.

Figures 1–7(b) through 1–7(d) show how channel service units (CSUs), digital service units (DSUs), and office channel units (OCUs) may be employed. Before the divestiture of AT&T in 1984, the CSU and and DSU were in separate boxes. They are responsible for coding the user traffic into self-clocking signals and performing a variety of testing and loop-back functions.

In the 1970s and early 1980s, the customer was provided an interface into a digital channel with a Western Electric 500A, a CSU and DSU, or a combination of the two (CSU/DSU). The DSU converts the user equipment signals into signals that are more efficient for use in a digital network. The DSU also performs clocking and signal regeneration on the channel. The CSU performs functions such as line conditioning (equalization), which keeps the signal's performance consistent across the channel bandwidth; signal reshaping, which reconstitutes the binary pulse stream; and loop-back testing, which entails the transmission of test signals between the CSU and the network carrier's office channel unit (OCU).

SUMMARY

Modern telecommunications and applications need increased carrier capacity for wide area transport service. In the past, the T1 system has provided this service and will continue to do so for many years. SONET represents second-generation digital carrier technology, which will eventually supplant the T1 technology. Fortunately, SONET is designed to support the T1 technology, which facilitates its placement into the pervasive and ubiquitous infrastructure.

2

Digital Transmission Carrier Systems

This chapter examines digital transmission carrier systems with emphasis on T1 and T3 (DS1 and DS3) technologies. The subjects of analog-to-digital conversions and pulse code modulation (PCM) are reviewed. A short tutorial is provided on analog systems, the telephone central office (CO), and the outside plant.

This chapter emphasizes the DS1 technology, because it is often the DS1 signals that become the inputs into the SONET multiplexers that create the SONET frame for transport over the SONET channel.

ORGANIZATION OF TELEPHONE SERVICES

Before we begin the examination of these systems, we should first understand the basic telephone service and terminology used by the public switched telephone network (PSTN). Telephone systems are in extensive use throughout the world, providing public access for interconnection between the telephone instruments connected to these systems. Both single line and multiline services are connected through dial-up switching on the local loops (see Figure 2–1).

The line connecting the customer premises equipment (CPE) to the CO consists of two wires. The connecting point between the CPE and CO is called the point of demarcation and is usually found in a box (the pro-

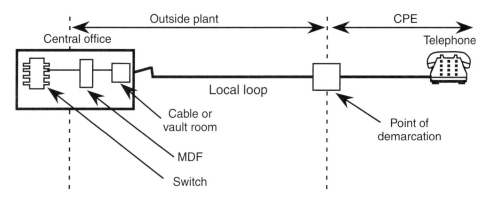

Figure 2–1   Examples of local telephone service.

tection block or station block) on the outside of a house. The outside plant facilities include the wires and supporting hardware to the CO.

At the CO, the lines enter through a cable room (aerial lines) or a cable vault (buried lines). The lines are then spliced to tip cables and directed to the main distribution frame (MDF); each wire is attached to a connector at the MDF.[1] From the MDF, the wires are directed to other equipment, such as switches.

The dial-up network also is called the Direct Distance Dialing (DDD) network (see Figure 2–2). With DDD service, the telephone messages are routed through a switch at the central office for local calls, through a switching center for out-of-area calls, and through DDD networks for long distance calls, which are routed through an interchange carrier (IXC or IC). Local exchange is the area served by a central office. As we just mentioned, the lines between the subscribers and the serving central office are called the local loop.

Figure 2–2 depicts several types of trunks, offices, and calls. Here is a brief summary [NORT95].

- Local office—a central office providing service in a local area, to which subscribers are directly connected; processes line-to-line, line-to-trunk, and trunk-to-line connections. "Line" refers to local loop lines, or subscriber lines.

---

[1]Even though the MDF is at the CO, it is usually considered part of the outside plant, and CO performance is usually measured between the MDFs.

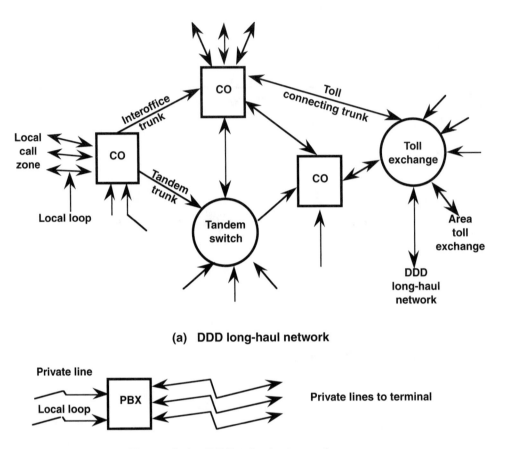

(a) DDD long-haul network

Figure 2–2   DDD telephone exchanges.

- Local tandem—a central office that connects only local offices.
- Tandem office—a central office containing only trunk circuits that serves as a switching point for traffic between central offices.
- Toll office (toll exchange)—a central office containing only trunk circuits (like a tandem office) that processes long distance calls and is responsible for toll call billing information.
- Toll tandem—a central office that connects only toll offices.
- Interoffice calls—calls between subscribers connected to different central offices.

- Intraoffice calls—calls between subscribers connected to the same central office.

TYPES OF SIGNALING

Telcos employ many types of signals for communications to operate the DDD network. The word signals is used in telephone service to identify a message that is transmitted between two parties.

Control Signaling

Control signaling describes the traffic used to indicate a system operation. These signals are used to "manage" a call. The central office's functions are activated by control signals. These signals emanate from the called and calling parties and from the central office switch.

The telephone instrument sends and receives three distinct signals through the local loop to/from the central office. First, the request for service signal is an off-hook state, and completion of service (or idle) is an on-hook state. The second control signal is the dial pulses or dial frequencies (a combination of two distinct frequencies for push button digits). This dial signal activates the switch at the central office to select the calling number for accessing the DDD network. The DDD network accepts and switches dial signals as either pulses or tones. Obviously, the third signal is voice information. In summary, the first two of the three signals activate or control the system, and the third is the voice traffic.

While there are only three signals that originate in the telephone instrument, there are many signals that originate in the central office. These signals are applied to the local loop and are detected by the subscriber instrument. They are (1) dial tone, (2) the ringer and ring-back signals, (3) the busy signal, and (4) the loud receiver off-hook signal or recording. Some signals, detected by the central office but not the subscriber, are DC (direct current or voltage polarity) signaling. The initial signal received by the central office is the DC current flow when the subscriber goes off-hook. This DC signal directs the central office to apply dial tone to the local loop.

E&M Signaling

Another form of DC signaling, called ear (E) and mouth (M) signaling, is used between one central office switch and another, but not in the local loop. E&M signaling was first used between switchboards on trunks.[2] In the past, these abbreviations were used to identify the transmit and receive connections, and their names were derived from the designations of the signaling leads on the circuit drawings. The presence and polarity of the DC voltage on these lines is used to advise the calling central office of the called central office's hook status (on-hook or off-hook).

DC signals are also often superimposed on voice and tone signals in two-way circuits that do not have an E&M lead. Superimposed ringing is defined as an AC current that is biased by being superimposed on a DC current. These DC signals are then identified as DX (distance) signaling.

An analog E&M tie line is used to connect private branch exchanges within a network. The lines can be two-wire or four-wire systems. For two-wire facilities, the wires are designated as T(tip) and R(ring). In four-wire facilities, the wires are designated as T&R (transmit pair) and T1 & R1 (receive pair).

Other Signaling

Some subscribers purchase telephone instruments for special applications or request special service applications from their local serving central office. With this arrangement, other signaling needs must be addressed. As an example, a subscriber may work or live in one area served by one central office but may want a telephone number out of another central office. This type of service is referred to as a foreign exchange (FX) line.

CONNECTING THE USER TO THE TELEPHONE SYSTEM

This section describes the interface options and line facilities for telco-provided private lines that are connected to a customer-provided PBX or station terminal equipment [ASCO94][BELL94a]. As shown in Figure 2–3, the interface options provide four types of facilities:

- Type I: A two-wire transmission interface with the channel signaling provided by the telco.

---

[2]E&M signaling is seeing decreased use in newer systems, where electronic switching is combined with the functions of the trunk circuit. Moreover, common channel signaling is replacing most trunk signaling in intraLATA networks. We discuss E&M in this chapter because it is still used in some systems.

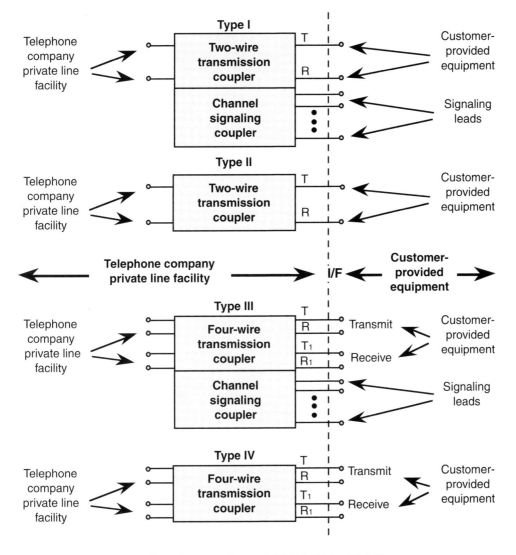

Figure 2–3   Interface options [ASCO94][BELL94a].

- Type II: A two-wire transmission interface without telco channel signaling. The customer must provide any channel signaling that is required using in-band signaling techniques.
- Type III: A four-wire transmission interface with the channel signaling provided by the telco.

- Type IV: A four-wire transmission interface without telco channel signaling. The customer must provide any channel signaling that is required using in-band signaling techniques.

Type I is the original E&M arrangement. On-hook signals use nominal −48V and local ground for on-hook signals on the M lead from the trunk circuit to the signaling facility. In the other direction, signaling is over the E lead using local ground for off-hook and open for on-hook.

The options available for a particular type of private line employing customer-provided terminal equipment at one or both ends will depend on the type of private line involved, the type of supervision and signaling required for the private line, the ownership of the terminal equipment at the distant end of the private line, and the availability of the telco facilities and equipment to serve a particular customer location.

The following sections describe the rules that the telco employs for use with the two-wire and four-wire interface options. Broad rules for the facility makeup are provided to cover those cases where the customer may want a four-wire interface option at one end of a private line and a two-wire interface option at the distant end.

Two-Wire Interface at Both Ends

The telco may supply any combination of two-wire or four-wire, and voice or carrier-derived facilities. This interface may include four-wire facilities out to the customer's premises, where it will be converted to two-wire at the interface by a telco-supplied four-wire terminating set.

Four-Wire Interface at Both Ends

The telco will supply four-wire facilities (voice or carrier-derived) from interface to interface. However, the customer may incur additional channel charges in accordance with telco tariffs.

Four-Wire Interface at One Site and Two-Wire at the Other Site

Intercity Private Lines.   Usually the telco provides four-wire facilities from the four-wire interface end to the toll center that serves the distant city end. However, where transmission considerations permit, any combination of two-wire or four-wire facilities (voice or carrier-derived) may be provided. The local channel from the toll center to the two-wire interface at the customer premises may be any combination of two- or four-wire facilities.

Intraexchange or Intracity Private Lines.   Operation with a four-wire interface at one end and a two-wire interface at the other on these private lines is not recommended. If the customer does order an intraexchange or intracity private line this way, the telco will place the four-wire terminating set required to convert the four-wire facilities to two-wire at its convenience. (This includes the customer's premises where the four-wire interface is ordered.)

Typical Applications.   Typical applications using the four interface options on a PBX tie trunk at a customer-provided dial or manual PBX are summarized here. The trunk circuit associated with a customer-provided PBX switching machine and/or attendant position converts the PBX and/or switchboard signaling into signaling suitable for use with the customer-provided in-band signaling unit, or with the telco-provided channel signaling circuit. The trunk circuit also connects the two-wire voice path switched through the PBX or the attendant position to the two-wire port of the terminating set or to the two-wire transmission coupler. For station terminations, the PBX tie trunk circuit would be replaced by a station line circuit. The line circuit performs the same functions as the PBX trunk and also provides the talking battery for the station.

For the type III and IV options, the function of the terminating set is to convert the PBX two-wire voice-path into four-wire facilities. The customer-provided in-band signaling units in type II and IV options convert the DC signaling from trunk and station line circuits into signals suitable for end-to-end in-band signaling over four-wire transmission facilities. In some cases, the customer may want to use equipment units that combine some or all of the functions of the trunk or line circuit, the terminating set, the pads, and the signaling unit.

The connecting arrangements provide the transformers, pads, and amplifiers necessary to couple the signal to the telco facility at the interface. In order to prevent the power of signals applied to the telco facilities from inadvertently exceeding the protective criteria, the connecting arrangements may also contain protective signal-limiting devices. The presence of the protective signal limiter, however, does not release the customer from the responsibility of meeting the protective criteria.

For type I and II options, the telco-provided facility leaving the customer's premises is a two-wire facility. In actual practice, with type I or II option interface, the telco, at its discretion, may use either a two-wire or a four-wire facility out to the customer's location. In the case where the customer requests a two-wire interface option, a four-wire facility, if provided, will be converted using a four-wire terminating set to two-wire on the telco side of the interface.

Where the customer chooses to provide his or her own communication channels to his or her premises, the telco will provide interface options to connect these channels to telco-provided PBXs. It will also provide interconnections with telco-provided terminal equipment if the terminal equipment is part of another telco service already provided to the customer at that location.

Since the telco is not providing the private channels in these cases, private line tariffs are not applicable. A number of connecting arrangements will be available and will be covered in local exchange tariffs for the connection of customer-provided channels with telco PBXs.

FREQUENCY DIVISION MULTIPLEXING (FDM) CARRIER SYSTEMS

We have only touched upon the telephone interfaces, equipment, and signaling procedures. For more detailed explanations, the reader is directed to the classic Bell Labs reference [BELL94a]. But we must now move on and address the primary material in this chapter: digital carrier systems. But before we move into the digital world, it is a good ideal to briefly review analog signaling and frequency division multiplexing (FDM).

In FDM, each information source is assigned a specific analog frequency band (channel) for the transmission of its information. FDM is a form of parallel transmission because it transmits multiple signals simultaneously on one path. In this way, individual channels may be combined on a pair of wires and simultaneously transmitted to a distant location.

Prior to 1962, telephone communications took place with analog electrical carrier waveforms, which are varied continuously in proportion to associated speech signals. Figure 2–4 provides an illustration of how these channels operate. At the transmit end, all signals are combined onto one physical channel. At the receive end, filters remove the desired signals through a demodulation process (which will be discussed below).

In spite of their legacy, analog systems are haunted by attenuation, noise, and crosstalk. An analog signal transmitted on a medium such as wire usually becomes distorted, due to signal loss, noise introduced into the signal, and the "pick up" of other signals from other channels. The receiver cannot correct the distortion, because it has no way of knowing the shape of the original signal.

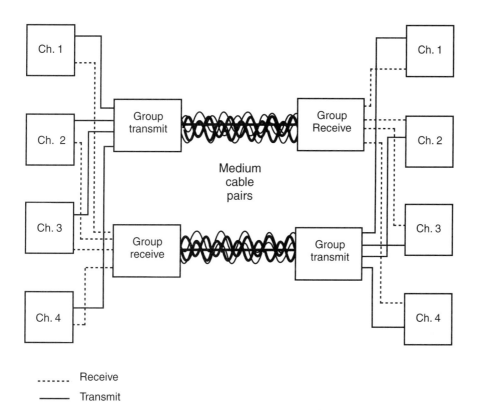

****** Receive

——— Transmit

Figure 2–4   Frequency division multiplexing.

Devices called field repeaters are used to make up for signal loss; they amplify or regenerate the signal.[3] Unfortunately, repeaters also strengthen any distortion associated with the original analog signal.

ANALOG-TO-DIGITAL CONVERSION

Classification of Speech Coders

In this section, several analog-to-digital (A/D) techniques are examined. All these systems are classified as waveform coders or source coders. This classification scheme is based on [ASCO94]. But, before we

---

[3]As a general practice, an analog field repeated is called an amplifier and a digital field repeater is called a regenerator.

explain these operations, let us review and amplify some thoughts on the attractive features of the digital technology.

The process of digitization was developed to overcome some of the limitations of analog systems. Digital systems represent the transmitted data through either the presence or absence of voltage pulses to convey the information. The analog signal is converted to a series of digital representations of the numbers and transmitted through the communications medium in pulse form as a binary code to represent the discrete voltage level of the amplitude of a PAM sample.

Of course, digital signals are subject to the same kinds of imperfections and problems as the analog signal: decay and noise. However, the digital signal is discrete: The binary representation of the samples for the analog waveform are represented by specific levels of voltages, in contrast to the nondiscrete levels of an analog signal. Indeed, an analog signal has almost infinite variability. As the digital signal traverses the carrier channel bank, it is only necessary to detect the absence or presence of a digital binary pulse—not its degree, as in the analog signal.

The mere absence or presence of a pulse can be more easily recognized than the magnitude or degree of an analog signal. If the digital signals are sampled at an acceptable rate and at an acceptable voltage level, the signals can then be completely reconstituted before they deteriorate below a minimum threshold. Consequently, noise and attenuation can be eliminated from the reconstructed signal. Thus, the digital signal can tolerate the problems of noise and attenuation much better than the analog signal. With these thoughts in mind, we now return to an examination of analog-to-digital conversion.

Waveform coders digitize the speech patterns on a sample-by-sample basis, which is the technique employed by pulse code modulation (PCM). The objective of PCM is to have the output waveform closely match the input waveform. Two types of waveform coders are used: (1) time-domain waveform coders utilize digitization schemes based on the time-domain properties of speech, and (2) spectral waveform coders utilize digitization schemes based on the frequency-domain properties of speech.

A source coder uses digitization schemes that describe the input voice signal in the context of a model. In effect, this technique models the speech signal in order to obtain a high level of quality at the receiver's ear.

Table 2–1 provides examples of speech coder types. Several of these systems are described in the following material.

Table 2–1   Types of speech coders.

Source Coders	
LPC	Linear Predictive Coding
RELP	Residual Excited Linear Prediction
RPE-LTP	Residual Pulse Excited–Long Term Prediction
CELP	Codebook Excited Linear Prediction
LDCELP	Low Delay Codebook Excited Linear Prediction

Time-Domain Coders	
PCM	Pulse code modulation
log PCM	μ-Law PCM, A-Law PCM
ADPCM	Adaptive Differential PCM
SB-ADPCM	Sub-band ADPCM
CVSD	Continuously Variable Slope Delta
DPCM	Differential Pulse Code Modulation
VQL	Variable Quantizing Level

Spectral Waveform Coders	
SBC	Sub-band Coding
ASET	Adaptive Sub-band Excitation Transform
ATC	Adaptive Transform Coding
HC	Harmonic Coding
TDHS	Time Domain Harmonic Scaling
ATC-HS	Adaptive Transform Coding Harmonic Scaling
SBC-HS	Sub-band Coding Harmonic Scaling

Time Division Multiplexing (TDM)

TDM, like frequency division multiplexing (FDM), allows two or more channels of information to share a common transmission medium. However, in TDM, rather than transmitting all information simultaneously (as in FDM systems), all channels take turns using the common medium.

In TDM carrier systems (see Figure 2–5), a channel is connected to the line briefly (for only about 5 millionths of a second). Then the line is used by the next channel. This procedure is repeated so rapidly that there is very little loss of message intelligence in any of the channels.

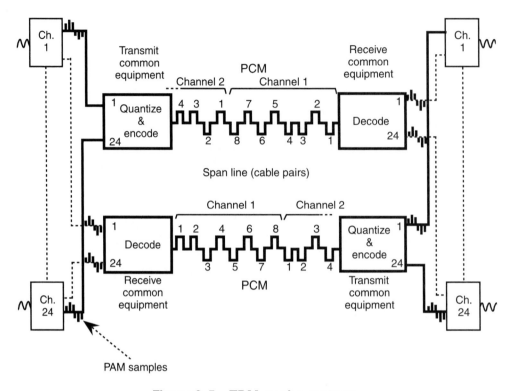

Figure 2–5   TDM carrier systems.

Since the time during which each channel is connected to the line is kept so short, many channels can share the same transmission facility.

These operations are digital in that binary 1s and 0s in the form of time slots with a presence or absence of pulses are sent over the transmission medium (not analog waveforms). Figure 2–5 identifies these images as pulse code modulation (PCM) signals, which are discussed in the next section.

Pulse Modulation

For this discussion we will be using Figure 2–6. Figure 2–6(a) shows three analog signals labeled Channels 1, 2, and 3. The solid bars in the figure represent the times each channel is sampled. These samples must be converted into a digital value. How this procedure is accomplished is explained next.

In contrast to the amplitude and frequency modulation techniques used in the older FDM systems, time division systems employ a tech-

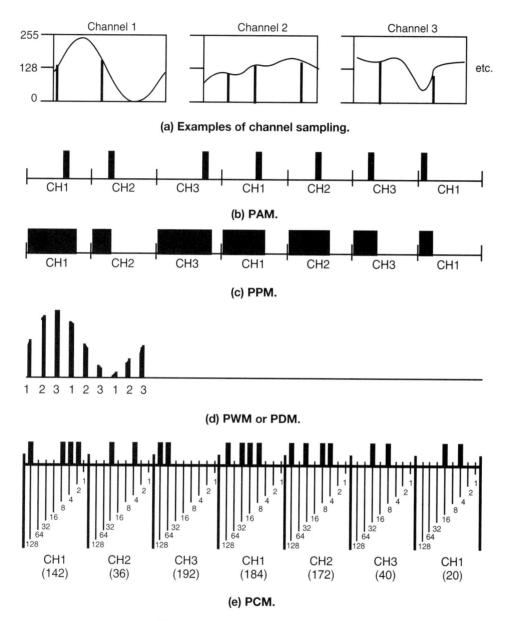

(a) Examples of channel sampling.

(b) PAM.

(c) PPM.

(d) PWM or PDM.

(e) PCM.

Figure 2–6   Pulse modulation.

nique called pulse modulation. Several pulse modulation types may be used in TDM: (1) pulse amplitude modulation (PAM), (2) pulse time modulation (PTM), and (3) pulse code modulation (PCM).

Figure 2–6(b) shows how PAM operates. The PAM sample is equal to the amplitude (height) of the analog signal at the instance it is sampled.

As depicted in Figures 2–6(c) and (d), PTM is a process whereby the instantaneous amplitude of the sample is used to vary some time-based parameter of a pulse train. Two examples of PTM are pulse position modulation (PPM) (Figure 2–6(c)) and pulse duration modulation (PDM) (Figure 2–6(d)), which is sometimes called pulse width modulation (PWM). In an assigned time slot, either the position of the pulse (PPM) or the duration of the pulse (referred to as width) convey information about the voltage level.

The primary disadvantage of PAM, PDM, and PPM is that the transmitted pulses are continuously variable. Either the amplitude, duration, or position will vary with each successive pulse. As we shall see shortly, PCM avoids these problems because it converts PAM samples into a digital code, so that all pulses have an equal duration during assigned periods of time (time slots).

PAM

We now focus in more detail on the PAM and PCM operations introduced earlier and shown in Figures 2–6(b) and (e). The first step to any analog-based TDM system is sampling. In PAM, a continuous signal, such as speech, is represented by a series of pulses called samples. As mentioned earlier, and as shown in Figure 2–6(b), the amplitude of each sample is directly proportional to the instantaneous amplitude of the continuous signal at the time of the sampling. Since the amplitudes of the samples are continuously variable, the problems of cumulative noise and distortion associated with analog signals are present in the PAM samples. However, as Figure 2–6(b) illustrates, the samples still have analog characteristics. Therefore, they are still subject to the same problems associated with a conventional analog waveform. To correct this problem, we need to translate the PAM signals into binary values. This process is called pulse code modulation (PCM) and is explained in the next section.

PCM

In 1938 Alec H. Reeves patented his invention of transmitting speech using coded pulses of a constant amplitude (similar to those used in telegraphy), which became known as PCM. With variations, PCM is still used today. In the transmitting direction, PCM transforms continuously variable speech signals (PAM samples) into a series of digitally coded pulses and reverses the process at the receiving end to recover the original analog signals. Thus, the transmitted information is a binary format with a 1 represented by a time slot of a set length with a pulse present. A 0 is represented by a time slot of a set length with no pulse present. The pulse is represented by a positive or negative voltage on the medium. Therefore, the presence or absence of pulses (voltages) conveys the information.

An example of this process is shown in Figure 2–6(e), for three channels. In this illustration, the solid bars represent the binary values of a PAM pulse for each sample. For example, the first sample in Channel 1 is a 142_{10}, the sample for Channel 2 is 36_{10}, and so on. Therefore, these solid bars can represent digital pulses on the line (i.e., voltages) and the lack of a solid bar represents binary zeros on the line (i.e., no voltage). The conversion process is now complete and the images represented in Figure 2–6(e) can be transmitted across the channel with relatively simple equipment, such as digital line drivers.

Moreover, since the shape of a pulse does not contain any information, the field repeaters may be regenerative. That is, they generate new pulses in place of old ones. Regenerative repeaters solve a major problem, called cumulative noise, that is associated with cable carrier systems. The receiver need only know the time slots that contain pulses. As we just learned, the absence or presence of pulses indicates the voltage level required to reproduce the amplitude for the PAM sample. The original analog signal can be reconstructed from the PAM samples at the receiving end if (a) they are sampled at the proper intervals (Nyquist Theorem) and (b) they are not distorted beyond recognition.

Sampling, Quantizing, and Encoding.   The process of creating a time division multiplexed PCM signal (derived from an analog-voice frequency voltage) requires three distinct operations: sampling, quantizing, and encoding. The PCM carrier channel banks (called D banks) perform these three steps, as shown in Figure 2–7. The channel bank is designed for 24 voice channels (in North America). Each channel supports one voice (analog) signal. The sampling takes place in the channel unit of the channel bank.

The channel unit contains AND logic gate-type circuitry. The AND gate requires two inputs for each output. One input is voice and the other is a clocking signal. Assume a person is talking on a particular channel

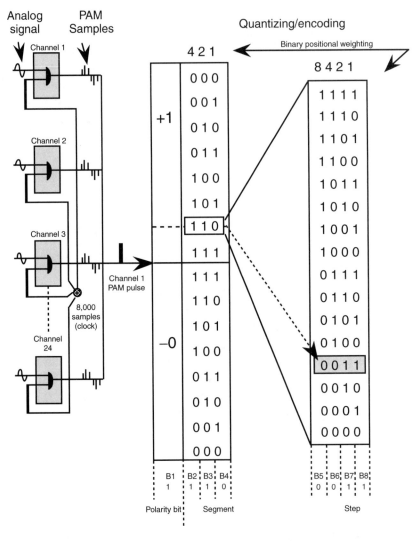

Figure 2–7   Segmented encoding.

unit. If the sampling clock is "looking" at that channel unit, the result will be an output from the gate (which is a PAM sample).

Sampling takes place at 8000 times per second using an analog-to-digital conversion process based on Nyquist sampling theory. The Nyquist sampling theorem states that when a signal is sampled instantaneously at the transmitter at regular intervals and at a rate at least twice the highest frequency in the channel, then the samples will contain sufficient information to allow an accurate reconstruction of the signal at the receiver. The voice bandwidth is 300 Hz to 3400 Hz. The accepted sampling rate in the industry is 8000 samples per second.

Next, the voltage amplitude of each sample, which may assume any value within the speech range, is assigned to the nearest associated value of a set of discrete values, where each value represents a certain voltage. This process is performed by the transmit board in the carrier channel bank and is known as quantizing. It is equivalent in mathematics to rounding off to the nearest whole number or integer. As a result, the PAM sample is rarely exact, which results in some distortion. This distortion can be measured and is called *quantizing noise* or *quantizing distortion*. The distortion is so minor that it is inaudible and poses no problem for voice communication. However, it can cause problems in data transmission, which is discussed later.

The third or final step *encodes* each discrete amplitude value into binary digital form, which equates to the quantum numerical value. Encoding is also performed by the transmit board in the carrier channel bank. PCM channel banks utilize an 8-bit binary word for each PAM sample. The bit utilization for signaling depends on the channel bank generation. (More will be said on this topic later.) Since eight bits are coded per sample, the bit rate for a conventional PCM signal is 64 kbit/s (sampling 8000 times per second × 8 bits = 64,000 bit/s). This signal is called a DS0 signal. (DS0 = digital signal at the zero level. Zero level is one channel and not a multiplexed channel.)

The distortion in the quantization is a function of the differences between the quantized steps. Ideally, one would like to use many quantizing steps in order to reduce the quantizing noise. Studies show that 2048 uniform quantizing steps provide sufficient "granularity" to represent the voice signal accurately. However, 2048 steps requires an 11-bit code (2^{11}), which translates into 88000 bit/s (8000 × 11). Since the voice signals in a telephone system can span 30 dB of variation, it makes sense to vary the distribution of the quantization steps. The variable quantizing levels reduce the quantizing noise.

As shown in Figures 2–7 and 2–8, this technique represents small amplitude signals with large step assignments to portions of high and low PAM signals. Smaller quantizing steps are used for intervals between those steps. The quantization error is reduced as the PAM signal level is reduced. As a consequence, a constant signal-to-distortion (S/D) ratio is maintained over a wide range of PAM signals.

However, if an acceptable signal-to-distortion (S/D) performance of the signal distribution is to be maintained, a logarithmic compression

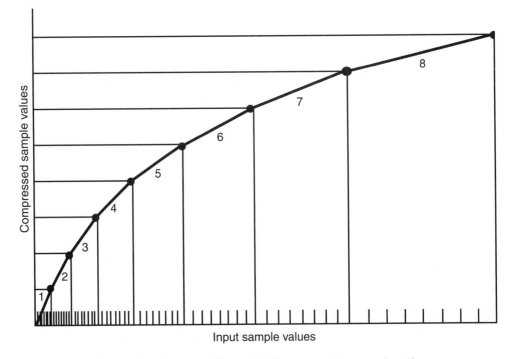

Figure 2–8   Companding with 8-segment approximation.

law must be used. The coding process to modify companding to make it near-linear for low sound levels is defined by a relationship in the form of the μ-law, or mu-law (used in North America and Japan), and the A-law (used in Europe). The laws are quite similar except that the A-law uses a truly linear relationship in the small-amplitude range. The minimum step size is 2/4096 for the A-law and 2/8159 for the μ-law. Thus, the A-law is inferior to the μ-law in the context of signal quality. In either case, the segments representing the low range of PAM signals are more accurately encoded than the segments pertaining to the high range of PAM signals.

The A-law functions similarly to the μ-law characteristic. Eight positive and eight negative segments exist as in the μ-law characteristic, but it is described as the 13-segment law.

As seen in the bottom part of Figure 2–7, the code of μ 255 PCM consists of: (1) a one bit polarity where 1 = a positive sample value and 0 = a negative sample value, (2) a 3-bit segment identifier(s), and (3) a 4-bit quantizing step identifier.

Segment Approximation

The nonlinear companding explained in the previous section is actually implemented in a stepwise linear process. For the μ-law, the m = 255 is used and the companding value is coded by a set of eight straight-line segments that cut across the compression curve (actually eight for negative segments and eight for positive segments; since the two center segments are collinear, they are considered one).

Figure 2–8 shows the segment approximation. With this approach, each segment is double the amplitude range of its preceding segment, and each segment is also one-half the slope of the preceding segment.

PCM Algorithms: μ-Law and A-Law

Newer techniques compress the higher amplitude signals to a smaller amplitude range for a given number of quantization levels. In other words, the smaller amplitude signals are expanded. On input, more gain is imparted to weak signals than to strong signals, which increases the number of available quantization levels and decreases the overall quantization distortion. After the signal is decoded, it is restored to its original amplitude level. The combination of compressing and expanding is called companding. In effect, large quantization intervals are assigned to large samples, and small quantization intervals are assigned to small samples.

The distortion in the quantization is a function of the differences between the quantized steps. This technique represents small amplitude PAM signals by larger coding variations than similar changes in large amplitude PAM signals; that is, more quantizing steps are used for low amplitude signals. The quantization error is reduced as the PAM signal level is reduced. As a consequence, a constant signal-to-distortion (S/D) ratio is maintained over a wide range of PAM signals.

However, if an acceptable S/D performance of the signal distribution is to be maintained, a logarithmic compression law must be used. Two common methods of modifying a true logarithmic law are described herein.

The coding process to modify companding to make it near-linear for low sound levels is defined in [BELL82]:

μ-law:

$$F_m^{-1}(y) = \text{sgn}(y)\, \frac{1}{m}\, [(1 + m)^{|y|} - 1]$$

where: y = the compressed value = $F_m(x)$ $(-1 \leq \times \leq 1)$; sgn (y) = the polarity of y; m = the companding parameter.

A-law:

$$F_A(x) = \text{sgn}(x) \quad \frac{A\,|x|}{1 + \ln(A)} \qquad 0 \le x \le 1/A$$

$$F_A(x) = \text{sgn}(x) \quad \frac{1 + \ln\,|A\,x|}{1 + \ln(A)} \quad 1/A \le x \le 1$$

Table 2–2 shows the bit and byte patterns for these systems [ASCO94].

OTHER ANALOG-TO-DIGITAL TECHNIQUES

Differential PCM (DPCM) and Adaptive DPCM (ADPCM)

Today's systems have more sophisticated approaches than the conventional PCM technique. One system that is an improvement over PCM is differential pulse code modulation (DPCM). It is not used in commercial systems today, but we will explain it here to lay the groundwork for other systems that are in use.

As illustrated in Figure 2–9(a), this technique encodes the differences between samples of the signal instead of the actual samples. Since an analog waveform's samples are closely correlated with each other (almost sample-to-sample redundancy), the range of sample differences requires fewer bits to represent the signal. Studies reveal that

Table 2–2 Comparison of µ-law and A-law.

Coded Numerical Value	Bit Number		
	µ-law 12345678	A-law 12345678	
+127	10000000	11111111	The left-most bit (Bit 1) is transmitted first, and
+96	10011111	11100000	is the most significant bit (MSB). This bit is
+ 64	10111111	11000000	known as the "sign" bit, and is a 1 for positive
+32	11011111	10100000	values and a 0 for negative values (both PCM
0	11111111	10000000	types).
0	01111111	00000000	
−32	01011111	00100000	Bits 2 through 8 are inverted between A-Law
−64	00111111	01000000	and µ-law PCM.
−96	00011111	01100000	
−126	00000001	01111110	In A-Law, all even bits (2, 4, 6, etc.) are inverted
−127	00000000	01111111	prior to transmission. The zero-energy code of 00000000 is actually sent as 01010101 (hex *55*).

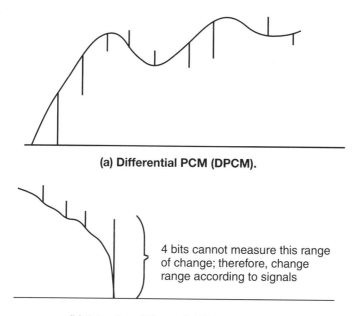

(a) Differential PCM (DPCM).

4 bits cannot measure this range of change; therefore, change range according to signals

(b) Adaptive differential PCM (ADPCM).

Figure 2–9   Differential PCM (DPCM) and Adaptive Differential (ADPCM).

the predictability between adjacent 8 kHz samples is 85% or higher. This redundancy in the PCM codes can be exploited to reduce the bit rate.

However, DPCM is subject to errors when an input signal changes significantly between samples. The DPCM equipment is not able to code the change accurately, which results in large quantizing errors and signal distortion.

The DPCM technology is enhanced by assigning 4 -bit signals to represent different ranges of the signal (see Figure 2–9(b)). For example, 4 bits can be coded to represent a change between samples. This technique is called adaptive differential PCM (ADPCM), because the systems increase or decrease the volume range covered by each 4-bit sample value.

ADPCM uses a differential quantizer to store the previous sample in a sample-and-hold circuit. The circuit measures the change between the two samples and encodes the change. Differential PCM achieves a smaller voice digitization rate (VDR) than do the conventional PCM techniques (32 kbit/s, for example). These systems have seen extensive use in digital telephony.

Some DPCM systems use a feedback signal (based on previous samples) to estimate the input signal. These systems are called adaptive predictive DPCM. The technique is quite useful if the feedback signal varies from the input (due to quantization problems) and the next encoding sample automatically adjusts for the drift. Thus, the quantization errors do not accumulate over a prolonged period.

Many systems store more than one past sample value, with the last three sample values commonly used. The previous samples are then used to produce a more accurate estimate of the next input sample.

Since DPCM and ADPCM do not send the signal but the representation of the change from the previous sample, the receiver must have some method for knowing where the current level is. Due to noise, the level may vary drastically or during periods of speech silence (no talking), several samples may be zero. Periodically, the sender and receiver may be returned (referenced) to the same levels by adjusting them to zero.

Sub-Band ADPCM (SB-ADPCM)

ITU-T Recommendation G.722 describes another digitization scheme, called sub-band ADPCM. With this system, the frequency band is split into two sub-bands, and these two bands are then encoded using ADPCM techniques and combined into an aggregate rate of 64 kbit/s. This technology is well-suited for public carrier services, since it provides high-quality speech (0 Hz–7 kHz). It can be transmitted over existing DS0 or ISDN channels.

Delta Modulation (DM) and Continuously Variable Slope Delta Modulation (CVSD)

Another A/D, D/A technique is delta modulation (DM) (see Figure 2–10(a)). It uses only one bit for each sample and follows the same concepts of DPCM by exploiting the sample-to-sample redundancy of the speech signal.

Delta modulation measures the polarity of difference of successive samples and uses a 1 bit to indicate if the polarity is rising and a 0 bit to indicate if the signal is falling. A pulse train supplies pulses to a modulator, which adjusts the polarity of the pulses to coincide with the amplitude changes of the analog signal.

This technique actually approximates the derivative of the analog signal and not its amplitude. The signal is encoded as a "staircase" of up and down sequences at each sampling time. The digital code can later be

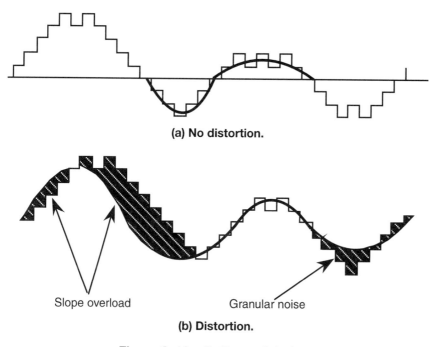

(a) No distortion.

Slope overload   Granular noise

(b) Distortion.

Figure 2–10   Delta modulation.

used to reconstruct the analog signal (analog-to-digital process) by
"smoothing" the staircase back to the original signal.

Delta modulation is simple to implement. However, it requires a
higher sampling rate than PCM or DPCM because each sample does not
carry much information. Many systems use 32,000 samples a second to
derive a 32 kbit/s digital signal.

Delta modulation assumes the encoded waveform is no more than
one step away from the sampled signal. However, a signal may change
more rapidly than the staircase modulator can reflect, producing a problem called slope overload (see Figure 2–10(b)). In contrast, a slow-
changing signal also creates distortions, called granular noise. The effect
of inaccurate representation of the waveform is called quantization noise
(it also occurs with PCM systems) and can be mitigated by measures that
are explained next.

One variation of delta modulation is continuously variable slope
delta modulation (CVSD), depicted in Figure 2–11. (Another term for this
technique is adaptive delta modulation.) CVSD transmits the difference
between two successive samples and employs a quantizer to change the
actual quantum steps based on a sudden increase or decrease of the

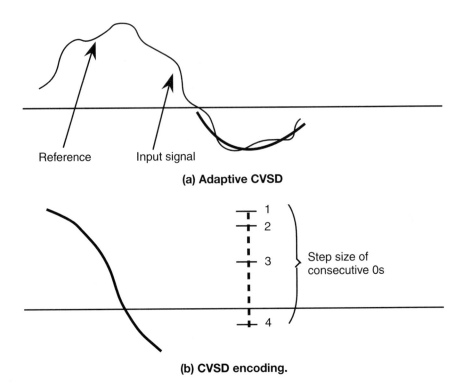

(a) Adaptive CVSD

(b) CVSD encoding.

Figure 2–11   Continuously variable slope delta modulation (CVSD).

signal. CVSD increases the staircase step size when it detects an increase in the waveform's slope and reduces the step size upon detecting a decrease in the slope.

CVSD does not send any information about the height of the curve (PCM) or the change in the height of the curve (ADPCM). It does send information about the changes in the shape of the curve.

A CVSD transmitter compares the input signal (its voltage) to a controlled reference signal. It increases or decreases the reference (bends up or bends down) if the input is greater or smaller than the reference. In effect, CVSD steers the reference signal to follow the input.

A CVSD receiver reconstructs the original signal by increasing the slope of the curve when a 1 is received and decreasing the slope when a 0 is received. A filter is then used to smooth the curve (waveform).

CVSD monitors the input signal for the occurrence of successive all ones (1111) or all zeros (0000). The former indicates the signal is rising too fast for the reference; the latter indicates the signal is falling too slowly for the reference. In other words, slope overload is occurring. These signals are used to produce an increased step-size voltage.

While CVSD systems exhibit some fidelity problems at the beginning of words and very strong syllables (slope overload), the technique generally produces high-quality signals. Some CVSD systems operate at rates less than 32 kbit/s with adequate (but poor quality) fidelity and crispness.

Voice Compression Techniques: Code Excited Linear Prediction

In addition to the waveform analysis techniques just discussed (such as PCM and delta modulation), the industry has devoted considerable research to a technique called parameter coding (or vocoding). Vocoders are not used on the telephone network because they are designed to encode speech signals only and cannot accommodate other analog signals, such as modem transmissions. In contrast, PCM can convey data or voice.

Vocoders do not preserve the character of the waveform; rather, the input waveform is processed into parameters that measure vocal characteristics. The speech is analyzed to produce a varying model of the waveform. Parameter coding then computes a signal that most closely resembles the original speech. These parameters are transmitted through the channel (or stored on disk) for later reproduction of the speech signal. Vocoders are commonly used for recorded announcements (e.g., weather information), voice output, and electronic video games.

Channel vocoders were developed in the late 1920s. Today the channel vocoders operate from a range of 1 to 2 kbit/s. These systems analyze the signal spectrum as a function of time. A series of band pass filters are used to separate the energy of speech into sub-bands. The bands are then filtered to determine the power levels relative to each other. The channel vocoders also determine the voiced and unvoiced nature of the pitched frequency of the input signal. The disadvantage of the channel vocoder is the difficulty of analyzing the pitch of the voice signal. Nonetheless, some of the vocoders today produce fairly high quality (if not synthetic) sound at 2400 bit/s.

In the past few years, voice compression techniques have given us the ability to carry voice images at bit rates as low as 2.4 kbit/s. One system is a variation of the channel vocoder, and is called the formant vocoder. This system takes advantage of the fact that most of the energy of speech is concentrated within a bandwidth of approximately 2 kHz. The formant vocoder encodes only the most significant short-time components of a voice signal. This technique provides a fairly intelligible speech signal with a fewer number of bits.

Linear predictive coding (LPC) is an example of vocoding. LPC is based on the fact that speech produces a vocal tract that is either voiced or voiceless. The vowel "e" in keep is a voiced sound; the "s" in sir is a voiceless sound. Both of these mechanisms are sampled to produce a stream of impulses. The impulses can then be stored as digital images for later use.

Another related technique is called vector quantization. (Variations of this technique are called code excited linear predictive coding, or code excited linear prediction [CELP], and vector-sum excited [LPC].) (See Figure 2–12.) The pattern of a speech signal is defined in 20 to 50 ms durations called speech segments or parcels. The segments are stored in a register in six PCM word blocks. These blocks are compared against a table of values (a code book). The entry in the table (library member) that is closest to the actual value is used as the transmitted value instead of the longer PCM block.

So, the library member whose value gives the best match to the signal is selected as the code word. The advantage of this approach is that each code word can be represented by fewer bits. For example, if a library has 4000 members, only 10 to 12 bits are required to represent and/or transmit the information about the full speech segment.

This technique is attractive because the codebook allows transmission at only 2.4 kbit/s. A high-quality 9.6 kbit/s telephone line supports

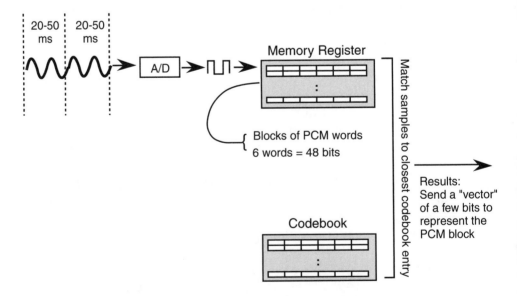

Figure 2–12   Vector quantization.

four time division multiplexed (TDM) 2.4 kbit/s LPC transmissions. This data rate is substantially lower than the waveform techniques of 64 kbit/s, 32 kbit/s, or 16 kbit/s. The main disadvantage of any type of compression is that the speech reproduction is not as high in quality as the PCM transmission quality.

NEWER DIGITAL VOICE SCHEMES

Voice compression is important in any system, but it is especially important in bandwidth-limited systems. As an example, in the new wireless mobile networks the voice signal is sampled every 20 ms, and 160 sampled values are stored in memory. These values are divided into four blocks of 40 samples each (each block is 5 ms), and the blocks are sorted in this order: 1,5,9 . . . 2,6,10 . . . 3,7,11 . . . 4,8,12, and so on. Using the code book method, the transmitter sends codes representing the differences between the sequences.

This approach produces a digitized voice signal of 13 kbit/s (260 bits every 20 ms = 13 kbit/s). However, due to the error-prone nature of mobile wireless links, this bandwidth requirement is more than doubled with the addition of error-correction and synchronization codes.

Convolutional Coding

If a certain amount of error can be tolerated on the channel, it is possible to reduce the amount of power required for the transmission of the signal, since a high-powered signal produces fewer errors than a low-powered counterpart. Convolutional coding provides the ability to correct certain errors at the receiver, and therefore permits a lower power transmitter than what would be required if convolutional coding were not used. The technique has been employed in conventional wire-based modems for a number of years (using Trellis Coding techniques), and is also applied to mobile modems.

Figure 2–13 is one example of convolutional coding. The k=9 value is the constraint length, which is the length of the register and one input bit. The R=1/2 value refers to the output of two symbols for every one input.

In a sense, the register has a memory: The symbol generated at each register shift is based on the new input bit, and the contents of the previous registers. This approach allows the receiver to perform a complemen-

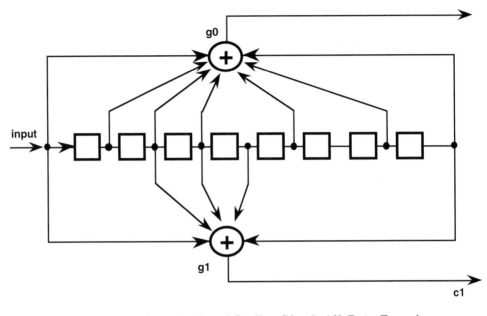

Figure 2–13   Convolutional Coding (K = 9, 1/2 Rate Encoder Example).

tary function and "correct" a bit if it does not fit with the expected results (the associated bits).

The Repetition Function

Another stage in many digital voice systems is the repetition function. As the name implies, it repeats the input data n times to equal an output rate of (say) 19.2 k symbols per second (ksps) for rate set 1, and (say) 28.8 ksps for rate set 2.[4] The number of times the data are repeated depends on the rate of the input to the repetition function. The effect of repetition is to add redundancy to the transmission, which helps combat the impairments to the bits that occur on (especially) mobile, wireless channels.

For example in some cellular phone systems, each convolutionally encoded symbol is repeated whenever the information rate is lower than 9600 bit/s (for 9600 bit/s, the code repetition rate is 1). If the code symbol is 4800 bit/s, the symbol is repeated one time (resulting in a code repeti-

---

[4]A symbol reflects the state of the signal during a specific time and is described in how many symbols (or different states) are represented per second. Each symbol is used to represent 1-n bits. The old term for symbol is baud.

tion rate of 2). If the data rate is 2400 bit/s, each code symbol is repeated three times (resulting in a code repetition rate of 4). For the 1200 bit/s rate, each symbol is repeated 7 times (resulting in a code repetition rate of 8). The idea is to provide a rate adaptation to have common input into the block interleaver.

Voice Quality Categories: A General View

A digital carrier service provider, such as a telephone company or an interchange carrier, must provide its customers with high-quality facilities.[5] Because this quality issue is so important, service providers have opted for systems that, while expensive, provide for superior voice quality characteristics.

In order to assess the quality of their facilities, carriers (and the manufacturers of the carriers' equipment) have developed voice quality categories. Table 2–3 provides one example of this practice.

Figure 2–14 shows voice quality categories just described in relation to the required bit rate, the type of coder, and the coding method.

Table 2–3   Voice quality categories.

Description	Characteristics
FM Broadcast	50 Hz–15 kHz. No perceptible noise.
High Fidelity	0 Hz–20 kHz. No noise.
AM Broadcast	50 Hz–6 kHz. No perceptible noise. Land lines may be equalized up to 8 kHz.
Toll Quality	200 Hz–3200 Hz. Standard telephone speech quality. Signal/noise ratio of > 30 dB, and total harmonic distortion below 2–3%.
Transparent Quality	Similar to toll quality. Difference can only be distinguished by direct A/B comparison.
Conversational Quality	Highly intelligible, but with noticeable distortion. Speaker can be understood and identified.
Synthetic Quality	More than 80% intelligibility. Sound is machine-like, and may not be able to identify the speaker.

---

[5]Sprint has capitalized on this aspect of digital carrier facilities with its commercials on the "pin drop" and the ability of a person to hear the sound of a pin dropping over a long distance circuit.

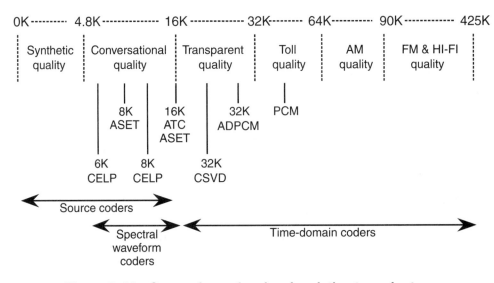

Figure 2–14   Comparison of coders in relation to coder type and signal quality.

THE NEW VOICE CODERS

Conserving Bandwidth with Voice Activity Detection (VAD)

The newer voice coders exploit the concept of silence suppression. The formal term for this operation is called voice activity detection (VAD). In silence suppression, packets are not sent when voice level activity falls below a certain threshold, which is about 50% of the time during a typical voice conversation.

This valuable tool, while reducing bandwidth consumption, can be a bit tricky to implement. It might lead to a problem called clipping, in which part of the speech is truncated and not carried in the VoIP packets. One way to combat clipping is to continue to sample and code the speech pattern and allocate the packet to the sample(s), but drop the packet if the voice energy does not meet a minimum threshold during an allotted time.

Table 2–4 shows the performances of several low bit-rate voice coders/decoders, as defined by the ITU-T. These machines are called codecs, a shortened form of coder/decoder. The column labeled "Voice BW (bandwidth) in kbit/s" is the bit rate of the codec, without the overhead of headers placed around the samples. The MOS (mean opinion score) is an assessment of the quality of the voice signal. Anything from 3.8–4.2 is

Table 2–4   Cisco support of ITU-T codecs.

ITU-T Codec Standard	Voice BW in kbit/s	MOS	Codec Delay in msec	Total BW, no VAD used	Total BW, VAD used
G.729	8.0	3.9	15.0	29.6	14.8
G.711	64.0	4.1	1.5	85.6	42.8
G.723.1	6.3	3.9	37.5	16.0	8.0
G.723.1	5.3	3.65	37.5	13.4	6.7

considered to be of acceptable quality. The next column contains the time it takes for the codec to process the voice sample. The key part of Table 2–4 are the last two columns. They show the bit rates for the traffic when VAD is not applied and when it is applied. The reason the bit rates in these columns are greater than those of the codec's output is because of the extra bits required for control headers (such as an IP header, in a voice over IP packet).

SUMMARY

The DS0 64 kbit/s rate has been the mainstay of digital networks since the 1960s, using conventional PCM techniques. Now, ADPCM and other techniques have become common, and 32, 16, 8 and 5 kbit/s systems are in place. These new systems provide equal quality to the PCM systems and allow more voice channels to be multiplexed onto the line.

APPENDIX 2A: CODING AND CODING VIOLATIONS

Chapter 4 examines the specific T1 coding schemes. For the newcomer, this appendix will lay the groundwork for that examination. The alternate mark inversion (AMI) code and duty cycle concepts are shown in Figure 2A–1. The reader may recognize this code as bipolar coding, and even though it is an old coding scheme, it is still used extensively in the industry.

A digital transmission system requires a 1 pulse to be sent as an opposite polarity from the preceding 1 pulse, regardless of the number of 0s between the two 1s (see Figure 2A–1(a)). The name alternate mark inversion is derived from the use of alternating polarities to represent binary 1s (marks).

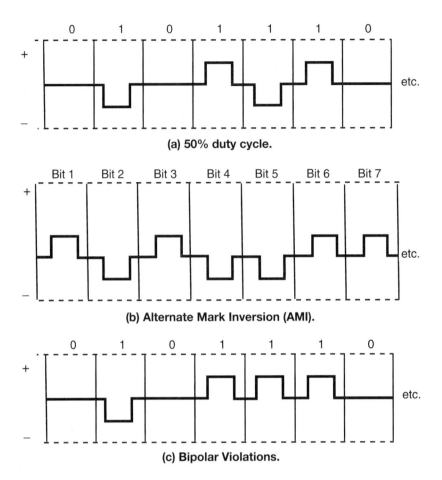

(a) 50% duty cycle.

(b) Alternate Mark Inversion (AMI).

(c) Bipolar Violations.

Figure 2A-1   Coding conventions.

This bipolar code performs well because it has no direct current (dc) component and therefore can be coupled with transformers. The scheme also makes efficient use of bandwidth. Figure 2A–1(b) illustrates a concept called the duty cycle, which describes how much of the time slot is taken by the pulse. The common practice in T1 systems is to employ a 50% duty cycle, which means the pulse takes up half of the slot time.

Most digital systems provide no separate clocking signal, a subject discussed at length in Chapter 3. The timing or clocking information is embedded in the data stream. At the receiving end, the clock is recovered from the data stream by the detection of 1 pulses. Obviously, if the data stream has insufficient 1 pulses embedded, the receiver can no longer produce reliable timing output.

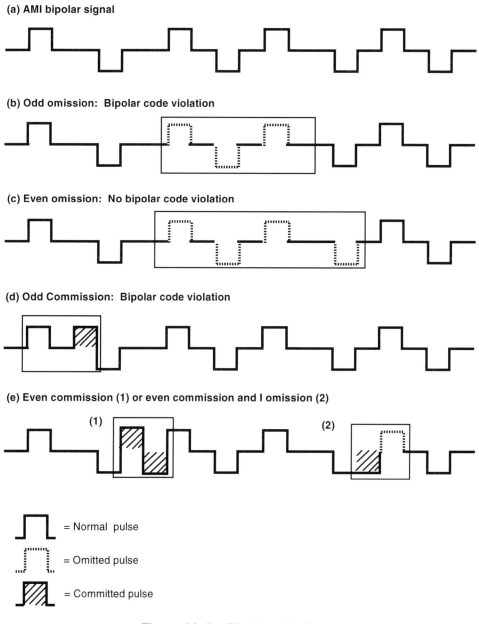

Figure 2A-2   Bipolar violations.

To overcome this problem, a certain number of 1s must be present to ensure proper timing. This concept is called 1s density. Most digital facilities require that no more than 15 contiguous 0s shall be present in the frame. An additional requirement is that there must be at least three 1s in every 24 bits. Moreover, T1 requires a ratio of no less than 12.5% of 1s versus 0s, even if the 15 consecutive 0 rule is met. Each pulse helps keep the clock aligned to a mid-bit sampling to eliminate or reduce systematic and waiting-time jitter. This convention is adequate to keep the receiver and the repeaters synchronized.

Due to noise, mechanical failures, and the like, the bits may become distorted, which can cause a "violation" of the AMI rule (see Figure 2A–1(c)). Bipolar violations or excessive errors are known as format errors because the errors are not in conformance with the required format.

A bit distortion may not cause a format error. As the examples in Figure 2A–2 show, the nature of the error determines if the bipolar violation is detected. The bipolar signal is altered with errors of omission (pulses are deleted) or errors of commission (pulses are added). The following possibilities exist:

- Odd omission: Creates a violation
- Even omission: Does not create a violation
- Odd commission: Creates a violation
- Even commission: Does not create a violation, or creates two violations

It is evident that, at best, only 50% of the errors can be detected. Unfortunately, the percentage is even worse if the signal passes through certain equipment before reaching the receiver. To illustrate, a T1 multiplexer may multiplex together two signals in which a code violation exists in each. In effect, the two errors "mask" each other when the multiplexer logic combines the signals into a single multiplexed stream.

The signal can be tested, but the transmission line must be taken out of service. Moreover, the majority of errors are transient in nature, and the testing routines often do not find any problem.

The errored bits cause problems in voice transmission, especially if the frame's control bits are corrupted. For data transmissions, the corruption is even more serious. Clearly, the problem begs for a solution, and later discussions in Chapter 4 examine several enhancements to address this problem.

3

Timing and Synchronization in Digital Networks

This chapter explains the synchronization and clocking functions used in T1 and SONET networks. Asynchronous, plesiochronous, and synchronous networks are examined. Clock variations and controlled and uncontrolled slips are analyzed and compared to each other. After these subjects are covered, systems that are pertinent to SONET are examined.

Since timing and synchronization are vital to a digital network, this topic is introduced early in this book. Because of the nature of the subject, it is necessary to use several terms and concepts that are covered in more detail in later chapters. Our approach is to give you enough information to understand timing and synchronization in relation to these terms and concepts, then concentrate on them later.

TIMING AND SYNCHRONIZATION IN DIGITAL NETWORKS

With the advent of digital networks and the transmission and reception of binary pulses (1s and 0s), it became important to devise some method for detecting these signals accurately at the receiver. Figure 3–1 illustrates the problem.

The ideal system is one in which the binary pulses arrive at the receiver in a very precise and concise manner. This means that the receiver knows the exact time that the signal (a binary 1 or 0) manifests itself at the receiver interface. This synchronization between the transmitter and

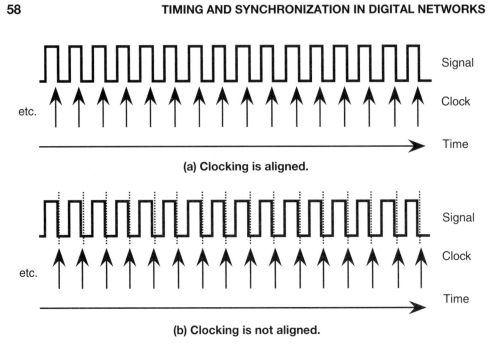

(a) Clocking is aligned.

(b) Clocking is not aligned.

Figure 3–1   Clocking and phase variation.

receiver is achieved when these machines know about each other's "clock," that is, at which frequency the sending machine sends its traffic to the receiving machine. Fortunately, it is a relatively easy task to determine this timing, because the receiver can derive (extract) the clock from the incoming bit stream by examining when the pulses arrive at the receiver. For example, in Figure 3–1(a), the signal and the clock are perfectly aligned when the signal reference mark occurs with the zero crossing in the physical clock wave form [REID95]. However, errors can occur if the clock is not aligned with the signal, as seen in Figure 3–1(b). This problem is usually called phase variation, and may translate into an incorrect interpretation of the binary 1s and 0s in the transmission stream.

Therefore, it is not enough that signals be aligned in the same frequency domain (the same rate of ticking at the clocks). The signals must also be aligned in the phase domain (the same instant the clocks emit the tick).

In older systems that operate at a relatively low bit rate, the clocking did not have to be very accurate because the signal on the line did not change very often (see Figure 3–2(a)). There is an inverse relationship between the number of bits on a channel (in a second) and the length of time the bit manifests itself at a receiver. For example, a signaling rate of

2400 times per second translates into a bit interval of 416 µsec (1 sec/ 2400 = .000416).

As the digital networks became faster and more bits were transmitted per second, the time the bits were on the channel decreased significantly (see Figure 3–2(b)). This meant that if there were a slight inaccuracy in the timing of the receiver's sampling clock, it might not detect a bit or, more often, it might not detect several bits in succession. This situation leads to a problem called slips. Slipping is the loss of timing and the resultant loss of the detection of bits.

Figure 3–2(c) shows some examples of the relationship between transmission speeds (in bits per second) and the related signaling interval. The first four entries in the list are the lower speed V Series modems published by the ITU-T. The 2400 baud example is the rate used by the newer V Series modems, such as V.29, V.32, and V.32 bis. Baud is the rate of signal change on the channel, also known as the symbol rate, unit interval, or signaling interval. These modems code multiple bits per baud and therefore achieve a higher bit rate than the symbol rate. The last entry in the list is the signaling rate for a T1 system: 1,544,000, which translates into a .000000648 second (648 µsec) signaling interval.

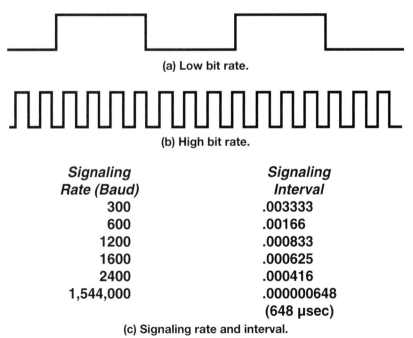

(a) Low bit rate.

(b) High bit rate.

Signaling Rate (Baud)	Signaling Interval
300	.003333
600	.00166
1200	.000833
1600	.000625
2400	.000416
1,544,000	.000000648 (648 µsec)

(c) Signaling rate and interval.

Figure 3–2   Signaling rate and signaling interval.

EFFECT OF TIMING ERRORS

The effect of timing errors (that result in bit errors) on the application depends upon the type of traffic. For data, the result may be reduced throughput, since a protocol at the sending machine will likely be required to retransmit the data. If modems are being employed, a timing error can result in a modem carrier drop. Certain types of encrypted data will require the resending of an encryption/decryption key. A fax transmission might result in a missing line or lines, or a distorted page. Errors in traffic containing video images may result in picture freezes or picture dropouts. The loss of voice images may result in an audible click at the receiver. Whatever the effect upon the application, it is desirable to reduce or eliminate timing problems and errors.

THE CLOCKING SIGNAL

In its simplest terms, a clocking signal carries information about time. As we explained earlier, this information is represented by the signal crossing a reference mark—in Figure 3–1, for example, when the signal crosses a certain voltage level. This crossing allows the receiver to determine when the clocking signals occur.

We just learned that different terms are used to describe the clocking signal. The one used in most literature is the unit interval (UI), which corresponds to one cycle of the clocking signal. Another term is the phase, which is measured in radians (and 1 UI = 2π radians). UI is equal to the reciprocal of the data rate. As examples, one UI for a DS1 1.544 Mbit/s rate is 648 nsec and one UI for a DS3 44.736 Mbit/s rate is about 22 nsec.

Timing (or Synchronization) Distribution

The operation of network synchronization, in which all nodes in the network are timed from the same clock source is known as either central timing distribution or central synchronization distribution. However, the idea of one single timing source (a central network clock) is not practical, since thousands of networks exist throughout the world in different countries, administered by different network operators. Consequently, there are many master clocks, yet they are sufficiently accurate that the frequency and phase differences between them are very small. There are still differences though, however small. Thus, the so-called synchronized networks can still experience timing errors. Nonetheless, the usual approach is to rely on a central clocking source in a network and have the other nodes base their timing operations on this source.

Clocking Rules

During the remainder of this chapter, you should keep the following general clocking rules in mind:

- Clocks should derive their timing reference from a clock that is a more accurate source (and never from a less accurate source).
- The number of cascaded clocks (nodes deriving their clocks from other nodes) should be minimized.
- A stratum level 3 clock (explained shortly) must have the stability characteristic such that when a stratum 3 entity is in a holdover mode, a link to a stratum 2 or 3 entity will not incur more than 255 slips during 24 hours following the loss of all reference links.
- Additionally, the average deviation from the nominal frequency over the first 24 hour period must be less than 3.7×10^{-7}. This characteristic equates to about 0.6 Hz at 1.544 MHz.

TYPES OF TIMING IN NETWORKS

Plesiochronous and Asynchronous Networks

The systems that existed in the early 1950s and 1960s were not synchronized to any common frequency source because they consisted of analog circuits and did not need a precise timing setup. However, as digital networks were deployed, and especially with the advent of the T1 technology, timing became a greater concern.

These early digital networks were not synchronized to a common frequency, and thus they were called asynchronous networks. Each machine in the network ran its own "free-running clock," and the clocks between two machines could vary by many unit intervals.

Today, T1 systems are plesiochronous because the timing is tightly controlled. The term plesio means "nearly." Each T1 portion of the network, as shown in Figure 3–3, is synchronized to a highly accurate primary reference source (PRS) clock. Because of the superior level of performance and the fact that this technique is fairly inexpensive, PRS clocks are a cost-effective way to improve network performance. In Figure 3–3, a portion of this network is referenced with PRS x and another

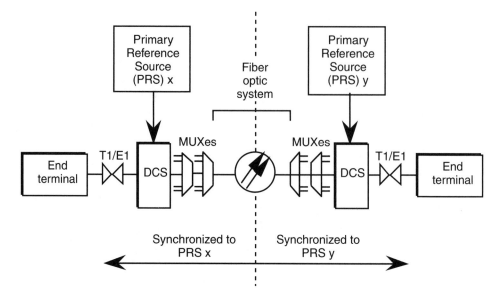

Figure 3–3   Plesiochronous networks [BLAI88].

portion is synchronized with PRS y. Thus, the term plesiochronous distinguishes this type of network from truly synchronous networks that have only one PRS. The distinction between synchronous and plesiochronous is not used much today.

Synchronous Networks

As we explained in Chapter 1, the synchronous network is distinguished by the use of one PRS, which is also known as the master clock. As shown in Figure 3–4, all components derive their clocking from this master clock. Timing is derived first from the master clock, and then from a slave (in this example, a toll office). The timing is then passed to digital switches, digital cross-connects, end offices, and so on. Therefore, timing is "cascaded down" to other equipment, such as channel banks and multiplexers.

Figure 3–4 also shows the employment of different types of clocks, called stratum n clocks. Each stratum n clock is required to perform within a certain degree of accuracy. The stratum 1 clock must meet the most stringent timing requirements whereas the stratum 4 clock need only meet the least stringent requirements.

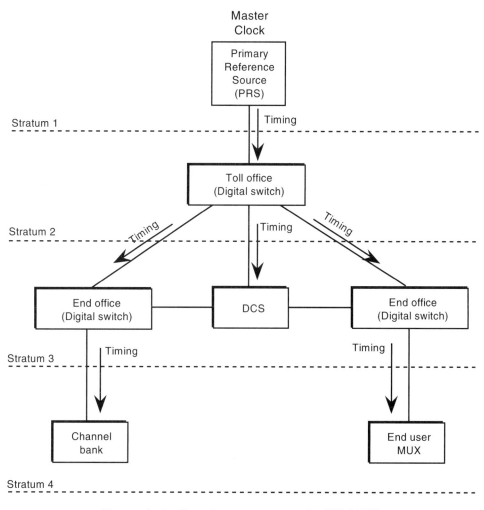

Figure 3–4   Synchronous networks [BLAI88].

The Synchronous Clock Hierarchy

Table 3–1 summarizes the synchronous network clock hierarchy and shows long-term accuracy for each stratum level, as well as typical locations of the clocking operations. Long-term accuracy for stratum 1 clocks is $\pm1.0 \times 10^{-11}$. The next level of accuracy is the stratum 2 clock, which is usually located in class 4 toll offices. The long-term accuracy for these clocks is $\pm1.6 \times 10^{-8}$. Next in the order of accuracy are the stratum 3 clocks typically located in the class 5 end office or a digital cross-connect system (DCS). The long-term accuracy of these clocks is $\pm4.6 \times 10^{-6}$. The

Table 3–1 Clock hierarchy for synchronous networks.

Clock Stratum	Typical Location(s)	Free Run Accuracy (Minimum)
1	Primary Reference Source (PRS)	$\pm 1.0 \times 10^{-11}$*
2	Class 4 office	$\pm 1.6 \times 10^{-8}$
3 and 3E[1]	Class 5 office, DCS	$\pm 4.6 \times 10^{-6}$
4 and 4E[1]	Channel bank, end-user mux	$\pm 32 \times 10^{-6}$

* = Also annotated as .00001 ppm (parts per million)

[1]Stratum 3E and 4E clocks are not part of ANSI standards (ANSI T1.101). They are used by Bellcore (GF-1244-CORE) and stipulate more stringent requirements with regard to wander and holdover (a loss of a previously connected external reference). These enhanced clocks are compatible with the ANSI T1–101 clocks.

last level of the synchronous network clock hierarchy is the stratum 4 clock. These clocks are usually located in channel banks or multiplexers at the end-user site. Their accuracy is $\pm 32 \times 10^{-6}$.

Summary and Clarification of Terms

The terms asynchronous networks, plesiochronous networks, synchronous networks, and (a new term) mesochronous networks are used in a variety of ways. To be precise, an asynchronous network is one in which timing between the network elements is not maintained. If the timing is maintained between the components, then is it not very accurate. As an extreme example, asynchronous data communications protocols have no common clocks but derive their timing from separate start and stop bits in the data stream.

In contrast, a synchronous network is one in which the network elements are aligned together with precise timing arrangements. All the payloads can be traced back to a common reference clock.

Another term used to describe a precisely timed network or networks is plesiochronous. The term is derived from plesio, a Greek term meaning "nearly". Many networks are actually plesiochronous networks in that they do not use synchronous timing, but very precise timing with variances that must fall within a very narrow range. AT&T uses this term to describe a system with multiple reference clocks. In summary, a plesiochronous network is a system in which the network elements are timed by different clocks achieving nearly the same timing.

A mesochronous network is used by some people to describe another type of clocking system. Strictly speaking, a mesochronous network's elements are timed to the same source, and all elements are exactly the

Table 3–2   Timing in networks.

Asynchronous network:
  • Network components are not synchronized to any clock. Each component runs with its own free-running clock.

Synchronous network:
  • Network components (and payload) are *traced* back to a common reference clock, perhaps through more than one clock. Timing is very precise.

Mesochronous network:
  • All components are timed to *one* single clock source. All timing is exactly the same.

Plesiochronous network:
  • Components are timed by separate clocks, but the clocks are almost the same.

---

same; in other words, an ideal world. Mesochronous networks are expensive, and hard to achieve. The four types of network timing are summarized in Table 3–2.

TIMING VARIATIONS

While synchronous networks exhibit very accurate timing, some variation will exist between the network elements within a network as well as network elements between networks. This variation is generally known as phase variation. Phase variation is defined as e(nt) [REID95], where t is the clock period, which is described as the continuous function of time, e(t). Phase variation is measured in UI, radians, or ns. Although phase variation can occur in synchronous networks, it is more of a problem in plesiochronous and asynchronous networks.

Phase variation, (e)t, is usually divided into jitter and wander. Jitter is defined as a short-term variation in the phase of a digital signal that includes all variations above 10 Hz. In effect, jitter is the short term for variation of the digital signal's optimal position in time. Causes of jitter include common noise, the bit stuffing processes in multiplexers, or faulty repeaters.

In contrast, wander is the long-term variation in the phase of a signal and includes all phase variations below 10 Hz. Wander may also include the effects of frequency departure, which is a constant frequency difference between network elements. Wander is almost inevitable in any network due to the slight variations in clock frequency differences, transmission delay on the path, or bit stuffing operations.

Jitter and wander are dealt with in many digital networks through the use of buffers. These buffers exist at each interface in any machine where the signal is processed (multiplexed, switched, etc.). Buffers act as windows to receive and transmit traffic. Additionally, for digital systems, they can be used to accommodate to frequency departure or phase variations. Buffers are carefully designed to handle the most common variations.

Frequency Accuracy

Most systems in North America describe clocking accuracy as the degree that a clock's frequency deviates from its ideal value. It is defined as:

$$FF_{os} = (f - f_d)/f_d$$

where FF_{os} = fractional frequency offset, f = actual frequency output of a clock, and f_d = ideal or desired frequency.

Dealing with the Timing Problems

A variety of methods are employed to deal with the timing problems just discussed. They are broadly classified as (a) elastic store, (b) phase-locked loop (PLL), and (c) a centralized network clock.

Elastic Store or Slip Buffer. Figure 3–5 provides an example of how a machine can establish synchronization between an incoming signal and an outgoing signal. Traffic is accepted from an input line and written into a buffer based on the frequency of the incoming signal. A locally generated clock determines the read frequency to this buffer. This read determines when the contents (1s and 0s) are placed onto an output line. This buffer is often called an elastic store because it is used to accommodate the different frequencies of the read and write operations. Other people call it a slip buffer. For example, if "writing into the buffer" is done more quickly than "reading from the buffer," then the buffer will overflow (the write operations overtake the read operations).

To handle this potential problem, a common practice is to read from the buffer at a slightly higher rate than the maximum expected write rate (which is the maximum rate sent from a transmitting machine). With this approach, the write operation cannot overtake the read. Periodically, the read is halted, and a bit is stuffed in the stream to handle the timing difference between the read and write operations. All inputs are read by the same clock, and their streams are bit-stuffed to equal a common rate, so they are synchronized together.

Phase-Locked Loop. Another approach used to deal with timing problems is the phase-locked loop (PLL). This technique keeps an ac-

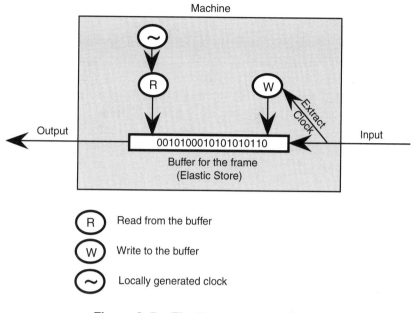

Figure 3–5   Elastic store operations.

count of the arrival of the bits and averages the arrival rate over a period of time. This average is used to generate a clock. PLL techniques are in use today and some SONET-based systems use this approach.

Centralized Network Clock.   The best solution to timing problems is to use a highly accurate network clock to serve as the primary reference source (PRS). This approach is simple, and overcomes the problems of slip buffers and PLL.

The next section explains in more detail how the slip operation is performed, since it is a prevalent technique used in many T1 systems. The subsequent sections of this chapter explain more sophisticated clocking mechanisms used in SONET.

SLIP OPERATIONS IN MORE DETAIL

Slips—Controlled and Uncontrolled

Buffers accommodate to problems in frequency departure and phase variation by either underflowing or overflowing. An underflowing buffer will repeat a block of data to compensate for slow timing. In contrast, an overflow buffer will throw away a block of data to accommodate to faster timing. Underflow or overflow operations are known collectively as slip. Obviously, slips result in errors within the network because the overflowing or underflowing results in either a frame being deleted in the transmission stream or being repeated.

Slips are either controlled or uncontrolled, the former being desirable and the later being highly undesirable. As stated, underflow and overflow buffers can result in a controlled slip. This term is used because this slip results in the deleting or repeating of a full frame (of 192 bits). This operation is possible because a buffer is actually larger than a frame size. The extra buffer space allows the most leeway to prevent frequency departure from creating slips on back-to-back frames.

As shown in Figure 3–6, the effect of a controlled slip results in one T1 frame being discarded or added, which means that 24 DS0 slots are deleted or added. Fortunately, these controlled slips do not affect the framing bit (the F bit) and therefore do not propagate to any subsequent back-to-back frames.

The reader may have noticed a controlled slip occurring occasionally in a voice circuit, which can usually be detected by a very quick popping or clicking sound. This rare aberration is usually only mildly irritating on a voice signal. For data signals, however, it results in the loss of data. Additionally, if (for example) a network element such as a DCS loses its master clock, it then must fall back to its internal clock, which is typically a stratum 3 clock. Loss of the master clock can result in a dramatic drop in the quality of the line and an increase in the bit error rate. Evidence has shown that, in the worst case, a DS0 channel will experience problems every 13 seconds when utilizing stratum 3 clocks.

The uncontrolled slip is also known as a change of frame alignment (COFA) or an unframed buffer slip (see Figure 3–7). This event occurs if only a portion of a frame is either repeated or deleted, and is the result of using unframed buffers.

Unframed buffers, while having the potential to present more problems, are used because they are less expensive than framed buffers. They are smaller (which decreases latency [delay] in the machine), and they are used in asynchronous multiplexers as a matter of course.

COFAs are the result of excessive jitter and wander of the inputs to the asynchronous multiplexers or any machine which uses unframed buffers. COFA affects multiple frames. The number of frames that are affected depends on how long it takes the receiving device to perform reframing operations (realigning onto a full frame). In many systems, the uncontrolled slip can result in an error of several thousand bits—some 40 to 50 times more serious than a controlled slip.

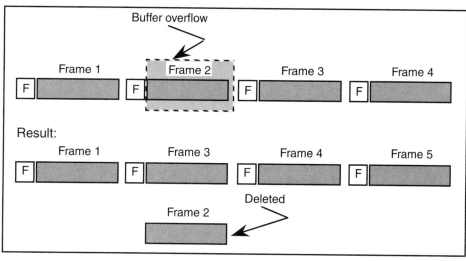

(a) Overflow.

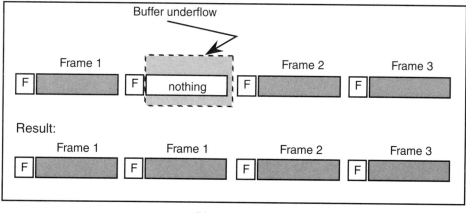

(b) Underflow.

Figure 3–6   Controlled slips for overflow and underflow.

Bit or Clock Slips

Another form of slip that exists in digital networks is called a bit slip or clock slip. This problem describes a phase variation of only one UI. For example, a T1 that operates at 1.544 MHz could experience a bit slip of 0.648 μsec. Figure 3–8 shows an example of a bit slip using differential Manchester code.

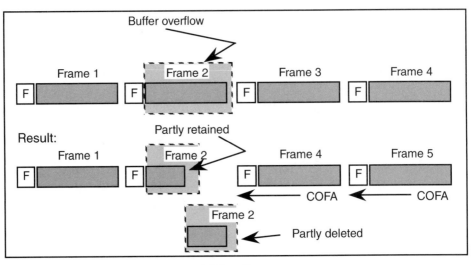

(a) Overflow.

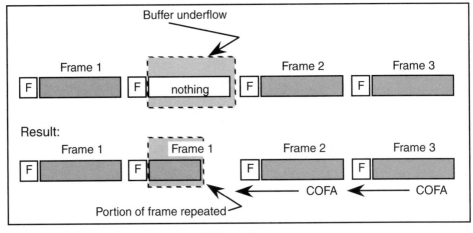

(b) Underflow.

Figure 3–7   Uncontrolled slips for overflow and underflow.

FREQUENCY DEPARTURES AND ACCURACIES

A one part per million (ppm) frequency departure is equivalent to a one µsec phase variation. In a T1 system, frequency departure can result in a control slip every 125 seconds. This value is derived from: 125 µsec/1 µsec = 125. Consequently, in a 24-hour day (in which 86,400 seconds exist) a 1 ppm network can experience 691 slips (86400/125 = 691).

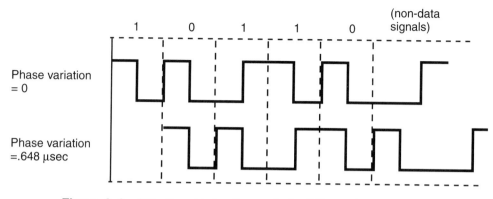

Figure 3–8   Bit slips. Note: Example is differential manchester code (used in several LANs).

Given these performance statistics, Table 3–3(a) shows the required Bellcore (GR-1244-CORE) performance of stratum 1, 2, 3, and 4 clocks with regard to wander, bit slips, and controlled frame slips. In the column labeled Controlled Frame Slips, derivation is shown with the four footnotes at the bottom of the figure. Please note the following points:

- 1 ppm frequency departure is equivalent to 1 µsec phase variation
- Frequency departure = 1 controlled slip every 125 seconds, where 125 µsec/1 µsec = 125
- With 86,400 seconds in a day, 1 ppm = 691 slips per day 86,400/125 = 691

Table 3–3(a)   Stratum clock requirements and performance examples.

Frequency Offset (ppm)	Wander (0.12 µsec increments)	"Bit Slips"	Controlled Frame Slips
00001 (stratum 1)	3.3 hr	18 hr	20.6 wk[1]
.016 (stratum 2)	7.5 sec	41 sec	2.17 hr[2]
4.6 (stratum 3)	26 ms	140 ms	27 sec[3]
32 (stratum 4)	4 ms	20 ms	3.9 sec[4]

[1] 125 / .00001 / 60 sec (per min) / 60 min (per hr) / 24 hr (per day) / 7 days (per wk)
  20.6 wk
[2] 125 / .016 / 60 sec (per min) / 60 min (per hr) = 2.17 hr
[3] 125 / 4.6 = 27.1 sec
[4] 125 / 32 = 3.9 sec

Table 3–3(b)　Other requirements.

Stratum	Holdover Stability	Pull-in/Hold-in Range
1	N/A	N/A
2	$\pm1 * 10-^{10}$/day	$\pm1.6 \times 10^{-8}$
3E	$\pm1 \times 10^{-10}$/day*	$\pm4.6 \times 10^{-6}$
3	<255 slips ($\pm3.7 \times 10-^{7}$)*	$\pm4.6 \times 10^{-6}$
SONET	Under study	$\pm20 \times 10^{-6}$
4E	NA	$\pm32 \times 10^{-6}$
4	NA	$\pm32 \times 10^{-6}$

Legend

Holdover:　　　Operating condition of a clock once it has lost a previously connected clocking reference. During this time the machine must exhibit the stability cited in this column.

Pull-in range:　The largest band of input signal frequency for which the clock will acquire lock. Assures that synchronization can be achieved with a clock of equal stratum level that may be operating at the limits of its permissible frequency offset, while the clock under test is operating at the opposite frequency offset limit.

Hold-in range:　The largest band of input signal frequency for which the clock will maintain lock. Specified so that a clock of a given stratum level will be able to maintain lock with a reference from a clock of the same stratum level as the upstream clock varies in frequency.

*For initial 24 hr

In addition to the requirements cited above, Bellcore establishes the following requirements for holdover stability and the pull-in/hold-in range (see Table 3–3(b)).

METHODS OF CLOCK EXCHANGE

Clearly, it is in the best interest of all concerned to use a common clocking source for all machines in the network. Some systems use this approach and some systems do not. This part of the chapter expands on our earlier discussions about clocking and describes several methods of achieving synchronization between machines.

Five methods of clock exchange can be employed in a network. They are as follows: (1) free-running, (2) line-timed, (3) loop-timed, (4) external, and (5) through-timed. Some systems use a combination of these methods. The reader should check vendors' offerings carefully, because each vendor most likely uses these operations in slightly different ways. In addition, the design of each network element may place limitations on how some of the clocking distributions operations are implemented.

Free-Running

The free-running method has each machine generate its own timing from a (highly stable) crystal oscillator. In most systems, this oscillator has a long-term accuracy better than ±4.6 ppm. Figure 3–9 shows a free-running/free-running configuration. We use the term free-running twice to connote that both machines on the line are running with an oscillator. With this approach, no external clocking source is used, which has its advantages and disadvantages. The advantage is the obviation of the expense of connecting to an external timing source. The disadvantage is the requirement for buffers to compensate for the delta between clock differences (i.e., an incoming DS3 signal and the outgoing signal to the other machine). Nonetheless, this approach is quite effective for point-to-point linear configurations with asynchronous (in this example, DS3) interfaces.

Line-Timed

The line-timed mode derives clocking from the signal on the incoming line. The clock extraction from this signal is fed into the local timing generator module, which in turns provides the timing to the outgoing signals. This configuration is shown in Figure 3–10. Line-timed mode is simple, but it does not perform very well in configurations where several machines are connected linearly to each other in a path. Clocking inaccuracies tend to accumulate at each node, and can lead to distorted signals.

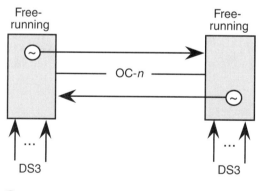

 = Free-running oscillator

Figure 3–9   Free-running/free-running configuration.

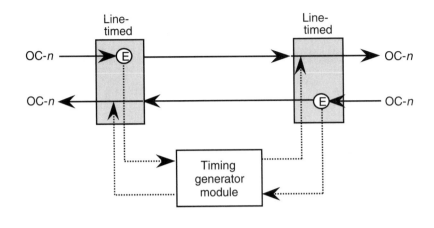

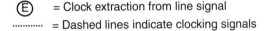

Ⓔ   = Clock extraction from line signal
.... = Dashed lines indicate clocking signals

Figure 3–10   Line-timed configuration.

Loop-Timed

Loop-timed mode is also called gateway or master/slave mode. It is used in systems where different timing generator modules are employed or where machines tied to different stratum levels must interact with each other.[2] The frequency sent from the master unit (in Figure 3–11(a), the free-running unit) is used to derive the clock at the slave unit (in Figure 3–11(a), the loop-timed unit). The slave unit loops the receive clock back across the line as the transmit clock. The loop-timed mode may also employ an external clock, as shown in Figure 3–11(b). The external clock is typically a stratum 3 level clock or better. This configuration in this figure is also called the phase-locked/loop-timed mode. Another configuration is shown in Figure 3–11(c). The slave unit can also furnish clocking utilizing a building integrated timing supply (BITS, described later in this chapter).

External

We introduced the external clocking mode in the previous section. As the name implies, the machines time their transmitted signals from internal oscillators that are locked to an external clocking source. This configuration requires local office clocks at each end terminal, so it is used in many

---

[2]Bellcore defines loop-timing as a timing mode for nodes that have only one synchronous interface. Therefore, it is a special case of line-timing. We consider this definition helpful but too restrictive.

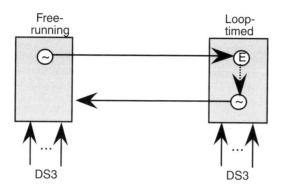

(a) Loop-timed at one end/free-running at the other end.

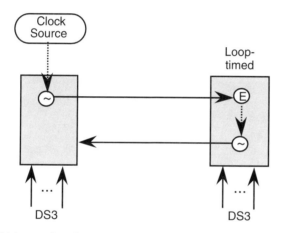

(b) Loop-timed at one end/external at the other end.

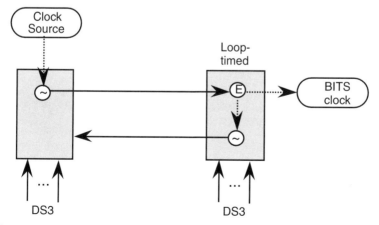

(c) Loop-timed at one end/external at the other end, and timing to BITS.

Figure 3–11   Loop-timing.

interoffice applications. The clock sources illustrated in Figure 3–12 must be stratum 3 or better, and they may emanate from more than one primary reference source (that is, they may be plesiochronous systems). Figure 3–12(b) shows that this configuration can provide synchronization outputs to the office BITS clock (or to other central office equipment).

Through-Timed

The last example of timing distribution is called through or through-timed mode. We use a ring topology for this example. Two configurations are shown in Figure 3–13. In Figure 3–13(a), a free-running clock distrib-

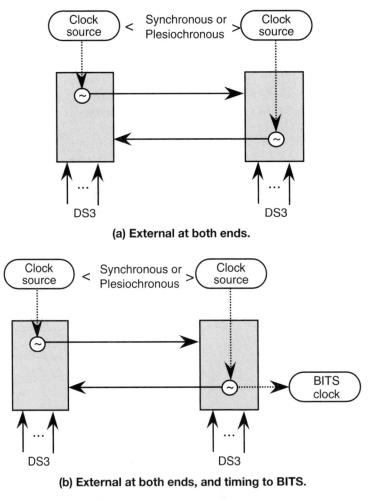

(a) External at both ends.

(b) External at both ends, and timing to BITS.

Figure 3–12   External timing.

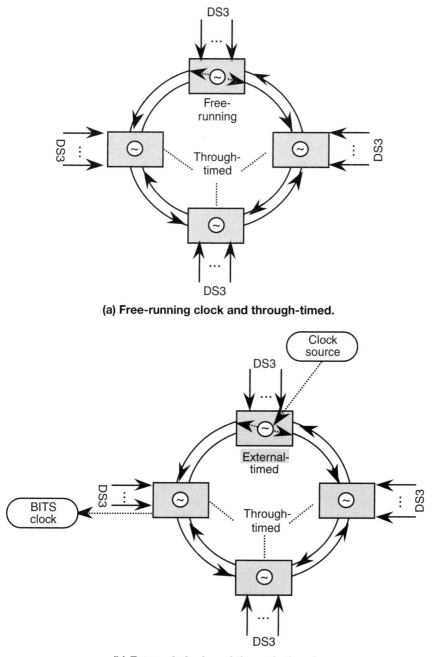

(a) Free-running clock and through-timed.

(b) External clock and through-timed.

Figure 3–13   Through-timed, continued.

utes timing signals to the other nodes on the ring. These nodes on the ring are through-timed. This term means that the network element derives its transmitted timing in the "east" direction from a received line signal in the "west" direction, and the transmit timing in the west direction from the received line signal in the east direction. Through-timing is typically employed when the network node is passing the signal transparently through the node and does not wish to change the timing. Through-timing is used in signal regeneration and echo cancellers.

Timing can be provided with an external clock as well, as depicted in Figure 3–13(b). This figure shows also that timing on the ring can be distributed to BITS.

DISTRIBUTION OF TIMING INFORMATION WITH SONET AND DS1 SIGNALS

Figure 3–14 shows a configuration for using both DS1 and SONET to distribute timing information. DS1 has been used over the years to distribute timing information throughout the network. As seen in this figure, the information is sent between the master (source) and slave clocks. These DS1 signals may also carry traffic. As networks have been upgraded to lightwave systems, SONET has become the preferred facility to

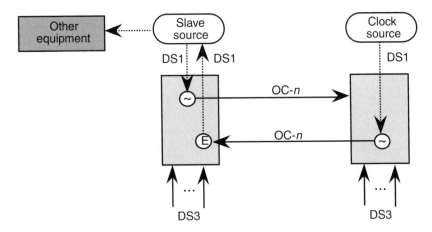

Figure 3–14 Using DS1 and SONET to distribute timing information.

transmit these signals between COs, interoffice networks, and access networks. The incoming OC-n signal provides timing information, which is traceable back to a highly accurate reference clock, exhibiting low jitter and wander. The DS1 timing signal can also be used to feed the local BITS clock, or if BITS is not available, the DS1 signal can be provided directly to other equipment.

DECOUPLING THE CLOCKS

Even though synchronous systems are closely aligned with regard to the timing between network elements, some timing discrepancies are inevitable. For example, the signals coming from different sources (networks with different clocks) may vary slightly. Even though the variation may be quite small, some adjustment must be made to accommodate to these differences.

Demultiplexing signals (from different machines) together can be done in a number of ways, including the following: (1) The synchronous payload envelope (SPE) can be decoupled from the synchronous transport signal (STS-1) frame alignment, or (2) extensive buffering can be provided to accommodate the differences in alignment similar to that performed in T1 networks. SONET approaches the problem by decoupling the SPEs from their STS-1 frames. This concept is called a floating payload. Through the use of pointers, the payload is decoupled from the STS-1 frame and then it is allowed to float within the payload area of an STS-1 frame.

In the example depicted in Figure 3–15, STS-1a and STS-1b use different system clocks. These modules are multiplexed into an STM-1z module, which also operates with a different clock. The tributaries are realigned in the STM-1z module by the use of pointers.

OTHER USES AND EXAMPLES OF POINTER OPERATIONS

From the previous discussion, it can be seen that pointers allow asynchronous operations to be serviced within a synchronous environment. This service is important, because current systems allow for the existence of more than one master network clock, and these clocks may operate at different rates.

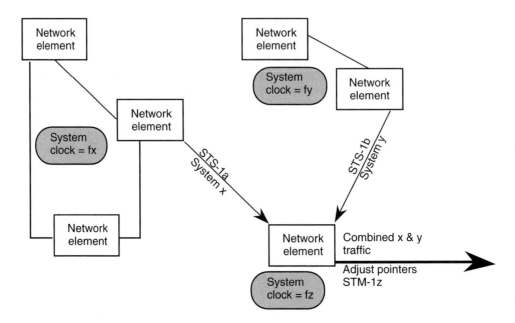

Figure 3–15   Resolving timing differences.

To illustrate the usefulness of pointers in resolving timing differences, refer to Figure 3–16. We assume an SPE frame arrives at add-drop multiplexer (ADM) B from terminal adapter (TA) A at 200 μsec, relative to B's sending SPE frames every 125 μsec. The value of 200 μsec (usually represented by t) is a function of when A sends its traffic, the

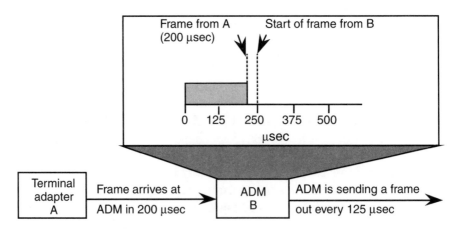

Figure 3–16   Resolving timing differences.

distance between terminal adapter A and ADM B, the size of the envelope, and the bit rate of the link.

A subtle but important point is that ADM B is not synchronized onto TA A's clock with regard to full frame alignment, but only in regard to frequency alignment (bit rate or clock rate). We know from previous discussions in this chapter that if A's and B's clocks are closely aligned, slip buffers are not needed to accommodate to timing differences.

However, the fact remains that B is tasked with receiving A's traffic whenever it arrives. But through the pointer capability, it doesn't care. In this example, B does not have to delay the transmission of A's traffic by 50 msec (to fit into the beginning of its next SPE). Rather, it multiplexes A's SPE into the immediate outgoing SPE and adjusts the pointer fields to show the position of A's payload in B's SPE frame. This example is an illustration of how payload (in this example, A's payload) may be located in more than one 125 msec envelope.

Floating Payloads and the SONET Pointer

As discussed in Chapter 1, the location of the payload (such as DS1 and DS3 signals) in the SONET envelope (frame) is identified by a pointer in the overhead (see Figure 3–17(a)). These pointers are labeled H1, H2, and H3, and are used for identifying the position of the payload in the envelope (or perhaps for adjusting the payload in the envelope). The dynamic alignment allows the payload to "float" within the frame. The pointers can adjust to both phase (time) changes and frequency (bit/frame rate) differences.

The pointer values can range from 0 to 782. The pointer indicates the relative position of the SPE within the payload. If the pointer is 0, the SPE begins in the byte adjacent to the H3 byte. Thereafter, the pointer value is adjusted to signify the relative position away from the H3 byte.

The pointer value is a binary number in bits 7 through 16 of H1 and H2. The first four bits of the payload pointer are used to indicate a change of the payload. These are called the n bits (for new data flag bits) and are used to indicate that a payload is new within the envelope.

If SONET encounters a timing difference in the payload or flags, it can adjust a pointer value to reflect this difference, as shown in Figure 3–17(a). For example, if the SPE that is being placed in the STS-1 envelope is "too slow" in relation to the STS-1 rate, the H1 and H2 bits are manipulated as the signal is sent through the SONET nodes. These operations will eventually reveal that the SPE is approximately one byte

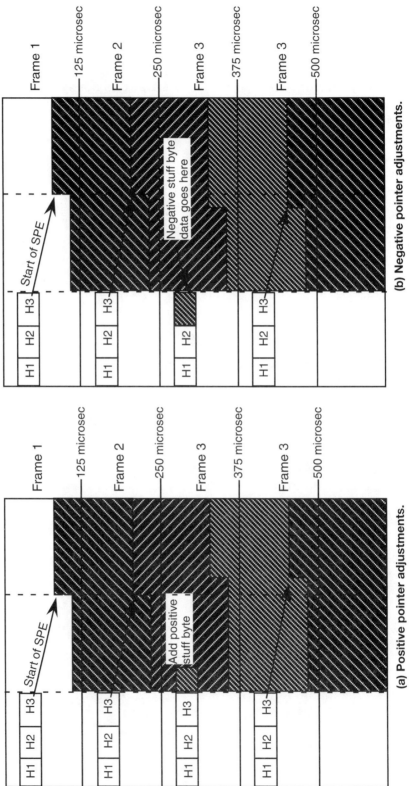

(a) Positive pointer adjustments.

(b) Negative pointer adjustments.

Figure 3–17   Pointer operations.

slower than the STS-1 rate, and positive byte stuffing will occur, which is shown in this figure. A byte is stuffed into the envelope, which allows the payload to "slip back." This concept is known as positive stuffing.

The stuffed byte contains no useful information. It follows the H3 byte. This figure also shows that the pointer is incremented by 1 byte to indicate the beginning of the SPE in the next relative position of the frame. The pointer is actually incremented by 1 in the next frame, and the subsequent pointers contain the new value.

Negative byte stuffing is the opposite of positive byte stuffing and is shown in Figure 3–17(b). In this situation, the SPE is too fast for the rate of the STS-1 frame. This situation requires that the SPE move forward into the envelope. To do so, the data is written in the H3 byte. Additionally, the pointer is decremented by one byte value in the next frame, with all subsequent pointers containing the new value. In essence, the SPE has been "speeded up" to match the alignment with the STS-1 frame.

While the use of pointers provides an effective means of adjusting to frequency and phase problems in the network, it also presents a problem known as payload output jitter. This timing impairment manifests itself on a received signal after recovery from a payload pointer change. This jitter, if excessive, can influence the timing in the network equipment that is processing the signal immediately downstream from where the change was made. Therefore, it is wise to design synchronous networks that use floating payload in a careful manner such that payload adjustments are rarely needed. Otherwise, jitter will accumulate through the network as payload adjustments are made.

LOCKED MODE

SONET does not require the use of floating payloads (known formally as the floating mode). The payload can be placed in a fixed position within the SPE, a concept known as the locked mode. The most common approach however is the floating mode.

BIT STUFFING FOR UNIFORMITY

Chapter 6 explains the mapping functions that SONET provides for DS1 and other payload, as well as a description on bit stuffing concepts. It should be sufficient to state here that bit stuffing not only provides for a uniform envelope, but the stuffing process also aids in aligning the tributary signal's bits with the payload capacity of the transport signal's bits. This feature is achieved by adding the extra stuffing bits to the signal stream within the mapping operations. Therefore, as depicted in Figure 3–18, a DS3 tributary signal operating at 44.74 Mbit/s is synchronized with a payload capacity of 49.54 Mbit/s. Then with the addition of the path overhead, the full STS-1 SPE is a composite bit rate of 50.11 Mbit/s.

It is important to distinguish between SONET bit stuffing and T1 bit stuffing, which was explained earlier in this chapter.

- T1 bit stuffing is used to compensate for timing differences between T1 machines.
- SONET bit stuffing is used to create a uniform SONET envelope.

Figure 3–18 also shows the payload demapping and desynchronization, wherein the SPE has its path overhead removed as well as the stuffing bits, which means the tributary signal is desynchronized from the

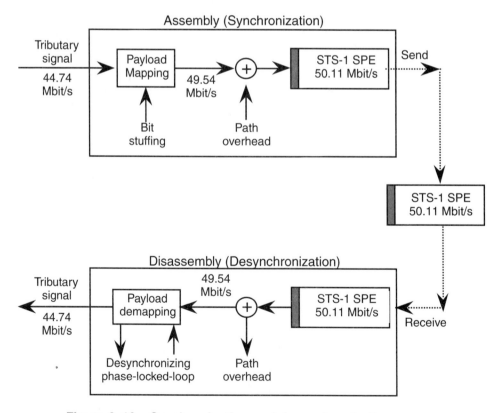

Figure 3–18   Synchronization and desynchronization.

composite SPE signal. The goal is to reproduce, as accurately as possible, the tributary signal in its original form. During the payload demapping (with the use of a phase-locked loop operation), payload pointer adjustments may take place during the desynchronization process.

TIMING DOWNSTREAM DEVICES

We have learned that synchronization can be provided with an external synchronization interface (ESI) and "cascaded" downstream to other nodes. An earlier discussion showed how this occurs in a ring configuration. Figure 3–19 shows several linear configuration options for downstream timing. These options are not all inclusive.

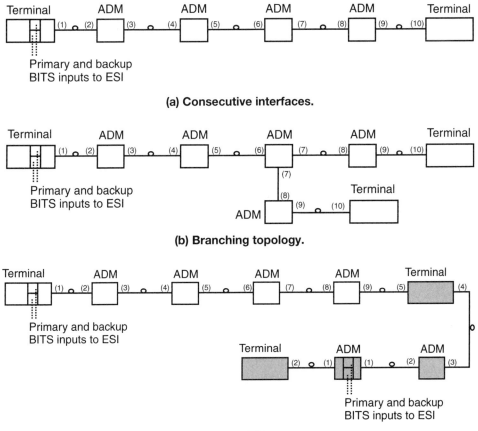

Figure 3–19   External synchronization interfaces (ESI).

The figure depicts where timing is inserted in the line and the number of interfaces (as (n)) that are clocked by building integrated supply timing (BITS). In Figure 3–19(a), a terminal provides primary and backup BITS to 10 external interfaces, with the timing cascading down through add-drop multiplexers (ADMs) to an end terminal. Figure 3–19(b) is provided to emphasize that timing signals can be branched across more than one link and to more than one end terminal. Figure 3–19(c) shows how two ESIs are terminated in one terminal. This configuration might occur if a terminal is connected to two different network providers. BITS does not define which ESI is the authoritative clock source—that issue must be resolved by the network providers. Some providers are reluctant to have their machines clocked by other providers. Others will not allow the customer to provide the clock.

SOURCE CLOCK FREQUENCY RECOVERY FOR ASYNCHRONOUS TRANSFER MODE (ATM) SYSTEMS

Clock recovery in an ATM network for constant bit rate (CBR) traffic can be provided by (1) a time stamp or (2) an adaptive clock. The first method is called the synchronous residual timestamp (SRTS). The SRTS information is carried in a serial bit stream in successive headers of the AAL PDUs. This value is used at the receiver to determine the frequency difference between a common reference clock (fn) and the local service clock (fs). A derived network clock frequency (fnx) is obtained from the fn. For example, assume an fn for SONET of 155.520 MHz. The fnx for fn $\times 2^{-K}$, where K is a specified integer. For a 64 kbit/s signal, K = 11, so the fnx is 155.520×2^{-11}, or 75.9375 kHz. The number of derived clock cycles (mq) is obtained at the sender and conveyed to the receiver in the time stamp field, which allows the receiver to reconstruct the service clock of the sender.

The term "residual" stems from the fact that this method actually sends a value that represents the residual part of the mq. The residual part is frequency difference information, and can vary. The time stamp represents y, where y = (N × fnx/fs × e) (N is the period of RTS in cycles of fs and e is the service clock tolerance ± e). This approach is used because it is assumed the nominal part of mq is known at the receiver (since the receiver and the sender both know fs), so only the residual part mq is conveyed.

The SRTS method assumes the availability of a common synchronous network clock from which sender and receiver can reference time.

Plesiochronous operations that do not have a common reference clock are not standardized and vary between vendors and countries.

For the adaptive clock method, the local receiver simply reads the buffer of the incoming traffic with a local clock. The level of the buffer (its fill level) controls the frequency of the clock. The measure of the fill level drives a mechanism to control the local clock.

SYNCHRONIZATION STATUS MESSAGES AND TIMING LOOPS

One of the overhead bytes of the SONET header (overhead bytes are discussed in Chapter 8) contains the synchronization status message (SSM). An SSM indicates the status and quality level of the SONET signal. It allows the network provider to define which clocking source (and its accuracy) is being used in the network.

The SSM operation is quite helpful in a situation where a SONET node (say node A) loses its synchronization clock from a primary source. Let us also assume that node A is providing clocking information to downstream node B; further, node B is also receiving clocking from yet another node, say, node C (and see Figure 3–19(c)) for this topology. The result is that node B is in a timing loop; it is receiving timing (now erroneous or, say, a stratum 3 clock) from node A and (correct, say, stratum 1) timing from node C. By the use of the SSM, node B knows that the timing from node C is preferred to that of node A, and can use C as its timing source instead of node A.

SSM operations have gone a long way toward solving the multiple ESI situation described earlier in this chapter.

EXAMPLES OF TIMING SUPPLY SYSTEMS

Use of Timing Supply Systems

Prior to the divestiture of the AT&T system in 1984, two synchronization networks operated in North America. The 4E switched synchronization network was managed by AT&T and provided a 2.048 MHz signal that was passed through analog facilities to 4E switches. This signal was known as the basic synchronization reference frequency (BSRF).

The second synchronization plan is called the Digital Data System (DDS) synchronization network. This timing was provided through T1 facilities and distributed through a 1.544 Mbit/s signal and passed between

Bell Operating Companies. The timing reference was extracted from incoming bit stream at the office receiving the signal. The T1 signal was used for timing references and was traceable to the primary reference source (PRS).

The Global Positioning System (GPS)

GPS was developed 32 years ago for military missions. Using satellite technology, it was conceived to locate (with great accuracy) stationary or mobile objects. The first systems were capable of accuracy to within 15 meters; newer systems are much more accurate. In addition to locating objects, GPS also provides time synchronization operations to an accuracy of 100 ns.

GPS consists of 24 satellites that are located in each of six planes, inclined at 55 degrees to the plane of the earth's equator at a distance of 20,200 km from the earth's surface. The satellites rotate around the earth every 12 hours. An earthbound unit determines time and position by tracking the time of arrival of signals from four of the GPS satellites. Each satellite generates time ticks from a cesium atomic clock at a 10.23 MHz frequency. The receiver determines the time of delay of the arrival of the signals and deduces the time from the calculations.

The Building Integrated Timing Supply

The building integrated timing supply (BITS) is now being employed throughout the United States to provide synchronization for digital networks. BITS has two timing references, a primary source called reference A and a secondary source called reference B. Regardless of the source reference, timing must be traceable to a stratum 3 clock or better.

BITS can provide timing for a wide range of equipment, such as channel banks, DCSs, SONETs, digital loop carriers (DLCs), signaling system #7 (SS7) components, asynchronous transfer mode (ATM) machines, frame relay nodes, and switched multimegabit data service (SMDS) devices.

BITS provides a composite clock for equipment with extractable timing of 64/8 kHz. It also provides DS1 timing as well as other timing, if needed. Figure 3–20 shows the 64/8 kHz composite clock. The term 64/8 refers to a 64 kHz bit clock and a 8 kHz byte clock that can be derived from the composite clock stream. The 64 kHz bipolar clock is derived with every eighth bit bipolar violation (BPV). Additionally, the 8 kHz byte clock is derived by counting the BPVs in the byte clock.

Therefore, two types of phase criteria must be satisfied: (1) bit phase and (2) byte phase. We learned earlier that phase is any stage in a series of changes. And two signals are said to be "in phase" when the two sig-

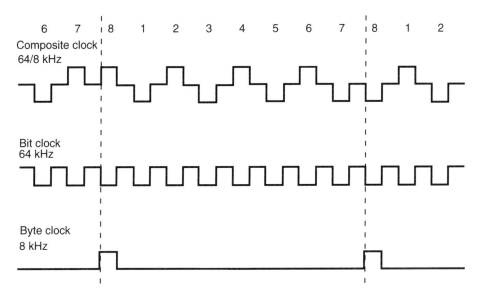

Figure 3–20   BITS clocks.

nals are in the exact same stage, that is to say, at the same percent of amplitude (rising or falling) at the exact same time.

Figure 3–21 shows how a composite clock clocks data across a channel unit in an office. The system clocks data in at one end and out at the other end. Therefore, if a 1 data bit is clocked out as a 0, then the results are in error. This error occurs when a transmitter's clock is out of phase

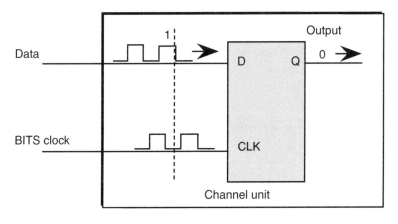

Out-of-phase condition

Figure 3–21   Bit sync.

with the receiver's clock. This situation can occur when two channel banks are referenced to two different composite clocks. While they both may be operating with the same frequency of 64 kHz, their signals are lacking phase sync.

While achieving correct bit phase synchronization is quite important, when used alone bit phase synchronization does not guarantee accurate sync operations at the machine. Figure 3–22 shows that byte clock phase synchronization must also be provided by the network. Figure 3–22(a) shows that the byte sent from the sender is in exact phase with the receiver's clock. Therefore, the sender and receiver have both the same frequency and the same phase relationships. Figure 3–22(b) shows that the sender's and receiver's frequencies are the same but their signals are out of alignment. Simply stated, the receiver is using a different set of 8 bits as a byte than the sender.

As we learned earlier, the byte BPV of the composite clock must be exactly the same with regard to amplitude polarity and the time at which it is measured. Figure 3–23 shows an out-of-phase signal from the perspective of transmitter and receiver.

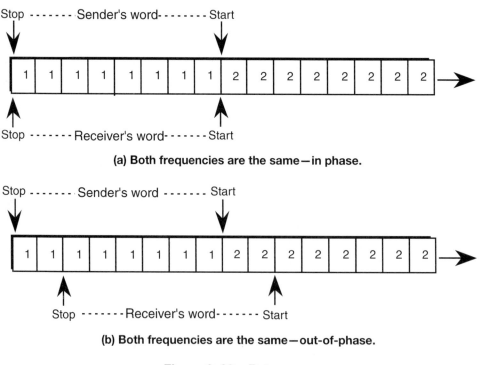

(a) Both frequencies are the same—in phase.

(b) Both frequencies are the same—out-of-phase.

Figure 3–22   Byte sync.

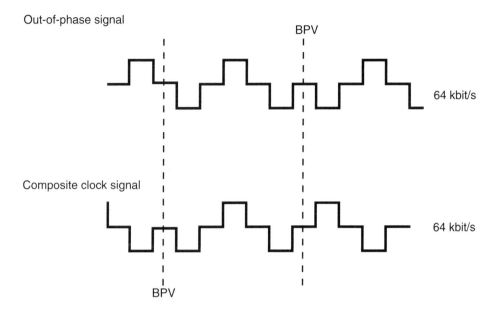

Figure 3–23   Composite clock and out-of-phase signal.

Be aware that phase sync failure will not cause office alarms; therefore, no protection switching operation is invoked nor is an alternate data path chosen. Additionally, carriers normally do not monitor loss of a composite clock, but they will receive information via customer complaints.

Without the use of BITS, a span slip will be passed to customers, perhaps through multiple offices. This creates a ripple effect throughout the network, but its effect depends on the type of traffic being transmitted. The impact of span slips on different types of signals is illustrated here:

Type of traffic	Result of slip
Digital data	Reduced throughput
Encrypted data	Resend key
Fax	Missing lines/distorted page
Video	Picture freeze, or dropouts
Voice	Audible click
Voice band data	Carrier drop

In contrast to a system that does not employ BITS, timing problems are filtered out at a tandem office and Bellcore standards allow no more than four slips per day per circuit.

The Network Time Protocol (NTP)

The NTP was developed for use on Internet computers to synchronize clocks between clients, servers, and other machines. It is not designed for the precise frequency clocking found in BITS or GPS, but is intended to be used for timestamping, such as job scheduling and echoes. We mention it here, because newcomers sometimes confuse timestamp clocking with frequency clocking.

Clocking information for a network is provided through the primary time server designated as a root. The time server obtains its clocking information from master sources. The master clocking sources are used to derive accurate clocks by the primary time server. Most of these clocks provide very accurate clocking synchronization on the order of less than 1 ms.

The primary time server, upon receiving clocking information from a master clocking source, uses the NTP protocol to coordinate all the clocks at the secondary time servers. Secondary time servers may, in turn, provide clocking for other secondary time servers. The NTP messages contain, as one might expect, timestamps that are used by the primary and secondary time servers to calculate clock offsets and correct clocking inaccuracies. The messages contain the following information:

- Time local clock updated: The time that the originator of this message has had its local clock updated
- Originate timestamp: The time that this message was originated
- Receive timestamp: The time this message was received
- Transmit timestamp: The time this message was transmitted after receiving it

All timestamps are 64 bits in length with 32 bits reserved for a whole number and 32 bits for the fraction. Timestamps are benchmarked from 1 January 1900.

SUMMARY

Synchronization and clocking functions are vital operations in digital networks. Older carrier systems are asynchronous in nature. Recent implementations are synchronous or plesiochronous. With these newer systems, clock variations and slips are tightly controlled.

4

The T1 Family

This chapter describes the T1 digital carrier technology. DS0, DS1, DS3, and DS4 signaling is emphasized, and we examine how these signals are processed with channel banks. The D generation of channel banks is described, as well as several vendors' systems. Appendix 4A provides detailed information on the bit and byte structures of the DS1C, DS2, and DS3 frames.

In the preface to this book, we stated that we had retained in this new edition some examples of older T1 and SONET technology. We mention this thought again to emphasize that many of our clients have asked us to retain this material, since it is helpful to understand how some of the technology came to be what it is, based on earlier "predecessors."

T1 LINE CONFIGURATIONS

Today, the majority of T1 offerings digitize the voice signal through a variety of analog-to-digital techniques. Whatever the encoding technique, once the analog images are translated to digital bit streams, the T1 system is able to time division multiplex (TDM) voice and data together in 24 user slots within each T1 frame.

Figure 4–1 shows a T1 configuration. There is no typical configuration for these systems. They can range from the simple point-to-point topology shown here, wherein two T1 multiplexers operate on one link, or

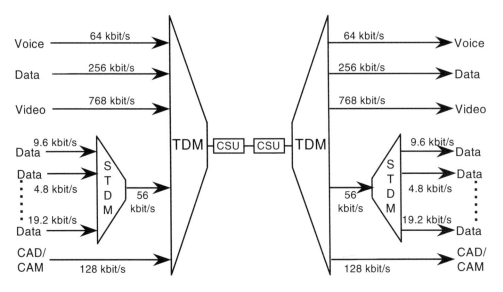

Figure 4–1   Possible topology for a digital carrier system.

they can employ digital cross-connect systems (DCS) that add, drop, and/or switch payload as necessary across multiple links.

Voice, data, and video images can use one digital "pipe." Data transmissions are terminated through a statistical time division multiplexer (STDM), which then uses the TDM to groom the traffic across the transmission line through a T1 channel service unit (CSU) or other equipment, such as a data service unit (DSU) or a combined DSU and CSU. The purpose of the CSU is to convert signals at the user device to signals acceptable to the digital line (and vice versa at the receiver). The CSU performs clocking and signal regeneration on the channels. It also performs functions such as line conditioning (equalization), which keeps the signal's performance consistent across the channel bandwidth; signal reshaping, which reconstitutes the binary pulse stream; and loop-back testing, which entails the transmission of test signals between the DSU and the network carrier's equipment.

The bandwidth of a line can be divided into various T1 subrates. For example, a video system could utilize a 768 kbit/s band, the STDM in turn could multiplex various data rates up to a 56 kbit/s rate and perhaps a CAD/CAM operation could utilize 128 kbit/s of the bandwidth.

THE DIGITAL NETWORK

The U.S. T1-based digital network has been under development for over 30 years. During this time, a hierarchy of transmission levels (low speeds to high speeds) has been implemented through time division multiplexers, channel banks, and digital cross-connects. These levels are designated by digital signal (DS) numbers ranging from DS0 to DS4.

DS1 Frame Format

Chapter 2 introduced the concept of digital signals, and Chapters 1 and 2 introduced the channel bank. In previous discussions, we learned that 24 channels (users) can be multiplexed together on one line (see Figure 4–2(a)). Each of these 24 channels is a 64 kbit/s signal. This signal is called a digital signal level 0, or DS0. The 0 means that the signal is not multiplexed (digital signal, level 0 of multiplexing). The multiplexed 24 DS0 signals are collectively called DS1 (digital signal, first level of multiplexing). Let us see how DS1 is formed.

A few simple calculations are needed at this point in the discussion in order to understand the DS1 signal. After each of the 24 channels in a channel bank (terminal) has been sampled, quantized, and encoded, the resultant pulse train (bit stream) is called a frame. A frame has a time duration of 125 microseconds (μsec) (1 second/8000 samples = .000125). The bit duration is 648 nanoseconds (nsec): 125 μsec/193 = 648 nsec.

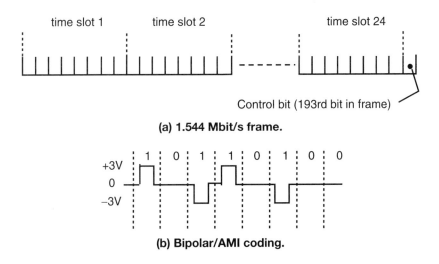

(a) 1.544 Mbit/s frame.

(b) Bipolar/AMI coding.

Figure 4–2   The T1 frame and coding scheme.

Further, each PAM sample is encoded into an 8-bit, 5.184 µsec word: 648 nsec × 8 = 5.148 µsec.

The frame contains 24 8-bit binary words, as depicted in Figure 4–2(a). At the end of channel 24, an additional bit (the F bit) is appended to the frame. This bit becomes the 193rd bit of a frame and is used for framing (synchronization), as well as a variety of operations and maintenance services.

These calculations provide an insight to the DS1 bit rate. We just learned that the pulse code modulation (PCM) terminal produces 24 eight-bit words, plus the F bit. The sampling rate of each channel in the system is 8000 times per second. Thus, 8000 × 193 bits per frame = 1,544,000 bits per second, or 1.544 Mbit/s: this is the DS1 line bit rate (see Table 4–1). This DS1 signal is transmitted onto the T1 TDM cable facilities.

Advantages of the Bipolar Code

The binary coded pulses transmitted onto the cable pair have a 50 percent duty cycle, which means the width of the pulses is one-half the time slot allocated to each pulse (324 nsec). In addition, this system employs bipolar transmission, which alternates the polarity for each successive binary 1. This technique is also called alternate mark inversion or AMI (see Figure 4–2(b)).

There are several advantages to the use of the bipolar pulse pattern over unipolar transmission. First, most of the energy of the bipolar signal is concentrated at one-half the pulse repetition frequency. Thus, the maximum frequency of DS1 signals is 772 kHz (with all 1s). Second, less energy is coupled into other systems in the same transmission cable because of increased crosstalk coupling loss. Third, bipolar pulses do not have a direct current (DC) component, thus permitting simple trans-

Table 4–1   Digital signal at the first level (DS1).

24	Channels or words
× 8	Bits per word
192	*Word bits* / frame
+ 1	*F* bit
193	Bits per complete frame
× 8000	Sampling rate/second
1,544,000	bit/s or 1.544 Mbit/s

former coupling at field regenerators. Fourth, the unique alternating pulse pattern can also be used for error detection, because errors tend to violate an ongoing, repetitive pattern.

For example, two consecutive pulses in the same direction (positive or negative) are referred to as bipolar violations (BPVs). Test equipment can be used to check for this condition, and protection switching will transfer to back-up facilities when errors exceed a threshold detected by the equipment.

INTRODUCTION TO THE D FAMILY CHANNEL BANKS

Carrier channel banks are utilized for interoffice and toll-connecting trunks at each end of a digital transmission system. Both channel banks are located in telephone company central offices. They convert speech signals into coded bits and may pass the signals to the Digital Data System (DDS) network. They can also provide fractional T1 (FT-1) to subscribers as well as other applications.

The various generations of channel banks have brought new features and applications to the customer. The new systems offer easier maintenance, with most of the provisioning performed by software instead of physical settings. The new channel banks also come in smaller packaging, which has resulted in less power consumption.

The D1, D2, and D3 channel banks are no longer manufactured. However, understanding their development and services gives us a better idea of where (and why) we are today with the D4 and D5 channel banks. D1, D2, and D3 are designations of the Western Electric Company, but many manufacturers make compatible channel banks which they refer to as D1-, D2-, and D3-types. Nortel describes its channel bank designation with a DE, as in DE4. Western Electric's (W.E. Co.) D4 and D5 channel banks are the most popular generation in use today. The D4 introduced a data port application, which is now one of the more popular features of these channel banks.[1]

As of this writing, the D5 channel bank is the state-of-the-art system. It uses extensive software provisioning and utilizes universal chan-

---

[1] A data port application allows the customer to send a digital payload from one point to another by utilizing the carrier channel banks' interoffice appplication. A data port can also be an avenue for the cutomer to connect to the DDS network.

nel units.[2] The extended superframe (ESF) format and B8ZS line coding for 64 kbit/s clear channel capabilities (CCC) are two of its features, and are explained later in this chapter. Nortel offers the DE4 and DE4E (an enhancement to the DE4), which support data port applications and have B8ZS line coding for 64 kbit/s CCC. Nortel's DE4E bank provides features and applications similar to the D5 channel banks. Ericsson, Siemens, and others manufacture D-type channel banks.

NORTH AMERICAN ASYNCHRONOUS DIGITAL HIERARCHY

When the digital network was in its early stages of development, common clocks (as a primary reference source) were not available. In order to synchronize the switches, terminals, and multiplexers to a common rate, bit stuffing was used to bring lower-rate signals into a common higher rate. Later in this chapter, we examine these operations. For the present, we emphasize that the rates in the digital multiplexing hierarchy (see Figure 4–3) are not integral multiples because the stuff bits are added to the payloads.

Five levels of multiplexing exist within the North American asynchronous digital hierarchy. Starting with the 1.544 Mbit/s DS1, each level of the hierarchy increases a facility's channel capacity. The current systems are capable of handling over 24,000 channels. There are several types of asynchronous digital multiplexers/demultiplexers that support this hierarchy, and they are described in this section.

A DS1 signal may be combined with another DS1 signal to produce a 3.152 Mbit/s signal containing 48 voice frequency (VF) channels. The multiplexer used for this operation is called an M1C mux, meaning first level in, combined level out. This level is called a digital signal at the first level combined, or DS1C.

The combination of four DS1s to produce a 6.312 Mbit/s bit stream is called a digital signal at the second level, or DS2. It supports 96 voice channels. The multiplexers used for this operation are called M12, meaning first level signals in, second level out.

Figure 4–3 shows the relationship of the digital signal cross-connect (DSX, also called a digital cross-connect) to the hierarchy. These compo-

---

[2]Universal channel units are not dedicated to a particular application, but are software programmable for one of several applications. This eliminates the need for telcos to keep many different types of channel units in stock for all the applications and service offerings that a customer may require.

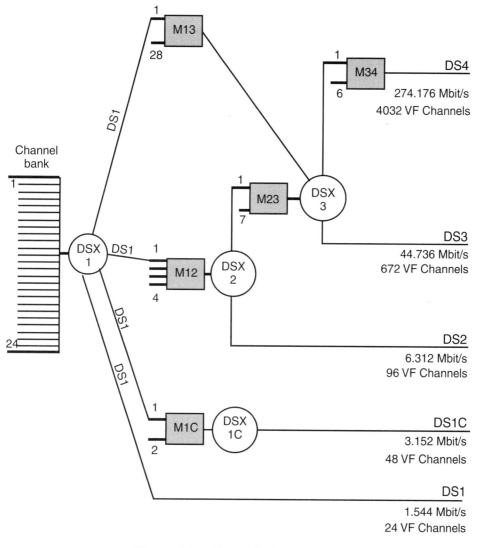

Figure 4–3   The digital hierarchy.

nents are equipment frames containing jack panels that serve as channel bank and multiplexer cross-connect interfaces in the telco office. The frames are named DSX-0, DSX-1, DSX-1C, DSX-3, and DSX-4 for each of the six DS rates (DSX-0 and DSX-4 are not shown in Figure 4–3). Each frame connects equipment that operates at the respective DSn rate. The DSX-0 is employed for connecting and terminating DDS equipment.

The DSX-1, DSX-1C, and DSX-2 have several common features, such as monitoring and patching jacks, accommodations for conventional telephone plugs, order-wire terminations, and tracer lamps (to identify the two ends of a cross-connection). As shown in Figure 4–3, the DSX-1 connects to a channel bank (and other equipment, as explained later). The DSXs are 110-ohm balanced points. The DSX-3 and DSX-4 are similar to the DSX-1, DSX-1C, and DSX-2, except they are 75-ohm coaxial interfaces.

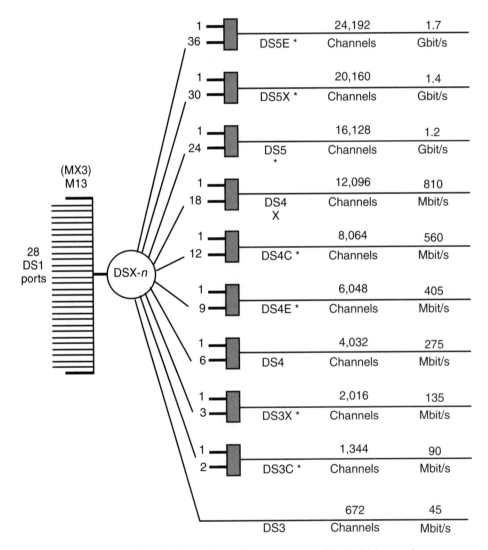

Figure 4–4 North American Synchronous Digital hierarchy.
Note: * = not standardized.

It is important to distinguish between a DSX and a DCS, which is also called a digital cross-connect. The DCS is considerably more intelligent. It is software controlled and uses time-slot interchange (TSI) to transfer slots between input and output lines. DCSs eliminate channel banks at interfaces where channels are transferred between carrier systems [BELL90b]. DCS operations are explained in more detail later in this chapter and in Chapter 5.

One of the most common type of multiplexers is the MX3. It accepts up to 28 DS1 signals, 14 DS1C signals, or 7 DS2 signals as inputs and creates a DS3 signal as its output. These multiplexers are called MX3 (with X designating the level in), meaning M13 for first level in and third level out or M23 for second level in and third level out.

The final (formally defined) level within the North American asynchronous digital network is the DS4, which produces a 274.176 Mbit/s signal with 4032 voice channels. An M34 mux is used for producing this digital level.

There are also several other common (but not standard) levels (shown in Figure 4–4). These are: (1) 90 Mbit/s DS3C, (2) the 135 Mbit/s DS3X, (3) the 405 Mbit/s DS4E, (4) the 560 Mbit/s DS4C, and (5) the 1.2, 1.4, and 1.7 Gbit/s systems. These systems accept DS3 as their inputs. The DS3C system accepts two DS3 inputs, the DS3X system accepts three DS3 inputs, and the DS4E system accepts nine DS3 inputs. The "E" indicates "extended." The signal is not high enough to be called a DS4C, which is a 560 Mbit/s system that accepts 12 DS3 signals as inputs. The reader should check the vendors' offerings for equipment operating above DS4, due to the lack of standards at these levels.

DIGITAL LOOP CARRIER SYSTEMS

The term digital loop carrier (DLC) system describes the outside digital facilities between a central office and the customer's site. Figure 4–5 depicts several examples of DLC configurations and topologies. As shown in Figure 4–5(a), the system consists of a feeder plant, a distribution plant, and the feeder-distribution interface. The feeder plant consists of the large number of physical wires and digital repeaters. Usually, they are located based on geography constraints and the customer locations. They often run parallel to roads and highways. The distribution plant consists of a smaller number of cables and connects to the customer's network interface (NI), which is usually located in a "box" attached to the customer's building. The serving area interface (interface plant) is the term

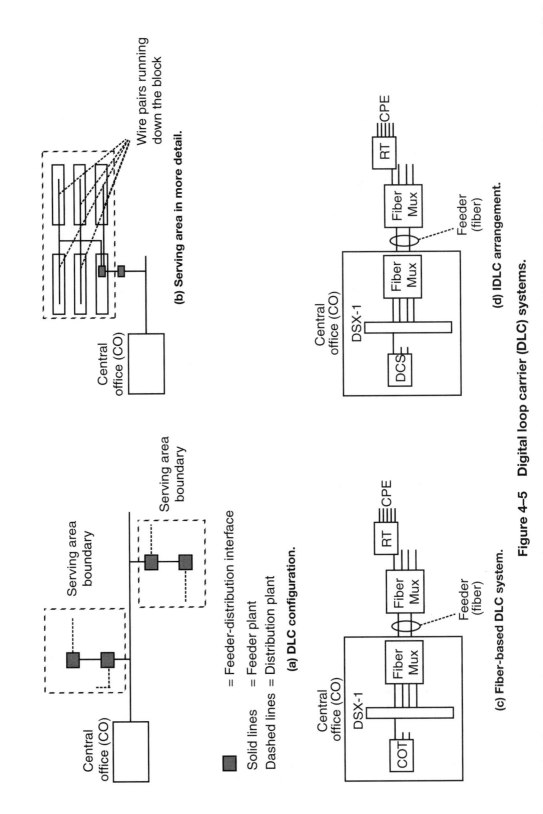

(b) Serving area in more detail.

(a) DLC configuration.

Solid lines = Feeder plant

Dashed lines = Distribution plant

■ = Feeder-distribution interface

(c) Fiber-based DLC system.

(d) IDLC arrangement.

Figure 4–5   Digital loop carrier (DLC) systems.

used to describe the manual cross-connections between the feeder and distribution plants. This interface is designed to allow any feeder unit to be connected to any distribution pair [BELL90b].

Figure 4–5(b) shows the serving area boundary in more detail. This term describes the geographical division of the outside plant into discrete parts. All wires in a serving area are connected to a single serving area interface to the feeder plant, which simplifies ongoing maintenance and record keeping.

Figure 4–5(c) shows an arrangement at the central office, where a central office terminal (COT) sends and receives 64 kbit/s signals to and from a remote terminal (RT). In this configuration, the COT is connected through a DSX-1 to a DS1-to-fiber multiplexer in order to use optical fiber on the feeder plant. The RT terminates the fiber and (on the subscriber side) distributes the signals to the subscriber through copper pairs.

Figure 4–5(d) shows an arrangement where the COT and DSX are eliminated. This system is called an integrated digital loop carrier (IDLC) system because it absorbs the functions of the COT. The IDLC does not need to do analog-to-digital conversions, which are performed in the COT operation. This approach is possible because IDLC systems terminate directly into the network in a digital CO. In effect, the COT is integrated into the DCS switch. To complete this overview of DLC, Table 4–2 provides a summary of the elements that make up a DLC system [BELL90b].

T1 LINE AND TRUNKS

T1 configurations are often organized with lines and trunks. Figure 4–6 shows the relationship of lines and trunks. The switch uses line and trunk identifiers to map incoming connections to outgoing connections. The figure shows a line side and a trunk side of a digital cross-connect switch. Each 64 kbit/s DS0 channel is associated with a DS1 number and a physical port (line) number. A mapping table correlates this channel with an outgoing channel. An end-to-end digital circuit is made up of a set of DS1 and DS0 at each physical interface between two end users.

Figure 4–6 shows the mapping table at the bottom of the figure. The top part of the figure shows two examples of how the cross-connect table is used. The two sets of arrows should aid you in these two examples. In the first example, DS0 #1 of DS1 #1 on line 1 is mapped to trunk 2, DS1 #1, and DS0 #5. In the second example, DS0 #2 of DS1 #1 on line 1 is mapped to trunk 1, DS1 #2, and DS0 #2. In newer machines, these

Table 4–2   DLC system elements [BELL90b].

Feeder Plant

Remote terminal

Digital line (T1 spans, radio, or optical fibers)

Structure (poles or conduit)

Repeaters (if used) (manholes, apparatus cases)

Lightguide interconnection terminal (if used)

Multiplexers (if used)

RT housing (controlled environment vault, hut, or cabinet)

Land for remote terminal (RT) housing

End Office

Main distributing frame (if used for DLC)

Office cabling

Digital signal cross-connect

Central-office terminal (if used)

Lightguide interconnection equipment (if used)

Multiplexers (if used)

Office repeater bays (if used)

Line interface modules (if used)

cross-connections are provisional (crafted) through software. Chapter 7 provides several examples of software-based provisioning.

D1 CHANNEL BANKS

As we explained earlier, this chapter describes all the D channel banks, even though some of them are no longer used. This approach is useful, because it allows us to explain why the modern channel banks are the way they are, and will give you an understanding of the hardware and software options as they pertain to the different generations of channel banks. This section is designed for the reader who needs detailed information on T1-based channel banks. Other readers can skip this material. An understanding of the material in Chapter 2 is essential before reading the remainder of this chapter.

After the introduction of the T1 system by Western Electric, many independent manufacturers began to produce similar T1-type equip-

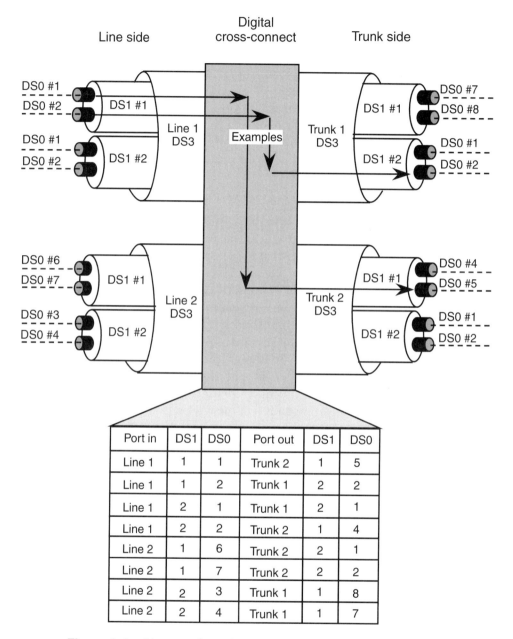

Figure 4–6   Lines and trunk: A digital cross-connect system.

ment. These systems became known as D1 channel banks. These systems are no longer deployed, but many of their operations are carried over to the new channel banks. For consistency, the present tense is used to describe all the channel banks.

The D1 channel banks, as well as D1A, D1B, D1C, and D1D, are considered first-generation channel banks. The other channel banks are of the second generation. While each channel bank is different, they all perform the same function, that of multiplexing DS0 signals into higher levels, and vice versa.

Basic Operations

The D1 generation bank uses 128 quantizing steps, which is adequate for direct or toll connecting trunks. As explained in Chapter 2, the number of steps used to represent a PAM sample determines the quality of the recovered voice signal at the receiver. The number of binary bits necessary to give a digital code representation of 128 steps is 7. Therefore, the D1 encoded "word" is a 7-bit word. A 7-bit code (bits 2 through 8) is used to represent each PAM sample. Built-in signaling arrangements are provided for loop-dial pulsing, multifrequency pulsing, revertive pulsing,[3] and ear and mouth (E&M) lead signaling.

An additional bit, called bit 1, is added to the 7-bit code representing each PAM sample to carry signaling information. This addition increases the number of bits per sample to 8 and provides 2-state signaling that is adequate for the two states of dial pulse and E&M signaling. For revertive pulse signaling, a 3-state signaling channel is required. This additional state is obtained by removing control of the least significant bit (last bit in the 7-bit code, called bit 8) from the encoder while dialing is in process and using this bit to transmit revertive pulses. When the called party answers, the returned answer supervision restores the encoder control of bit 8.

Each sampling gate output is time division multiplexed with PAM samples from other channels to form a PAM signal. The channels are sampled in the following order: 1, 13, 2, 14, 3, 15, and so on. This technique is called the alternate sequential sampling sequence, and its purpose is to distribute the load evenly to the compressors. The compressor is an amplifier that amplifies low-level inputs more than high-level inputs by the use of logarithmic compression (discussed in Chapter 2).

---

[3]Revertive pulsing is an old techniqque used to support panel-type switching systems. It is no longer used and is not covered in this chapter.

The compressed PAM samples are then fed into the encoder. Each PAM sample, which has a continuous range of possible levels, is encoded into 1 out of 127 possible levels that are linearly spaced (each of which is represented by a 7-bit code). Code 0000000 is suppressed to prevent the regenerator clocks from dying and causing loss of synchronization between channel banks. The encoder output train of unipolar PCM pulses is combined with signaling and framing pulses and converted to a bipolar pulse train in the transmitting converter circuit. The transmitting converter inverts (reverses polarity of) every other pulse that is present in the unipolar pulse train without regard to the number of pulse positions between pulses. The converter output train of bipolar PCM pulses is connected to an outgoing repeated line.

For on-hook signals, bit 1 is transmitted, and for off-hook signals, bit 1 is inhibited. When bit 8 is not controlled by the encoder for voice, it is normally absent. But when revertive ground pulses occur, bit 8 is present.

The 24 8-bit words (one signaling bit position plus seven bit positions for each coded sample in each frame) together with the framing bit position make a total of 193 bit positions per frame.

The 193rd pulse position has a repetitive pattern of 1,0,1,0,1,0,1,0 . . . and so on, when the channel bank is "in frame," that is, in synchronization.

At the receiver, the entire process is reversed. The bipolar pulse train from the incoming line enters the receiver at the receiving converter circuit. When the framing pulse is found, the receiver locks on to the signal and is in synchronization (in frame). If the framing detector does not find the framing pulse, a receiving alarm circuit is activated and a message is sent to the sending channel bank to activate a transmit alarm. If the framing pulse is found, then decoding takes place. The decoding is the reverse function of encoding, which takes place in the receive section of the channel bank.

Demise of the D1 Channel Bank

In spite of its popularity, the D1-type (the original Western Electric D1/D1A was modified for D1B and D1C versions) channel bank did not have the necessary transmission quality to be applied in the intertoll networks. Shortly after the introduction of the D1, it became desirable to connect several T1 transmission spans together in tandem, but the quantizing noise produced by the 7-bit encoding was too high for satisfactory performance. Moreover, providing signaling information in every code word (8000 bit/s) was not required for a channel because signaling information did not change that rapidly.

D1D Channel Banks

To solve the shortcomings of the D1A, D1B, and D1C channel banks, a fourth modification was made to the D1 series. It is called the D1D. The sampling sequence remains the same alternate sequential sampling (see Table 4–3), but the modified D1D uses segmented encoding and the superframe format (discussed shortly).

Table 4–3   Time slot assignment.

Time Slot	D1D Channel Number Assignment	D2 Channel Number Assignment	D3 Channel Number Assignment
1	1	12	1
2	13	13	2
3	2	1	3
4	1	17	4
5	3	5	5
6	15	21	6
7	4	9	7
8	16	15	8
9	5	3	9
10	17	19	10
11	6	7	11
12	18	23	12
13	7	11	13
14	19	14	14
15	8	2	15
16	20	18	16
17	9	6	17
18	21	22	18
19	10	10	19
20	22	16	20
21	11	4	16
22	23	20	22
23	12	8	23
24	24	24	24
	ALTERNATE SEQUENTIAL	RANDOM	SEQUENTIAL

D2 CHANNEL BANKS

The D2 channel bank was introduced into the telephone networks in the late 1960s, particularly for service in the intertoll network. In addition to providing better transmission characteristics, it offers features tailored to intertoll and special service usage, as well as enhanced maintenance operations. The D2 bank introduced the concept of a frame grouping, which is the organization of 12 DS1 frames into the "superframe." Figure 4–7 and Table 4–4 show the structure of the superframe, and a later section is devoted to an analysis of the superframe.

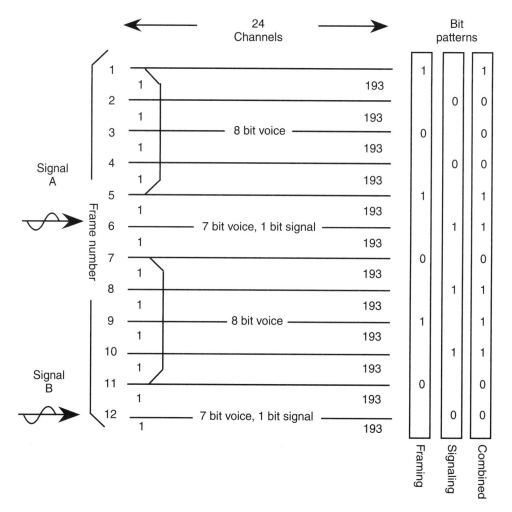

Figure 4–7   The superframe.

Table 4–4 Format for 12–frame superframe [BELL90b].

| Frame No. | Bit No. | F Bits | | Bit Use per Time Slot | | |
		Terminal Framing (Ft)	Signaling Framing (Fs)	Information Bits	Signaling Bit	Signaling Channel
1	0	1	—	1-8	—	—
2	193	—	0	1-8	—	—
3	386	0	—	1-8	—	—
4	579	—	0	1-8	—	—
5	772	1	—	1-8	—	—
6	965	—	1	1-7	8	A
7	1158	0	—	1-8	—	—
8	1351	—	1	1-8	—	—
9	1544	1	—	1-8	—	—
10	1737	—	1	1-8	—	—
11	1930	0	—	1-8	—	—
12	2123	—	0	1-7	8	B

D2 uses 256 quantizing steps; therefore, the D2 word is 8 bits. Ideally, to allow for the least amount of quantizing distortion, all 8 bits of a word should be used for voice encoding. However, signaling for each channel (such as dial pulsing and supervision) must also be transmitted. Since dial pulsing and supervision happen so seldom, they can be transmitted at a lesser signaling rate than the voice signals. The D2 scheme represents a compromise: 8 bits of voice are transmitted on five of six frames in the superframe, and 7 bits of voice and 1 bit of signaling are transmitted every sixth frame in the superframe for each 24 channels. Figure 4–7 shows the format of the superframe.

Table 4–4 provides more information on the superframe. The frame number and bit number are shown, as well as the bit use per time slot [BELL90b]. The Ft and Fs bits are explained shortly.

The D2 channel bank employs the conventional sampling, quantizing, and encoding operations, which we introduced in Chapter 2. For this discussion, we focus on encoding. The encoder makes three decisions that result in an 8-bit binary word. First, the encoder determines if the polarity of the pulse is positive or negative (see Figure 4–8, which is an extension of Figure 2–6, in Chapter 2). In this example, the result is positive and the first bit of the binary word becomes 1. With the second decision, the encoder determines in which of the eight segments on the positive

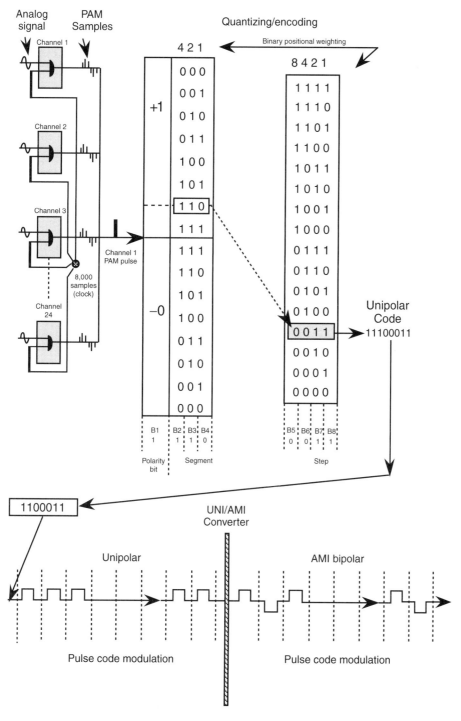

Figure 4–8 Segmented encoding.

side of the quantized PAM sample resides. In this example, the quantized PAM sample is in segment six. The next three bits are assigned the positional weighting base 10 values of 4, 2, and 1; so, segment six can be represented as 110.

Finally, the encoder decides to which of the sixteen steps (within the segment) that the quantized PAM sample is closest. As before, the four remaining bits are assigned the positional weighting values of 8, 4, 2, and 1. In this example, the sample is closest to step 3. So, the next four bits are 0, 0, 1, and 1. Thus, the quantized and encoded 8-bit binary word is 1110011. This value is the binary equivalent 227_{10}, which is the sample voltage level value.

At the receiving end of the system, the channel bank reverses the process; that is, it will decode the 8-bit binary word and recreate the PAM sample. The quantizer scale in the D2-type channel bank is actually a nonlinear scale. We learned in Chapter 2 that logarithmic compression is used to maintain an acceptable constant signal-to-distortion ratio over the full range of PCM signals.

Robbed Bit Signaling

Signaling is a procedure used for indicating to the receiving end equipment the digits that are dialed by the calling customer at the transmitting end and the special signaling for that customer's circuit. As stated earlier, signaling is accomplished during every sixth frame, where one bit of each channel's eight bits is used as a signaling bit. In other words, five frames convey eight bits for voice, while the sixth frame conveys seven bits for voice plus one bit for signaling. The one bit for signaling is the "robbed bit."

But, why is the robbing performed on every sixth frame? Why not every fifth or seventh frame? The decision is based on the old telephone rotary dial. A telephone rotary dial generates 10 pulses per second. The central office equipment is adjusted to accept pulses as fast as 12 pulses/sec. Since sample signaling occurs at one-sixth the rate of the sample of the customer's voice, then one-sixth of 8000 samples per second equals 1333 signal pulses per second, which is more than enough samples for each dial pulse. Since 0s are sent during the time the springs (rotary dialing operation) are closed and 1s are sent while the springs are open, this approach is more than enough time to accomplish the goal of setting up a switch train or establishing a path to the out-called party.

However, if the customer has a dual tone multifrequency (DTMF) instrument (touch tone), then the signaling is sent over the voice frequency path and the signaling bit only shows the on-hook/off-hook states.

The D2 is packaged as a 96-channel terminal, although it functions as four nearly independent 24-channel terminals. Each 24-channel transmission package, called a digroup, operates over a separate 1.544 Mbit/s T1 line. However, the independent manufacturers have designed D2-compatible channel banks as 24-channel terminals, and they are completely self-contained. All these terminals have the higher transmission qualities of D2 signaling, as well as the features applicable to intertoll and special service usage.

The Superframe

The D2 generation channel bank's framing is called a superframe format (refer back to Figure 4–7). To review briefly, the superframe consists of 12 frames that produce the full pattern required to synchronize the T1 machines. The synchronization pattern occurring in the odd-numbered frames is 1010, and so on, skipping the even-numbered frames. These are the synchronization bits for the channel banks. The voice clock synchronization pattern occurring in the even-numbered frames has a different pattern: 001110. Thus, the combined S bit pattern is 100011011100 for the superframe. It is called the S bit because it is shared between framing and signaling.

Alarm Methods

The D2 superframe provides for several alarms that are also implemented in the new channel banks: (1) red alarm, (2) yellow alarm, and (3) alarm indication signal (AIS). These terms also apply to the second-generation channel banks. We discuss alarms briefly here and in more detail in Chapter 8.

The receive alarm is a function of the 193rd bit pattern. This is a local alarm, meaning the local channel bank is not receiving its framing. It is also referred to as alarm red because the LED is red in color. However, instead of the 193rd pulse position containing a repetitive pattern of 1,0,1,0,1,0,1,0,1,0 . . . , and so on to keep the channel bank in-frame (synchronized; as it is in the D1 generation channel banks), the D2 system uses the odd frames of the superframe for this same pattern.

The difference in alarming methods pertains mainly to the transmit alarm. The transmit alarm in the D1 generation banks is initiated when a terminal receives 0s in the bit-1 and bit-8 time slots of every channel. The terminal that has the receive alarm automatically suppresses these bit positions. This alarm is generally referred to as a remote alarm (the remote terminal sends the message to go into the alarm condition) or yellow alarm (the LED is yellow in color).[4]

In the D2 generation channel banks, bit 2 of the 8-bit word is inhibited for all 24 channels. Again, the terminal that has the receive alarm automatically suppresses this bit in every word, which causes the remote terminal to go into a yellow alarm condition. This condition lasts for the duration of the alarm condition or for at least one second.

The DS1 AIS is an unframed all-1s signal. An unframed all-1s pattern is used by some equipment as an alarm condition. When a device loses synchronization, it sends all 1s to keep the network up and to indicate that there is a problem in transmission between two locations. The AIS is removed when the condition triggering the AIS is back on line.

D3 CHANNEL BANKS

The D3 channel bank was conceived as a technical update to the D1 channel bank. It is designed to be used in the same type of service and packaged as a 24-channel entity. However, it was soon realized that with the availability of new technologies such as integrated circuits, it was a relatively simple and inexpensive to make the D3 operations compatible with those of the D2. This approach affords greater flexibility for the D2, and enables it to be used in intertoll service, as well as direct and toll connecting service.

The modified D1D, D2, and D3 channel banks each use the segmented encoding method and have the identical superframe format, which was covered in the section on D2 channel banks. They also provide the necessary transmission quality to be applied in intertoll networks. The only difference is the manner in which they handle the sampling sequence for polling the channel units. The modified D1D uses alternate sequential sampling, the D2 uses random sampling, and the D3 uses sequential sampling (see Table 4–3). All the systems discussed so far have the common characteristics shown in Table 4–5.

D4 CHANNEL BANKS

The D4 generation of channel banks grew out of the emerging digital hierarchy. The telephone equipment manufacturers, in an effort to meet the customers' needs, decided to include an on-board multiplexer in the

---

[4]The yellow alarm is called the remote alarm indication (RAI) by the ITU-T and other organizations.

Table 4–5   Common characteristics of D1n, D2, and D3 channel banks.

1. Line rate	1,544,000 bit/s
2. Line code	AMI (bipolar)
3. Line frequency	772 kHz (maximum)
4. Line impedance	100 Ohms-Nominal
5. Pulse height	6 volts (peak-to-peak)
6. Duty cycle*	50%*
7. Pulse width	324 ns
8. Time slot width	648 ns
9. PCM word width	5.18 µs
10. Frame width	125 µs
11. Channel units	200 to 3400 Hz

Notes:
1. Any variation in the alternating signal will result in a bipolar violation (BPV).
2. Line repeaters and decoders require positive/negative transitions in order to maintain timing.
3. At least 12.5% of the bits must be 1s for synchronization to be maintained.
4. At least 1 bit in 15 must be a 1, and at least 3 bits in 24 bits in the data stream must be a 1 in order for the channel bank to maintain frame structure.
5. Zero code suppression (ZCS) insures that the DS1 signal will not have more than 15 consecutive zeros in a row.
6. The option in selecting this line code is referred to as AMI or ZCS, depending on the vendor for the fourth or fifth generation channel bank.
* Pulse width takes up half of the time slot
ns = nanosecond
µs = microsecond

D4 channel bank to provide for the first three levels of the hierarchy. This approach obviates purchasing an external multiplexer.

Operating Modes

The modes of operation in the D4-type channel banks pertain to the use of these different on-board multiplexers (see Figure 4–9):

Mode 1: This mode combines two digroups to provide a single 48-channel DS1C line signal of 3.152 Mbit/s for transmission over conventional T1C-type span lines. The DS1C line interface units (LIU) are set up in such a manner that mode

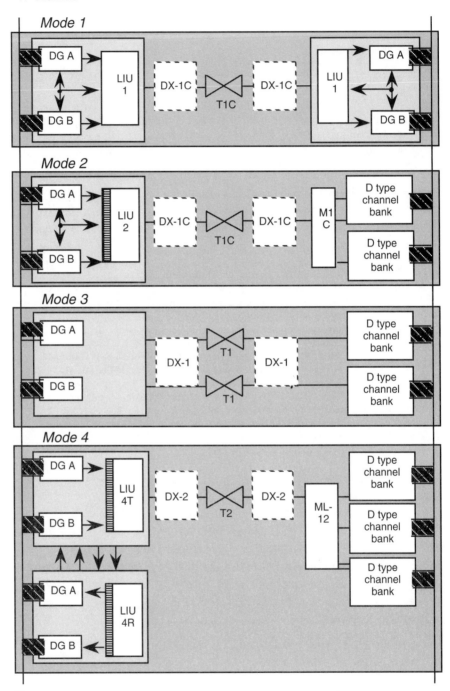

= Synchronizer/desynchronizer

Figure 4–9   Modes 1, 2, 3, and 4. Note: Mode 5 is like Mode 4, but uses optical fibers for the link.

1 cannot be demultiplexed to DS1 by an M1C multiplexer. Furthermore, it cannot be multiplexed to the DS3 level. Mode 1 is not recommended as a standard, because the two digroups must be synchronized with each other.

Mode 2: This is the preferred mode. It produces a single 48-channel DS1C line signal. However, the frame format is M1C, and the two incoming digroup signals are not required to be synchronized. Mode 2 provides asynchronous operation of 48 channels over a 3.152 Mbit/s facility (T1C line). The LIU is similar to the LIU in Mode 1, and a synchronizer/desynchronizer unit performs bit stuffing (in the same manner as the M1C unit).

Mode 3: This mode is used with the T1-compatible carrier system. The two digroups function independently over separate T1 facilities (1.544 Mbit/s). The far-end terminal can be any combination of D1D, D2, D3, and D4 channel banks (mode 3) or other compatible terminals.

Mode 4: This mode consists of four digroups (two D4 systems) multiplexed together to generate a single 96-channel signal. The mode four systems' output is DS2 or a 6.312 Mbit/s and it is compatible with the DS2-type digital line.

Mode 5: Mode 5 is the same as mode 4 except the link is fiber. It is not used much, because fiber usually is employed for higher speeds.

VENDORS' D4 CHANNEL BANKS

Today, there are several D4 channel bank manufacturers. While they are compatible, they have different packaging arrangements, and different nomenclature regarding their common cards. Moreover, different testing procedures are employed on each system. The examples provided here are Nortel Networks' and AT&T's D4 and DE4/DE4E.[5]

---

[5]AT&T transmission products (which were split off into Lucent) still carry the AT&T brand name. However, all new documentation which supports the AT&T products (such as DDM2000 and FT2000) uses the Lucent name instead of AT&T. Field technicians often refer to AT&T and Lucent equipment synonymously. The new shelves, replacement cards, and updated documentation use the Lucent name instead of AT&T.

AT&T's D4

The AT&T D4 carrier system is packaged as a 48-channel entity. It uses the same quantizing and encoding method as the D2 and D3 generation channel banks and can sample in any of the three sequences that have been discussed. It can be configured as two independent digroups and can be interfaced with two different T1 facilities. It can also be equipped with an on-board multiplexer to work with DS1C or DS2.

Nortel Networks' DE4 and DE4E

The DE-4 channel bank is packaged as two DE-3 channel banks on one backplane. The common equipment in this channel bank is similar to that of the older banks, and the DE-4 can be equipped with the older channel units. The main difference in the DE-4 channel bank is that space is made for an onboard multiplexer, called a line interface unit (LIU). Each half section (24 channels) is called a digroup, with the lower one designated "A" and the upper one "B" (see Figure 4–10).

The Nortel DE-4 enhanced (DE4E) channel bank is a 48-channel digital carrier terminal used for two-way transmission of voice and data-port signals over DS1, DS1C, or DS2 facilities. (Western Electric's D4 has dataport application, Nortel's DE4 does not.) In addition to providing high quality toll-grade transmission for voice circuits, the enhanced bank provides the following features:

1. Full-fill data capability for local loop applications or access to the DDS network.
2. Provision for 64 kbit/s clear channel capability (with B8ZS line coding as an option).
3. Capability of future upgrading for extended superframe format and/or low bitrate voice (LBRV) feature provides compressed encoding of the voice channel signal processing.

The DE4E channel bank is composed of two digroups. Digroup A is the bottom 24 channel group, and digroup B is the top 24 channel group. When the channel bank is equipped for voice or data circuits, it may be configured for DS1, DS1C, or DS2.

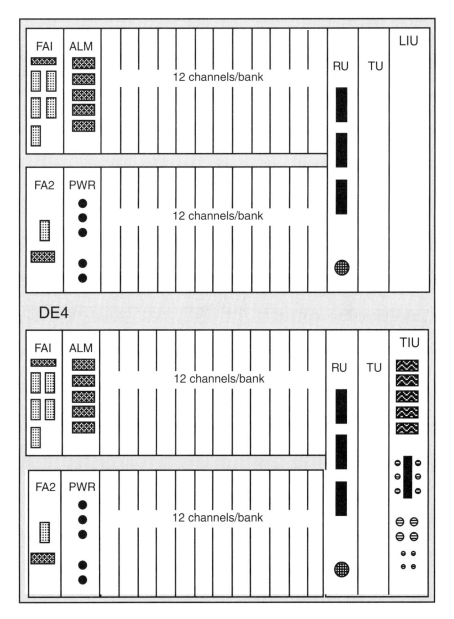

Figure 4–10   The Nortel DE4.

OTHER D4 FEATURES

During the mid-to-late 1980s customers showed interest in dataport, DDS, and clear channel capabilities (CCC). Consequently, all manufacturers and vendors began making their D4 or D5 generation channel banks capable of supporting AMI or B8ZS. These channel banks can also be configured for either SF or ESF formats.

B8ZS

A minimum of one pulse in eight is required by the network span repeaters. B8ZS inserts intentional bipolar violations (BPVs) to represent a string of eight consecutive 0s. The principal characteristics of B8ZS are as follows:

1. B8ZS does not limit the number of 0s allowed in the data stream.
2. Each block of eight consecutive 0s is removed and bipolar violations are inserted in the fourth/fifth and seventh/eighth bit positions.
3. Multiplexers must be equipped to detect B8ZS codes and convert them to eight consecutive 0s, because they cannot pass bipolar violations.
4. B8ZS is required for 64 kbit/s clear channel applications.

Clear Channel Capability

To provide CCC, a DS1 signal with unconstrained information bits is altered to meet the pulse density requirements cited in Table 4–5. The recommended long-term method used for providing CCC is bipolar with 8-zero substitution (B8ZS). This method permits CCC by replacing each all-0 octet with a signature octet that contains a line signal pulse sequence with bipolar violations (BPVs).

- If the last one bit is coded as -1, the 8-zero string is replaced by the pattern, 000–1+10+1–1 (see Figure 4–11).
- If the last one bit is coded as +1, the 8-zero string is replaced by the pattern, 000+1–10+1+1.

This deliberate production of a specific bipolar violation pattern allows recognition that an 8-zero string is intended, provided that the

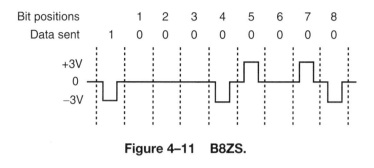

Figure 4–11   B8ZS.

equipment receiving the DS1 signal has been optioned to recognize it as such. This substitution allows the DS1 signal to pass an 8-zero string without depriving the T1 generators of power for their clock.

Zero-Byte Time Slot Interchange (ZBTSI)

ZBTSI is another method for providing bit sequence independence for networks with restricted transport capability (stemming from the use of the alternate mark inversion line code). Two kbit/s of overhead information is required for the ZBTSI algorithm to function properly. This requires the use of the ESF to carry the information within the data link. For more detailed information on ZBTSI, see Bellcore Technical Reference TR-TSY-000499, Issue 31.

Acceptance and Maintenance Testing for DS1 Service. Acceptance and maintenance testing for DS1 service is performed on carrier POT-to-POT basis (POT stands for point of termination) using the errored second (ES) performance parameter, one or more ESF errors. These tests are typically performed utilizing a quasirandom signal source (QRSS). QRSS is a specific bit error rate test (BERT) pattern injected into a T1 system facility sent to a device to test the facility's ability to pass the pattern correctly. BERT is the percentage of received bits in error as compared to the total number of bits received. In addition to QRSS, the 3-in-24, 1-in-8, and all-1s test patterns (see Table 4–6) are acceptable diagnostic stress tests for DS1 service.

These tests are not mandatory but are performed upon request according to the AMI/B8ZS testing matrix as shown in Table 4–7. All locations have the test equipment to perform these tests. In these instances, appropriate loopback techniques are utilized.

Table 4–6   Test pattern definitions.

Test	Pattern
3-in-24	F01000100000000000000100
1-in-8	F01000000 . . . (1:7) bit 2 = 1
All 1s	F11111111 . . . .
QRSS	Framing bit may be randomly phased. (See TR-NPL-000054 and ANSI T1.403-1989)

Extended Superframe Format

All D4 channel bank vendors offer a model that is capable of ESF (see Table 4–8). The ESF format consists of 24 consecutive frames. Each 193rd bit times 8000 frames per second yields 8000 bits, which is divided into these three categories:

1. 2 kbit/s terminal synchronization: As previously discussed, there are 193 bits in each frame of the extended superframe, which is comprised of 24 frames. The 2 kbit/s terminal synchronization relates to the use of six of the flag bits. They are called framing pulse synchronization-framing extended (FPS/FE) bits. The synchronization is inserted into the 193rd bit of every fourth frame

Table 4–7   AMI and B8ZS testing matrix.

Acceptance Tests			Immediate Action Limits	
Test	Duration	E/S limits	Duration	E/S Limits
3-in-24 (AMI)	5 min.	7	5 min.	60
1-in-8 (B8ZS)	5 min.	7	5 min.	60
All 1s	5 min.	7	5 min.	60
QRSS	15 min. (4–15 min. test)	20	5 min.	60

3-in-24   The pattern consists of three 1s in a 24-bit word with no more than 15 consecutive 0s. This pattern contains the minimum number of 1s and the maximum number of 0s. Valid for all types of T1 carrier system testing.

1-in-8   This pattern consists of a repetitive 10000000 pattern and is a valid test for types of T1 carrier systems and facilities.

Table 4–8   Format for 12–frame superframe [BELL90b].

Frame No.	Bit No.	S Bits (193rd)			Bit Use per Time Slot						
		Extended Super Framing	Data Link	Block Check/ CRC	Information Bits	Signaling Bit	Signaling Options				
							T	2	4	16	
1	0	–	M1	–	–	–	–	–	–	–	
2	193	–	–	C1	1-8	–	–	–	–	–	
3	386	–	M2	–	1-8	–	–	–	–	–	
4	579	0	–	–	1-8	–	–	–	–	–	
5	772	–	M3	–	1-8	–	–	–	–	–	
6	965	–	–	C2	1-7	8	–	A	A	A	
7	1158	–	M4	–	1-8	–	–	–	–	–	
8	1351	0	–	–	1-8	–	–	–	–	–	
9	1544	–	M5	–	1-8	–	–	–	–	–	
10	1737	–	–	C3	1-8	–	–	–	–	–	
11	1930	–	M6	–	1-8	–	–	–	–	–	
12	2123	1	–	–	1-7	8	–	A	B	B	
13	2316		M7	–	–	–	–	–	–	–	
14	2509	–	–	C4	1-8	–	–	–	–	–	
15	2702	–	M8	–	1-8	–	–	–	–	–	
16	2895	0	–	–	1-8	–	–	–	–	–	
17	3088	–	M9	–	1-8	–	–	–	–	–	
18	3281	–	–	C5	1-7	8	–	A	A	A	
19	3474	–	M10	–	1-8	–	–	–	–	–	
20	3667	1	–	–	1-8	–	–	–	–	–	
21	3860	–	M11	–	1-8	–	–	–	–	–	
22	4053	–	–	C6	1-8	–	–	–	–	–	
23	4246	–	M12	–	1-8	–	–	–	–	–	
24	4439	1	–	–	1-7	8	–	A	B	B	

Notes:
1. Block check (or CRC-6 cyclic redundancy, check code 6).
2. C1 to C6 cyclic-redundancy-check code.
3. Option T—Transparent mode (bit 8 used for information—no signaling bits) for 64 CCC.
4. Option 2—2-state signaling (channel A).
5. Option 4—4-state signaling (channels A and B).
6. Option 16—16-state signaling (channels A, B, C and D).
7. Data link may be subdivided.

in a repetitive framing pattern sequence: 0 0 1 0 1 1 (frames 4, 8, 12, 16, 20, and 24, respectively), when the channel bank is in a normal condition.

2. 2 kbit/s cyclic redundancy check/blocked check (CRC/BC): This signal operates in frames 2, 6, 10, 14, 18, and 22) of the ESF. All of the data bits in one ESF (24 * 193 = 4632) are considered to be one binary number. This number is divided by another binary number, called a constant (which equates to the decimal value of 64). The six least significant bits (LSBs) of the remainder are sent as CRC bits during the next ESF. At the receiving end, the constant is applied to the 4632-bit ESF, and the six LSBs of the remainder are stored and compared with the CRC bits received during the next ESF.

3. 4 kbit/s data link control channel: This signal operates in every odd-numbered 193rd bit (in frames 1, 3, 5, . . . 23). The data link bit is used to report cyclic redundancy check (CRC) violations to the distant end as well as system alarms and commands (loop back, testing, provisioning, etc.).

The Data Link Channel. One option on the data link channel is based on the well-known High Level Data Link Control (HDLC) protocol and Link Access Procedure D (LAPD), published by the International Standards Organization (ISO). The HDLC standard forms the basis for many layer 2 protocols for other technologies, such as ISDN and X.25. The aggregated bits of the DL channel create a frame, as shown in Figure 4–12. The address field contains identification information about the frame, the control field uses the HDLC unnumbered information format, which means that the channel does not offer any sequencing (numbered) operations for the frames on this channel. The information field (I field)

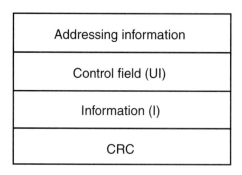

| Addressing information |
| Control field (UI) |
| Information (I) |
| CRC |

Figure 4–12   The DL channel format.

contains the diagnostic information pertaining to ESF operations. The CRC field is part of HDLC, but is considered a separate operation in the ESF system.

ANSI T1.403 (1995) describes the use of the ESF data link. Two formats within the channel are permitted. The bit-patterned format can carry various messages, called code words. These messages are used for RAI/yellow alarms, activating/deactivating loopbacks between a channel bank and customer equipment and a variety of other functions. The second format uses the HDLC/LAPD frame format shown in Figure 4–12.

Examples of ESF Operations. Table 4–9 shows the structure for the performance report message and some examples of messages that are coded in the I field. It is evident that the message is used for monitoring and reporting on the state of the link. The contents of the I field are interpreted as follows: The "Bits" designation is a tag for each bit in the

Table 4–9 Performance report message structure.

Value	Interpretation
00111000	SAPI = 14, C/R = 0 (from customer), EA = 0
00111010	SAPI = 14, C/R = 1 (from Carrier), EA = 0
00000001	TEI= 0, EA = 1
Control	*Interpretation*
00000011	Unacknowledged information transfer (UI)
I Field	
Bits	*Interpretation*
G1 = 1	CRC error event = 1
G2 = 1	1<CRC error event $\leq$ 5
G3 = 1	5<CRC error event $\leq$ 10
G4 = 1	10<CRC error event $\leq$ 100
G5 = 1	100<CRC error event $\leq$ 319
G6 = 1	CRC Error event 3 320
SE = 1	Severely errored framing event $\geq$ 1 (FE shall = 0)
FE = 1	Frame synchronization bit error event $\geq$ 1 (SE shall = 0)
LV = 1	Line code violation event $\geq$ 1
SL = 1	Slip event $\geq$ 1
LB = 1	Payload loopback activated
U1, U2 = 0	User study for synchronization
R = 0	Reserved (default value is 0)
NmN1 = 00,01,10,11	One-second report Modulo 4 counter
FCS	INTERPRETATION
VARIABLE	CRC 16 Frame Check Sequence

I field. Bits G1 and G6 contain information on the number of CRC errors that have been detected by a receiver during certain time periods. The other bits, SE through N1, provide a variety of provisioning and alarm signals. ANSI T1.403 (1989) provides several examples of the use of the ESF data link, if the reader wishes more information.

The CRC Operations. Let us take a closer look at the cyclic redundancy code 6 (CRC-6) and how it is used in the ESF. Error checking codes overcome many of the limitations of BPV monitoring. The CRC-6 code built into the ESF framing format makes performance monitoring possible at any point in a DS1 facility, including T1 span line outputs, DS1 outputs of multiplexers and terminals (including channel banks), digital switches, and DSXs (digital cross-connect systems).

The CRC-6 code identifies 63 out of 64 (98%) ESFs with one or more errors. CRC-6 is the only available method that verifies the 95% error free second (EFS) specification of customer premise DS1 facilities (that pass through multiplexers).

CRC-6 works by treating the ESF as a number represented in binary form (4632 bits long, or 193×24). This number could be as small as zero (all 0s) or as large as 2^{4632} (all 1s). The number is then divided by 64, which will always give a remainder between 0 and 63 (63 being the largest number that can be reported in the 6 CRC bits). The value of that remainder is reported in the CRC bits of the following ESF. Meanwhile, at the far end, the CRC operation is repeated and the remainder stored in memory. When the following frame arrives, the CRC bits are evaluated and checked against the previous frame's value (stored in memory). If the numbers do not match, a CRC error is recorded. The calculations shown in the following example is accomplished in hardware, so there is no noticeable time delay caused by CRC-6 checks. Box 4–1 shows an example of the CRC operation.

D5 CHANNEL BANKS

The D5 channel bank is the latest generation of D channel banks. The D5 digital terminal system is microprocessor-based and software-driven. Its plug-in units have no mechanically adjustable attenuators, switches, or shorting pin options. Instead, all channel units, common equipment transmission parameters, and options are established electronically with software utilizing the EIA-232 interface and a craft interface unit (CIU) or personal computer (PC). All D5 provisioning can be performed re-

---

Box 4–1   The Error Check

Assume the numeric value of an ESF is 122,070
Divide 122,068 by 64
The answer is 1,907 with a remainder of 22
Convert the remainder or 22 in base 10 to binary (base 2)
The result is a 010110 binary number
The next extended superframe CRC bits would be:

LSB	Frame 2 = 0	
	Frame 6 = 1	
	Frame 10 = 1	
	Frame 14 = 0	
	Frame 18 = 1	
MSB	Frame 22 = 0	

0	1	0	1	1	0	Add the columns with 1 s in them
32	16	8	4	2	1	16 + 4 + 2 = 22 remainder

LSB = least significant bit
MSB = most significant bit

---

motely from a remote switching control center or centralized operation center. The remote center also can audit equipment status, monitor transmission and equipment performance, receive alarms, and obtain enough information to make a dispatch decision for maintenance problems. Only limited central office and facility forces need to be utilized, which maximizes efficiency.

In other channel banks, loop testing is time consuming and expensive because it requires the coordinated action of a technician at the customer's premises and one or more testers at the serving central office. The D5 system offers a more cost-effective and accurate method of loop testing. It makes use of a portable test set, called a transponder, which is connected to the network interface loop (loop termination) at the customer's premises. Measurements are made automatically, and the results are used by the system controller to calculate optimum balance, gain, and equalize settings, and to automatically adjust the channel unit to these values. Each loop is measured in less than five minutes (on average) and the transponder operator needs no coordinated assistance from the central office. The results of these adjustments are reported automatically to the switching control center and the craft interface unit at the D5 office. In almost every case, substantial savings in craft time and improved loop transmission performance result from transponder provisioning.

The D5 system contains D5 channel banks (up to 20). Their operation is controlled by a microprocessor-based system controller that contains the operating program and channel unit database. The preprogram data for each channel unit and for the bank common equipment is stored in the nonvolatile bubble memory and backed up by magnetic tape.

Each D5 channel bank has a capacity of 96 channels (four digroups), giving a maximum system capacity of 1920 channels. Each can transmit and receive in the DS1 (1.544 Mbit/s) format over four T1 carrier lines, or in the DS1C (3.152 Mbit/s) format over two T1C lines. The frame formats and channel sequencing are compatible with:

- D1D, D2, D3, and D4 channel banks
- Digital carrier trunk used with the AT&T #5ESS switch
- DDS interfaces
- AT&T digital access and cross-connect system (DACS)

ESF, SF, and B8ZS/AMI options are provided. The B8ZS option provides a 64 kbit/s CCC and is compatible with the ISDN B channel.

The D5 system controller administers the provisioning and maintenance activities of all D5 common units and channel units through a bank controller unit in each bank that interprets communications to and from the system controller. Timing signals are derived in a bank clock and a bank synchronizer unit that provides independent timing for each individual digroup (24 channels) and external DDS synchronization, when needed.

Summary of the Use of the Eighth Bit

The D4 and D5 channel banks use the 8th bit with a four-state and sixteen-state scheme, respectively. For the D4 bank, the A bit is sent in the 6th frame and the B bit is sent in the 12th frame. For the D5 channel bank, the A and B bits are sent as in the D4 scheme, then the C bit is transmitted in the 18th frame and the D bit is transmitted in the 24th frame. In summary, Table 4–10 shows these operations.

Table 4–10   Use of the 8th bit.

D4 Super Frame:

Frame	2-State	4-State	
6	A	A	
12	A	B	

D5 Extended Super Frame

Frame	2-State	4-State	16-State
6	A	A	A
12	A	B	B
18	A	A	C
24	A	B	D

SUBSCRIBER-TYPE SYSTEMS

Subscriber-type PCM systems are available that use the same quantizing and encoding processes as the D2, D3, and D4 systems explained previously (see Figure 4–13). These systems are also software programmable for voice and data circuits just as the D4 and D5 channel banks are. They are capable of SF/ESF, AMI/B8ZS, and ADPCM (LBRV) operations. The main difference is that one terminal is located in the central office while

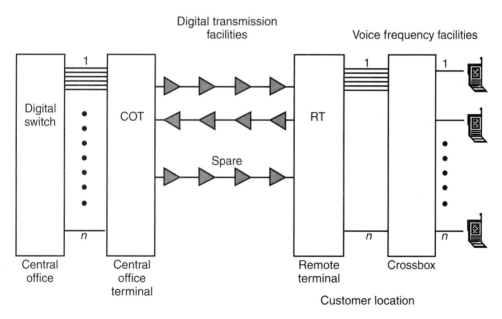

Figure 4–13   Basic subscriber system arrangement.

the other is in the field near or on the customer's location. They may also be referred to as a pair gain system, a digital loop carrier, or a subscriber loop carrier. Some of them can also extend a leased DS1 and or DS3 to the customer premise for his or her own use.

Subscriber-type systems support a wide variety of applications by various operating companies. One of the more popular uses is providing service to developing areas for new subdivisions where an existing cable plant is insufficient. A system can provide the service immediately and permanently, or it can be moved to another location (if growth in the area eventually justifies a central office). Regardless of whether the service is permanent or temporary, a subscriber system is easy to engineer and install on short notice. An example would be a new industrial park experiencing sudden and unexpected growth, resulting in demands for service exceeding available loop plant. The system can be installed and operating within a few weeks. Also, many companies use these systems to provide temporary service to large functions, such as business conventions or sporting events.

There are other reasons to justify the placement of a subscriber loop carrier in the loop plant. First, the copper pairs serving the subscribers will be much shorter, thus overcoming distance limitations in providing the newer services. Second, shortening the customer loop decreases the exposure to power-line interference with its resultant degradation and noise impact on these circuits. Flexibility is further enhanced by the 1200-ohm loop capability of the remote terminal. Third, electronics allow for the future ability to provide new services quickly. The distance from the central office to the remote terminal is limited only by the copper DS1 span line performance. Today, most of these systems employ fiber optics, so there is very little distance limitation. Subscriber loop carriers provide applications for videoconferencing and local area network (LAN) links.

Subscriber carrier systems provide several functions that channel banks do not because they are in the local loop. These are as follows: ringing, coin collection, party lines, remote terminals, and subscriber line testing, as well as batteries for back-up power and fan units when not installed in a controlled environment.

GR-303

GR-303 was published by Bellcore under the title *Integrated Digital Loop Carrier* (IDLC) *System Generic Requirements, Objectives, and Interface.* This publication sets forth the requirements for the installation, operations and maintenance of the ADSL, HFC, ATM, and wireless technologies on the local loop. The GR-303 technology has been widely deployed throughout the United States.

Figure 4–14 shows the functional view of the IDLC architecture. In this particular installation, IDLC includes the DSX-1 frame over which the physical cross connects occur for the DS1 signals. The remote digital terminal (RDT) provides the interface between the customer access lines (CALs) and the DS1 facility. The digital transmission facility (DTF) interface terminates one DS1 facility and provides several digital terminal services, such as frame alignment, multiplexing/demultiplexing, signaling insertion, and signaling extraction.

The DTF facility also includes power feed, fault location with loopbacks, and signal regeneration. These functions operate in the line terminal equipment (LTE) card which is installed into the RDT or LDS. These LTE functions can also be installed in other external equipment such as office repeater bays (ORBs) located either at the central office or at the RDT.

While the ORB is part of the DTF, it is installed as a separate piece of equipment (located in the central office or the RDT). In addition the office regenerators (ORs) provide the signal characteristics that are needed for the connection of the DTF to the DSX-1 frame. These functions must

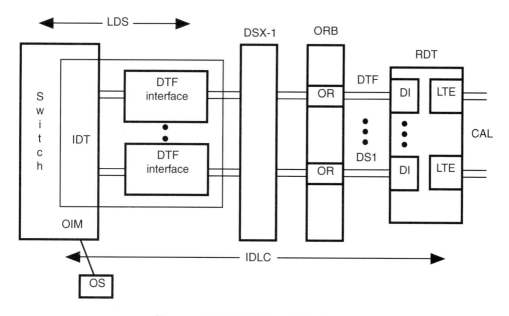

Figure 4–14   IDLC architecture.

include DC powering for all line repeaters, equalization, and signal regeneration, impedance matching, and metallic pair termination.

The integrated digital terminal (IDT) is a piece of equipment that replicates the functions of previous UDLC systems COT, with the exception of D/A and A/D conversions.

The GR-303 interface provides for five major types of services. The first service is DS1 facility operations, which is used to support the signals across the interface with DS1 alarms, loopbacks, and protection switching. Call processing is the second major function, which allows setup and clearance of calls, timeslot assignment, and use of autoband signaling (with some options). The third function is information transport and is for the support of the transport of user traffic—voice, video, data, etc. The fourth function is IDLC System/Terminal Operations, and encompasses provisioning, performance monitoring, etc. The fifth function is part of the DS1 facility operations and is called loop testing. Loop testing is controlled in a proprietary fashion between lines, in the CO, or in a remote maintenance center at an RTU at the RDT location.

FINAL THOUGHTS ON THE D CHANNEL BANKS

People who are trained in software engineering and data switches often find the T1 family (especially channel banks) prosaic and inefficient. We agree. But remember, the new generations have had to support the services and formats of the older generations. They are cumbersome because they must be backward compatible. (Most any technology that is backward-compatible carries the older technology as a technical albatross.) For this reason, SONET makes a clean break from the past, but still provides clever mechanisms to support the older T1 family of products.

Also, the pair gain, digital loop carrier, and subscriber loop carrier and devices (as implemented with GR 303) are currently the new systems being deployed in the field and in the serving central office. (Whether they are referred to as pair gain, digital loop carrier, or subscriber loop carrier depends on the vendor.) Typically, these systems have a build-in OC-3 SONET multiplexer to interface with fiber for transport of the customers traffic from the local loop to the serving central office. The RT (remote terminal, or remote digital terminal) is located at the customer premises and the COT (central office terminal) is located in the central office.

We are getting ahead of ourselves. Let us wrap up some of the other important aspects of T1 before moving to SONET.

FRACTIONAL T1 (FT1)

Some customers require more than one DS0, as in data port applications, but not a full DS1. Fractional T1 can be the answer since it provides 4 to 23 DS0s in a DS1, and is cost effective for numerous applications (see Table 4–11). FT1 uses the standard DS1/T1 signal. The DCS can perform grooming for the number of DS0s that the customer needs at any given time.

DIVIDING AND FILLING THE T1 CHANNEL

Most T1 vendors now offer various services for dividing the T1 channel into "smaller pieces," often called enhanced PCM. Some of the options are shown in Figure 4–15. The use of enhanced PCM schemes allows a user to obtain more bandwidth for the T1 channel.

In addition, most vendors have capabilities that allow the customer to use the T1 channel for voice, video, and data. The manner in which this traffic shares the channel differs among vendors. Most vendors allow the dynamic allocation of the slots in the T1 frame and compress periods of silence, sending only talkspurts (spoken periods only) across the channel. These concepts are shown in Figure 4–16.

Table 4–11 Examples of fractional T-1 use.

Examples:
X-ray transmission
Main frames
Video teleconferencing
Digital fax
Direct interchange carrier (IXC) connection
Computer-aided design (CAD)/computer-aided manufacturing (CAM)

Customer Benefits:
Growth to six DS0s (possibly to 12 DS0s)
Digital voice, data, video
High speed
Economical
Security
Standard DS1 interface

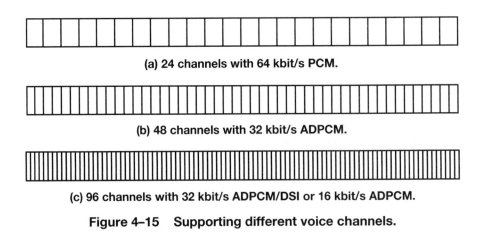

(a) 24 channels with 64 kbit/s PCM.

(b) 48 channels with 32 kbit/s ADPCM.

(c) 96 channels with 32 kbit/s ADPCM/DSI or 16 kbit/s ADPCM.

Figure 4–15   Supporting different voice channels.

COMPENSATING FOR CLOCK DIFFERENCES IN A T1 SYSTEM

In Chapter 3, we examined timing, clocking, and synchronization. We will now apply some of these ideas to the T1 system. Recall that in an asynchronous or plesiochronous system, timing differences usually occur between the different network elements (multiplexers, digital cross-connects, etc.). We also have learned that as signals are multiplexed into higher rates, the pulses of the signals become narrower at each stage of the multiplexing operation, which allows for more pulses per second.

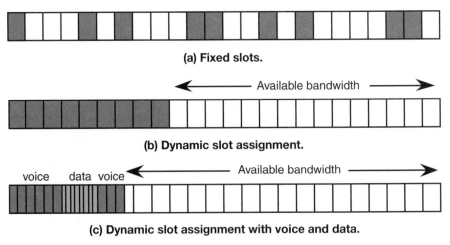

(a) Fixed slots.

(b) Dynamic slot assignment.

(c) Dynamic slot assignment with voice and data.

Figure 4–16   Assigning bandwidth.

The T1 approach to synchronizing different inputs (say, DS1 inputs) to a common frequency at the output (say, DS2 output) is to use a bit rate of each input that is higher than a maximum expected input rate. With this approach, all inputs can be rate-adapted to this common higher rate and then fed into the common DS output. How is this done? It is accomplished through the simple technique of bit stuffing. Figure 4–16 shows an example of this operation.

The basic idea of bit stuffing is to provide at the receiving machine a means to increase the bit rate of each incoming stream to a common rate. Thus, in Figure 4–17, the DS1 signals arrive at a multiplexer at different rates, but at rates that must be lower than the rates that are generated at the multiplexer. Each incoming signal has its bit stream stuffed to raise its rate to a common rate of all incoming streams. In this manner, asynchronous streams are synchronized to a common stream at the multiplexer. Bit stuffing consumes about one percent of the bandwidth on the channel.

Figure 4–18 shows stuffing operations in more detail. At a transmitting multiplexer, the clock is extracted from the incoming DS1 signals and used to write into an input buffer at the DS1 clock rate. This operation is labeled "E&W" in Figure 4–18. A locally generated clock is used to read (labeled "R" in the figure) from this buffer at a higher rate than the maximum input rate. When the read operation is about to overtake the write, the read-out operation is halted briefly and a stuffing bit is inserted into the bit stream (labeled "S" in the figure). This operation ensures that all incoming streams are synchronized to a common frequency. The figure shows that the additional framing bits (labeled "F" in the figure) are also added to the stream.

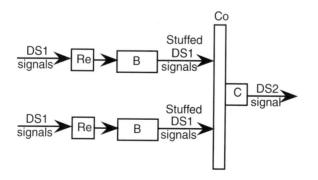

Figure 4–17   Bit stuffing.

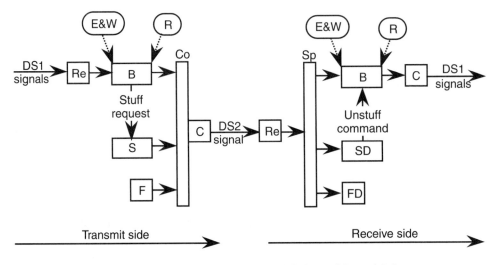

Figure 4–18   Typical T1-based multiplexer/demultiplexer.

At the receiving multiplexer, the process is reversed. As before, the clock is extracted from the incoming DS2 signals and used to write into the input buffer at the DS2 rate. However, the locally generated read clock operates at a lower rate than the input stream. The stuffing bits are removed at the receive buffer by stopping the write clock for the exact time interval that is taken up by the stuffing bit. The framing detector detects the framing signals and removes them. The read clock is derived from the input streams (after unstuffing has occurred), and any accumulated jitter is removed by a locally generated oscillator before the bit streams are sent out as DS1 signals.

SUMMARY

Digital transmission carrier systems have been in existence for over thirty years. These have evolved from rather primitive D1-type channel banks to sophisticated, self-provisioning D5 channel banks. Notwithstanding, their underlying asynchronous architecture is based on an old technology. SONET updates this archaic technology by restructuring the asynchronous input to a structured frame that allows for enhanced communications between the network elements.

APPENDIX 4A: FRAME FORMATS

Frame Formats

In the main body of this chapter, we learned how a DS1 frame was developed and we introduced the equipment that created DS1C and DS2 signals. Now, let us examine their frame formats.

DS1C Formats. As shown in Figure 4A–1(a), bit interleaving is used for each port following each control bit. As shown in Figures 4A–1(a) and (b), the DS1C bit stream is organized into a block of 52 bits, with 26 bits from each DS1 input signal. A control bit precedes each block, designated as an M, C, or F bit. The 24 control bits are distributed

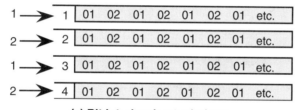

(a) Bit interleaving technique.

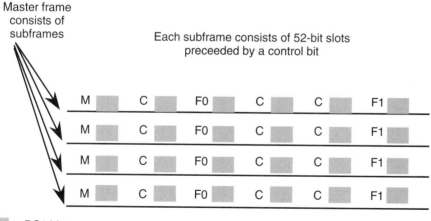

= DS1 bits

(b) Basics of asynchronous rate exchange (for DS1C).

Figure 4A-1   Note: Asynchronous multiplexing uses bit interleaving. A bit from port 01 (DS1 signal) and a bit from port 02 (another DS1 signal) then a bit from port 01, then a bit from port 01, etc.

in the M frame and are called a control sequence or word. The 1272-bit block is called an M frame.

Figure 4A–2 provides more information on the DS1C frame format, and Figure 4A–3 shows the flow of bits in the DS1C frame. The 4 Mbits reside in the first, seventh, thirteenth, and nineteenth positions of the control sequence. Its sequence is 011X, and 011 identifies the M frame format and the start of the four 318-bit subframes. The X bit is used as a maintenance channel to send alarm conditions from the receiving terminal to the sending terminal. A value of 1 is no alarm and a value of 0 is an alarm.

The F-bit sequence is made up of alternate 0s and 1s for a pattern of 010101 and resides in every third bit of the control sequence. It is used by the receiving terminal to identify the frame and control bit time slots.

The C-bit sequence is used to identify the presence or absence of stuff bits in the DS1 parts of each subframe. These bits are coded according to the following rules:

- C bit = 111: A stuff bit (pulse) is to be inserted into the subframe
- C bit = 000: No stuff will occur

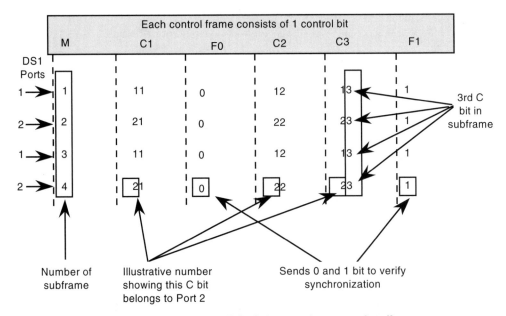

Figure 4A-2   The DS1C format in more detail.

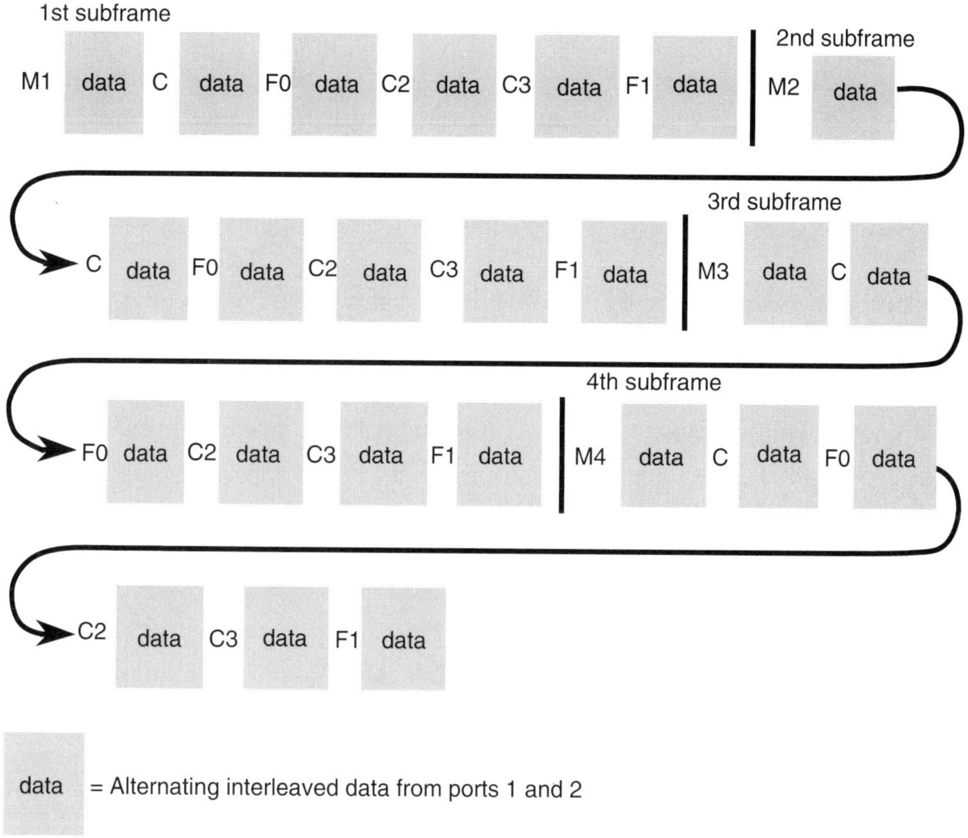

1st subframe

M1 data C data F0 data C2 data C3 data F1 data | 2nd subframe M2 data

3rd subframe

C data F0 data C2 data C3 data F1 data | M3 data C data

4th subframe

F0 data C2 data C3 data F1 data | M4 data C data F0 data

C2 data C3 data F1 data

data = Alternating interleaved data from ports 1 and 2

Figure 4-A3   DS1C master frame bit flow.

- Stuffed time slot: Third information bit following third C bit in the subframe
- Stuffing for 1st DS1 signal: First and third subframes
- Stuffing for 2nd DS1 signal: Second and fourth subframes
- Maximum stuffing rate is 4956 bit/s for each DS1 signal and nominal rate is 2264 bit/s

The standards committee did allow for AMI or B8ZS line code options for DS1C. However, AMI was the selected choice by the vendors as well as the Telcos and these organizations never implemented the option for B8ZS.

The DS2 Frame Format. The basic difference between the M1C and the M12 multiplexer is that the M12 has four DS1 inputs (ports), not just two. Remember, M12 means first level in and second level out. As shown in Figure 4A–4, the master frame is still divided into four subframes and each subframe is divided into six control frames. Synchronization of the frame DS1 signals together is still a requirement because these inputs may have originated from different sources with different clocks.

The DS2 frame is 1176 bits, and is divided into four 294-bit subframes. Each control frame has 49 time slots instead of 52 time slots. Each control frame still begins with a control bit for the multiplexer and is followed with 48 information bits, a bit interleaved from each of the four ports twelve times. Instead of a port stuffing in two subframes, the M12 stuffs port #1 in subframe #1, port #2 in subframe #2, port #3 in subframe #3, and port #4 in subframe #4. Instead of the stuffing following the third C bit, as was done in the M1C frame, the stuffing is in the last F1 control frame in the subframe for that port. For example, if port #1 needs to stuff, then the three C bits will all be all 1s and we stuff for port #1 in subframe #1 and the time slot that is designated for stuffing is the first time slot following the last F1 in subframe #1 because that is port #1 information time slot. Three of the ports will have to do stuffing, the fastest DS1 port will not do any stuffing.

It should be noted that the decoder in the receiving multiplexer only needs to detect at least two of the three C bits as being logic 1s to denote that stuffing was done. This is true of DS1C, DS2, and DS3 multiplexers.

B6ZS Line Code—DS2. The DS2 line code is bipolar with 6-zero substitution (B6ZS) (see Figure 4A–5). In the B6ZS line code, any series of six consecutive 0s is replaced by a specific code containing bipolar violations (BPVs). Where a 6-zero byte is encountered:

- If the last one bit was coded as +1, the 6-zero byte is replaced by the pattern, $0 + 1 - 10 - 1 + 1$
- If the last one bit was coded as –1, the 6-zero byte is replaced by the pattern, $0 - 1 + 10 + 1 - 1$

The DS3 Frame Format. Seven DS2s make up a DS3 signal, so there are seven DS2 ports as inputs into the multiplexer and a master frame is divided into seven subframes (as shown in Figure 4A–6). Each port has its own subframe for stuffing, just as was done in the DS2

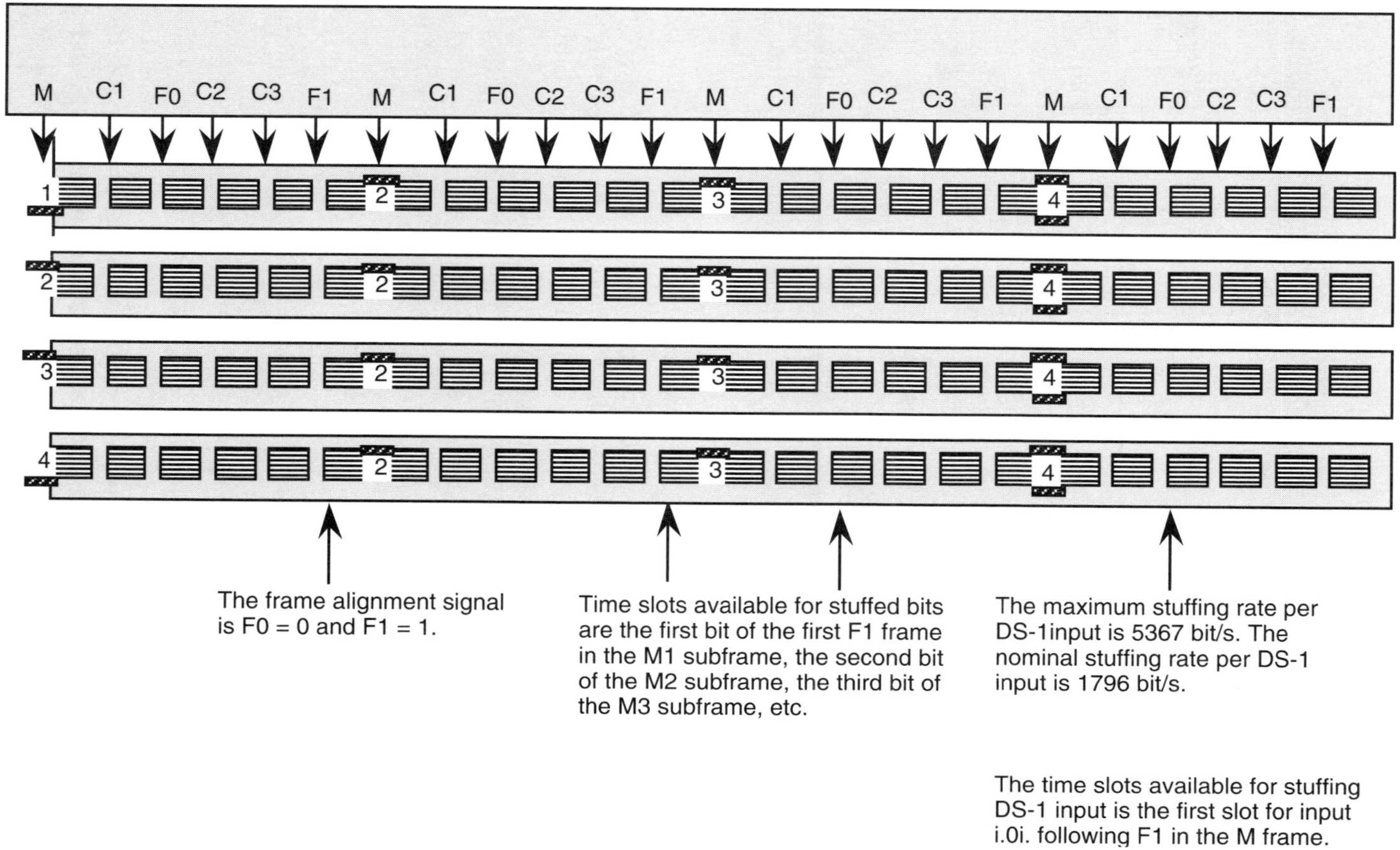
M C1 F0 C2 C3 F1 M C1 F0 C2 C3 F1 M C1 F0 C2 C3 F1 M C1 F0 C2 C3 F1
1 2 3 4
2 2 3 4
3 2 3 4
4 2 3 4
The frame alignment signal is F0 = 0 and F1 = 1.
Time slots available for stuffed bits are the first bit of the first F1 frame in the M1 subframe, the second bit of the M2 subframe, the third bit of the M3 subframe, etc.
The maximum stuffing rate per DS-1input is 5367 bit/s. The nominal stuffing rate per DS-1 input is 1796 bit/s.
The time slots available for stuffing DS-1 input is the first slot for input i.0i. following F1 in the M frame.

Figure 4A-4 Asynchronous DS2.

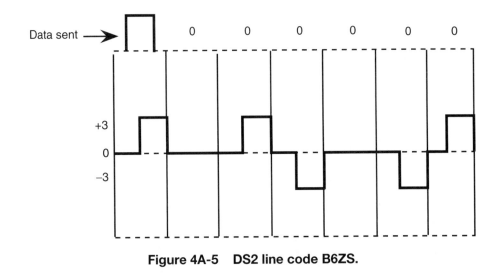

Figure 4A-5   DS2 line code B6ZS.

frame. Stuffing is the first information bit following the last F1 in the subframe that belongs to the port needing to stuff. Two additional control bits signify the start of subframes 1, 2, 3, and 4. The "X" bits begin subframes 1 and 2 as per technical advisory #34 of technical reference 43804; in any one M frame, the two X-bits must be identical. The "P" bits signify the start of subframe 3 and 4. The P bits are for odd or even parity and will be logic 1s if the digital sum of all information bits is odd and logic 0s if the digital sum of all information bits is even.

The electrical DS3 signal is made up of 672 voice channels (DS0s) and its line code is B3ZS. The characteristics of a DS3 signal must meet the ITU-T and ANSI standards in order to be compatible with other vendors.

The DS3 signal in the North American Digital Hierarchy was the last level where standards were set. Therefore, it was only natural that the decision was made for all DCSs into higher level fiber multiplexer be made at the DS3 rate. The frame formats we have covered meet these standards. Because of the timing, framing, and synchronization bits required in asynchronous transmission, the DS3 bit rate used is not a direct multiple of the DS1 or DS2 signals. Once the signals are multiplexed above DS1, the DS0 signals cannot be directly extracted. Anytime a DS0 or DS1 signal must be accessed (cross-connected, etc.), the DS3 or DS-n (any signal higher than DS3) signal must be demultiplexed to a DS1 signal. Using asynchronous multiplexing techniques, there is no end-to-end overhead channel for administrative or maintenance purposes. This in-

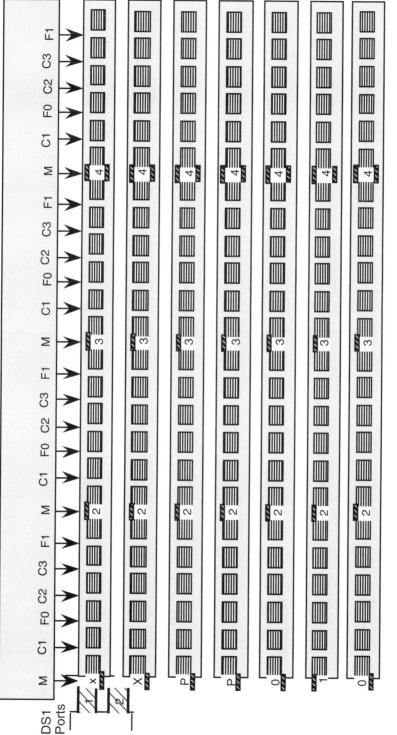

Figure 4A-6 Synchronous DS3.

formation sets the stage for the next chapter on SONET. But first, let us look at two examples of asynchronous multiplexing shelves.

DS3 Alarm Indication Signals. The AIS is used for transmission downstream upon the detection of a digital signal failure. There are two types of AIS signals available at the DS3 signal level:

- Blue signal: A framed 10101010 pattern
- All 1s: An unframed pattern of all ones

The type of AIS signal to be generated depends upon the application. The blue signal is recommended for most standard applications while the all-1s signal should be used for all applications requiring an unframed DS3 signal (such as clear channel applications, video, etc.).

Parity. Parity is an online error checking method used for minimizing transmission errors in received data signals (DS3).

Parity can be declared in one of two ways: even or odd. It is generated at the transmit side, where a parity bit is added to the data stream so as to make the total number of 1s even or odd. The parity bit can be a 1 or 0.

When parity errors are detected, they are put into a counter-register, where the system uses them to compute the bit error rate. When the bit error threshold (strap select option) is exceeded, protection switching occurs. The parity is checked at the receive side.

Parity can be an unreliable source for error checking because it doesn't have a way of computing the total number of bit errors, it just

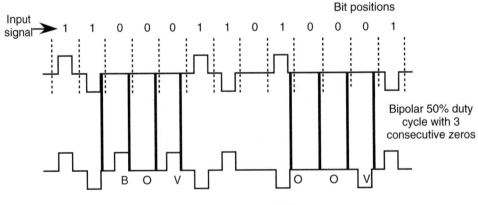

Figure 4A-7   B3ZS.

Table 4A–1   Coding rules for B3ZS.

Binary Signal	101	000	11	000	000	001	000	1.....
Case 1								
Odd	B0B	00V	BB	B0V	B0V	00B	00V	B...
	+0–	00–	+–	+0+	–0–	00+	00+	–
Case 2								
Even	B0B	B0V	BB	B0V	B0V	00B	00V	B...
	+0–	+0+	–+	–0–	+0+	00–	00–	+

shows that there is possibility of bit errors. Instead of parity, a more sophisticated checking system, CRC-6, could be used.

B3ZS Line Code.   The line code is bipolar with 3-zero substitution (B3ZS) (see Figure 4A–7). In the B3ZS format, each block of three consecutive 0s is removed and replaced by either of two codes containing BPV. These replacement codes are B0V and 00V, where B represents a pulse conforming with the bipolar rule and V represents a pulse violating the bipolar rule. The choice of these codes is made so that an odd number of bipolar conforming pulses (B) will be transmitted between consecutive bipolar violation pulses (V).

Table 4A–1 assumes the polarity of the last pulse transmitted was negative (–). If the last pulse transmitted had been positive (+), the resulting bipolar signals would be inverse of that shown. Case 1 assumes an odd number of pulses have been transmitted since the last bipolar violation.

5

SONET Operations

This chapter expands on the material in previous chapters, and describes the basic operations and features of SONET. The subjects of payload mapping, SONET envelopes, topologies, and equipment, introduced in Chapter 1, are examined in more detail in this chapter.

EXAMPLE OF SONET INTERFACES

Figure 5–1 shows an example of SONET interfaces and multiplexing schemes. The reader may wish to review Table 1–1 in Chapter 1 if the terms used in this part of the chapter are not familiar.

The service adapters act as the interfaces into and out of the network. They can support signals ranging from DS1/CEPT1 to B-ISDN, as well as ATM cells. Additionally, sub-DS1 rates (such as DS0) are supported. The purpose of the service adapter is to map these signals into synchronous transport signal 1 (STS-1) envelopes or multiples thereof. As explained in Chapter 1, in North America, all traffic is initially converted to an STS-1 signal (51.84 Mbit/s or higher). In Europe, the service adapters convert the payload to an STS-3 signal (155.520 Mbit/s).

Lower speed signals (such as DS1, and CEPT1) are first multiplexed into virtual tributaries (VTs, a North American term) or virtual containers (VCs, an European term), which are sub-STS-1 payloads. The purpose of the VT/VC is to keep the various payloads organized within the

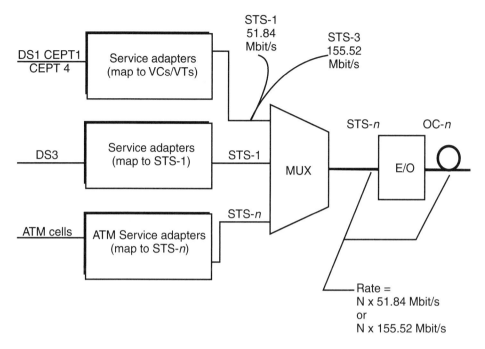

Figure 5–1   SONET multiplexing.

SONET envelope. Several STS-1s can be multiplexed together to form an STS-n signal. These signals are sent to an electrical/optical (E/O) converter, where a conversion is made to an optical carrier-n (OC-n) optical signal. Thereafter, all traffic is transported through SONET in homogenous, synchronous envelopes.

SONET Configuration

Figure 5–2 shows a simplified diagram of a SONET configuration. The bottom part of the figure relates the configuration to some terms used later in the chapter. Three types of equipment are employed in a SONET system: (1) path terminating equipment, (2) line terminating equipment, and (3) section terminating equipment (a regenerator). These components are introduced in this section and described in more detail later in the chapter.

The path terminating equipment (PTE) is a terminal or multiplexer that is responsible for mapping the user payload (DS1, CEPT1, FDDI, etc.) into a SONET format. Some vendors call this equipment a service adapter (a term we introduced in Figure 5–1). The PTE must extend to

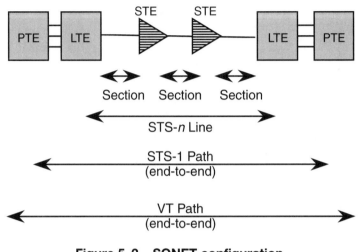

Figure 5–2   SONET configuration.

the network elements that assemble and disassemble the payload for the user customer premises equipment (CPE).

The line terminating equipment (LTE) is a hub that provides services to the PTE, notably multiplexing, synchronization, and automatic protection switching. It does not extend to the CPE, but operates between network elements. Thus, the customer never "sees" this part of the SONET configuration.

The section terminating equipment (STE) is a regenerator that also performs functions similar to HDLC-type protocols: frame alignment and scrambling, as well as error detection and monitoring. It is responsible for signal reception and signal regeneration. The STE may be part of the LTE.

OAM at the Three Components

Each of these components utilize substantial operations, administration, and maintenance (OAM) information (overhead). Path level overhead is inserted at the SONET terminal and carried end-to-end to the receiving terminal. The overhead is added to DSn signals when they are mapped into virtual tributaries (VTs) and removed when the DSn signals are extracted from the SONET envelope.

Line overhead is used for STS-n signals. This information is created by LTE, such as STS-n multiplexers. The SONET line concept is important to network robustness, because a line span is protected in case of line or equipment failure, or a deterioration of conditions. Functions operate at the line level to provide for alternate paths—an operation called protection switching—and part of the line overhead is used to implement protection switching.

The section overhead is used between adjacent network elements such as the regenerators. It contains fields for framing of the traffic, the identification of the STS payload, error detection, order wires, and a large variety of network-specific functions.

CONFIGURATION POSSIBILITIES

One of the attractive aspects of SONET is its ability to use multiple fibers between equipment. For example, two fibers can be connected between two machines, say, a terminal adapter at a customer office and a terminal adapter at the central office. The advantage to having multiple fibers between the two locations is that one can be utilized as a back-up to the other. In a SONET system, the fiber that carries the user traffic is called the working copy, and the fiber that acts as a back-up to the working copy is called the protection copy.

Automatic Protection Switching (APS)

If more than one fiber is available between the machines, provision can be made for automatic protection switching or APS. This feature permits the network to react to failed lines, interfaces or poor-quality signals by switching to an alternate facility (as illustrated in Figure 5–3). Protection-switching operations are initiated for a number of reasons. As an example, the network manager may issue a command to switch the working facility operations to the protection facility for purposes of maintenance, testing, etc. Or, more commonly, APS operations are initiated when connections are lost or the signal quality deteriorates.

APS can be provisioned for a 1:1 or a 1:n facility. With the 1:1 option, each working facility (fiber) is backed up by a protection facility (fiber). With a 1:n option, one protection facility may service from one to a maximum of 14 working facilities.

As a general practice, the 1:1 operation entails the transmission of traffic on both the working and protection facilities. Both signals are monitored at the receiving end (the tail end) for failures or degradation of signal quality. Based on this analysis, the working or protection facility can be selected and switching operations can be sent back to the sender

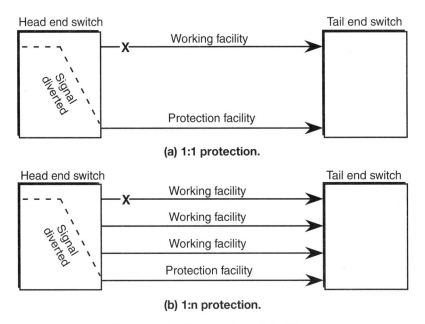

(a) 1:1 protection.

(b) 1:n protection.

Figure 5–3   Protection switching.

(head end) to discern which facility is being employed for the transmission of the traffic.

For the 1:n APS, the switching is reverted. That is to say, the traffic is sent across the working facilities and the protection facility is only employed upon the detection of a failure. So the protection facility is not employed until a working facility fails.

Achieving Structural Diversity

Ideally, one would like to have the working and protection fiber in different paths (different feeders) between the network elements. This option is not always possible, but (as seen in Figure 5–4(a)) it may be possible to place two fiber cable sheaths in the same conduit structure, and separate them physically within the conduit.

Since many systems and their conduits are laid out in a grid structure, it may be possible (as in Figure 5–4(b)) to place the working and protection fibers in separate conduits for at least part of the feeder connection.

Yet another possible alternative (see Figure 5–4(c)) is to use different feeders for the working and protection fibers. Finally, Figure 5–4(d)

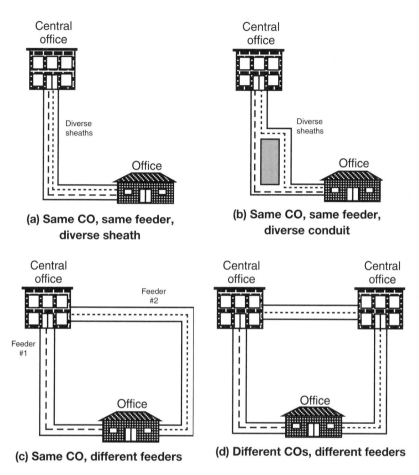

Figure 5–4   Structural diversity in the access network.

shows another possible way to separate the cables. Since some feeder routes in densely populated areas may intersect or be situated close together, it may be feasible to use two dual paths to two separate central offices, and have the ring connected through these offices.

SONET LAYERS

Before we examine further aspects of SONET configurations, it is necessary to introduce the important concept of SONET layers (also called levels). The SONET layering concept is based on the Open Systems Interconnection (OSI) Model.

Figure 5–5 shows the relationship of the user layers and the layers associated with SONET. The user layers run on top of the SONET physical layer. The physical layer is modeled on three major configuration entities: transmission path, digital line, and the regenerator section. Remember that we explained these three configuration entities earlier in this chapter in the section titled "SONET configuration."

The section and photonic layers comprise the SONET regenerators. The photonic layer is responsible for converting the electrical signal to an optical signal and then regenerating the optical signal as it is carried through the network. This stack may vary in different implementations. For example, at a switch, the SONET path layer might not be accessed because it is intended as an end-to-end operation. The manner in which the layers are executed depends on the actual design of the equipment.

In accordance with the OSI Model, traffic to be transmitted into the network is passed from the user layer (for example, an ATM layer) to the path layer. Here, a header is attached to the traffic, certain operations are performed, and then the traffic is passed to the line layer. Once again, the line adds a line header, performs certain actions, and passes the traffic to the section layer. As before, the section layer adds a header to the traffic, performs certain actions, and passes the traffic to the photonic layer. The

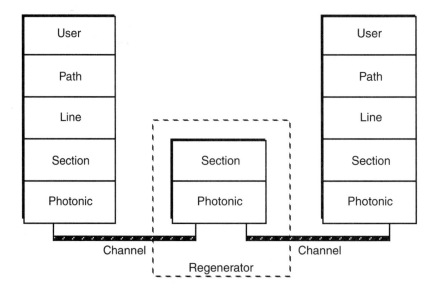

Figure 5–5   A SONET/ATM layer configuration. Note: Layer stacks may vary at multiplexers, switches, and other line-terminating equipment.

photonic layer adds no header, but it encodes the bits, places a synchronization flag in front of them, and transmits them onto the channel.

So, three of the SONET layers add a header to the payload, resulting in three headers. At the receiving machine, the process is reversed; each layer strips off its respective header and uses it to determine what actions that layer is to take.

The purpose of the layering concept, and its association with the configuration components, is to partition activities and responsibilities among the three major components (divide and conquer). This modular approach greatly facilitates the ability to add or remove payload and headers, because from a protocol standpoint (logical operations), the three components are somewhat independent of each other. These ideas are shown in Figure 5–6. The header, created by a component (and its associated layer) are examined only by the peer component (and its associated layer).

SONET Signaling Hierarchy

Table 5–1 shows the SONET multiplexing signaling hierarchy as related to the OC and STS levels. STS-1 forms the basis for the optical carrier-level 1 (OC-1) signal. OC-1 is the foundation for the synchronous optical signal hierarchy. The higher level signals are derived by

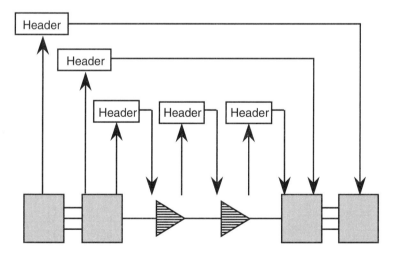

Figure 5–6   Headers and SONET components.
Notes:
(a) Headers created at an entity and used only by a peer entity.
(b) These operations are based on the OSI layered approach.

Table 5–1   SONET signaling hierarchy.

OC Level	STS Level	Line Rate (Mbit/s)
OC-1*	STS-1	51.840
OC-3*	STS-3	155.520
OC-9	STS-9	466.560
OC-12*	STS-12	622.080
OC-18	STS-18	933.120
OC-24	STS-24	1244.160
OC-36	STS-36	1866.230
OC-48*	STS-48	2488.32
OC-96	STS-96	4876.64
OC-192	STS-19	9953.280

*Currently, the more popular implementations
(Note: Certain levels are not used in Europe, North America, and Japan)

multiplexing together the lower level signals. As stated earlier, the high level signals are designated as STS-n and OC-n, where n is an integer number. As illustrated in Table 5–1, OC transmission systems are multiplexed by the n values of 1, 3, 9, 12, 18, 24, 36, 48, 96, and 192.

As the technology develops, multiplexing integrals greater than 192 will be incorporated into the standard. Presently, signal levels OC-3, OC-12, and OC-48 are the most widely supported multiples of OC-1.

BEYOND OC-192

It is anticipated that in the near future, standardized systems designated as OC-768 will enter the marketplace operating at 40 Gbit/s. The standards groups are working on the definition of standards for this rate, as well as OC-3072 at 160 Gbit/s.

SONET Envelopes

We have learned that the basic transmission unit for SONET is the STS-1 synchronous payload envelope (SPE or frame). SDH differs in this regard because it starts at the STS-3 level. All levels are comprised of 8 bits (1 octet) that are transmitted serially on the optical fiber. For ease of documentation, the payload is depicted in a two-dimensional map (see

Figure 5–7). The map is comprised of N rows and M columns. Each entry in this map represents an individual octet of a SPE and is shown as 0. The transmission starts with a flag (F), which is placed in front of the envelope to identify where the envelope begins.

The octets for the envelope are transmitted in sequential order, beginning in the upper left-hand corner (0_1) through the first row, and then through the second row, until the last octet is transmitted—from the last row in the last column (0_n).

As explained earlier, the SPE is the method SONET uses for transmitting user information. The user information is called payload in a SONET system, and SONET allows payloads from different users to occupy the same envelope. SONET keeps track of where each user's traffic is located in the payload of the SPE through the use of VTs and VCs.

The envelopes (frames) are sent contiguously and without interruption, and the payload is inserted into the envelope under stringent timing rules. Notwithstanding, a user payload may be inserted into more than one envelope, which means the payload need not be inserted at the exact beginning of the payload part of the envelope. It can be placed in any part of this area, and a pointer is created to indicate where it begins. This approach allows the network to operate synchronously, yet accept synchronous or asynchronous traffic.

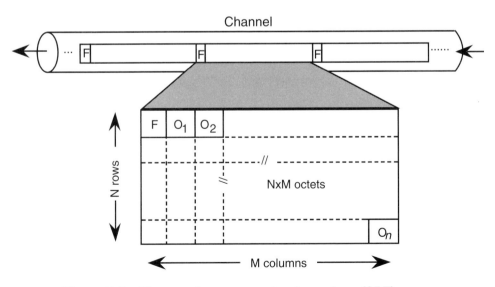

Figure 5–7 The synchronous payload envelope (SPE).

EXAMPLES OF PAYLOAD MAPPINGS

Chapter 1 explained that SONET is backwards compatible in that it can carry the payloads of current systems, such as DS1 and DS3. Figure 5–8 shows two examples of payload mapping. In Figure 5–8(a), 24 DS0 channels are multiplexed into a conventional DS1 payload through a DS1 multiplexer. The next stage of multiplexing and mapping occurs when 1 to n DS1 streams are multiplexed together through a SONET service adapter. This output is an STS-1 stream. Next, 1 to n STS-1 streams can be further multiplexed into a STS-n stream. This signal is then converted into an OC signal.

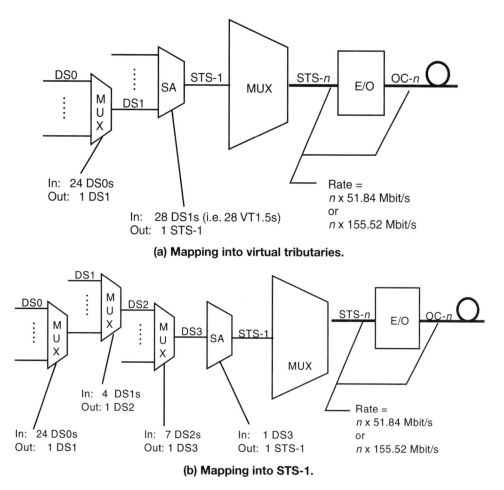

(a) Mapping into virtual tributaries.

(b) Mapping into STS-1.

Figure 5–8   Examples of payload mapping.

Figure 5–8(b) is similar to Figure 5–8(a), except it shows the asynchronous multiplexing hierarchy operations that lead to the DS3 payload. The intermediate rates are DS2 and DS3.

THE SONET ENVELOPE IN MORE DETAIL

Chapter 1 introduced the SONET envelope. This discussion expands on that subject. Figure 5–9 depicts the SONET STS-1 envelope. It consists of 90 columns and nine rows of 8-bit octets (bytes), and carries 810 octets, or 6480 bits. SONET transmits at 8000 frames/sec. Therefore, the frame length is 125 μsec. This approach translates into a transfer rate of 51.840 Mbit/s ($6480 \times 8000 = 51,840,000$).

The first three columns of the frame contain transport overhead, which is divided into 27 octets, with nine octets allocated for section overhead and 18 octets allocated for line overhead. The other 87 columns comprise the payload, or STS-1 SPE (although the first column of the envelope

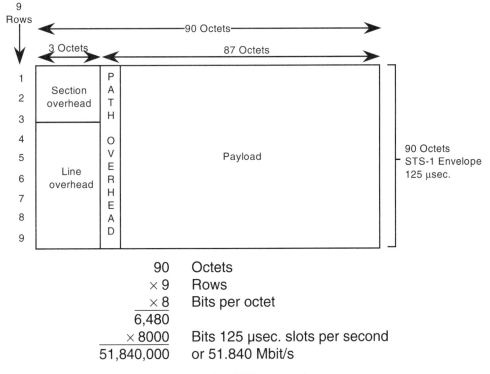

$$
\begin{array}{rl}
90 & \text{Octets} \\
\times 9 & \text{Rows} \\
\times 8 & \text{Bits per octet} \\
\hline
6{,}480 & \\
\times 8000 & \text{Bits 125 μsec. slots per second} \\
\hline
51{,}840{,}000 & \text{or 51.840 Mbit/s}
\end{array}
$$

Figure 5–9   STS-1 envelope.

capacity is reserved for STS path overhead). In certain parts of the world, the section overhead in this envelope is also known as region overhead, and the line overhead is also known as the multiplex section. The frame consists of two distinct parts: the user SPE part and the transport part.

Since the user payload consists of 86 columns, or 774 octets, it operates at 49.536 Mbit/s (774×8 bits per octet $\times 8000 = 49,536,000$). Therefore, the user payload in the STS-1 envelope can support information ranging from VTs (1.544 Mbit/s) up to the DS3 rate (44.736 Mbit/s).

The SDH envelope begins at STS-3. As shown in Figure 5–10, it consists of three STS-1 envelopes and operates at a bit rate of 155.52 Mbit/s ($51.840 \times 3 = 155.52$ Mbit/s). The STS-3 SPE has sufficient capacity to carry a broadband ISDN H4 channel.

The original SONET standard published by Bellcore had no provision for the European rate of 140 Mbit/s. Moreover, it was inefficient in how it dealt with the European 2.048 Mbit/s system. Therefore, Bellcore and the ANSI T1 committee accommodated the European requests by accepting the basic rate for SDH at 155.52 Mbit/s. Other higher multiplex-

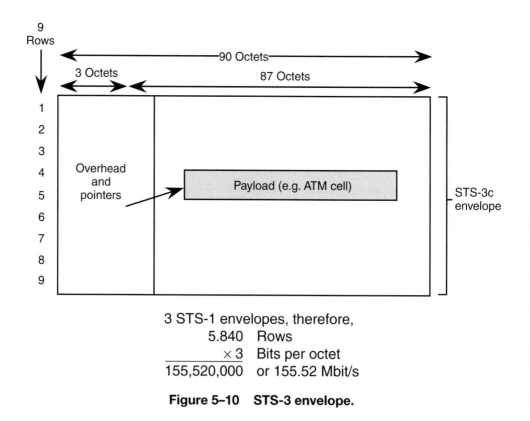

Figure 5–10   STS-3 envelope.

ing rates were also approved. All parties worked closely together to accommodate the different needs of the various administrations and countries. This cooperative approach resulted in a worldwide multiplexing structure to cooperate with the North American, European, and Japanese carrier systems.

Payload Pointers

SONET/SDH uses a new concept to deal with timing (frequency and phase) variations in a network. This concept is called pointers and was introduced in Chapters 1 and 3. The purpose of pointers is to allow the payload to "float" within the VT payload. The pointer is an offset value that shows the relative position of the first byte of the payload within the SPE. During transmission across the network, if any variations occur in the timing, the pointer need only be increased or decreased to compensate for the variation.

Several options are available in how the payload is mapped into the frame. The option discussed in the previous paragraph is called the floating mode, for obvious reasons.

Another option is called the locked mode. With this approach, pointers are not used and the payload is fixed within the frame. The payload cannot float. This approach is much simpler, but it requires that timing be maintained throughout the network. When all signals have a common orientation, the processing of the traffic is efficiently performed.

The Control Headers and Fields

Figure 5–11 provides a general view of the control fields that are used by SONET equipment for control and signaling purposes. Our approach is to discuss these fields in a general manner in this chapter, and in more detail in Chapter 9.

The section overhead and line overhead make up the transport overhead that consumes nine rows of the first three columns of each STS-1 payload. This equals 27 octets that are allocated to the transport overhead. Nine octets are allocated for the section overhead and 18 octets are allocated for the line overhead. On a more general note, headers are used to provide OAM functions such as signaling control, alarms, equipment type, framing operations, and error-checking operations. The payload pointers are also part of this header. There are also several octets that are available for the network vendor (i.e., not defined). The network vendor octets differ among vendors and can create interworking problems at the OAM level.

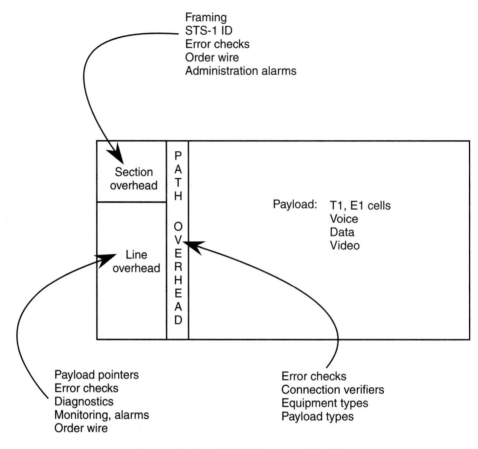

Figure 5–11   SONET control fields.

SONET EQUIPMENT AND TOPOLOGIES

This section is intended to be a general introduction into SONET equipment, with more detailed explanations provided in Chapter 8.

The terminal multiplexer, add-drop multiplexer (ADM), and building integrated timing supply (BITS) are shown in Figure 5–12. The terminal multiplexer is used to package incoming T1, E1, and other signals into STS payloads for network use. The architecture of the terminal multiplexer consists of a controller, which is software driven; a transceiver, which is used to provide access for lower speed channels; and a time slot interchanger (TSI), which feeds signals into higher speed interfaces.

The add-drop multiplexer (ADM) replaces the conventional back-to-back devices in DS1 cross connections. The ADM is actually a synchronous multiplexer that is used to add or drop DS1 signals onto the

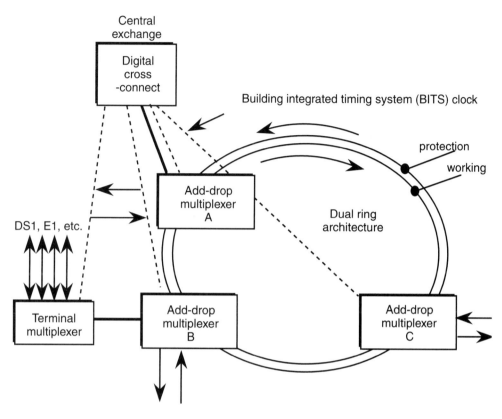

Figure 5–12   SONET equipment.

SONET ring. The ADM is also used for ring healing in the event of a failure in one of the rings. This means that ADM can be reconfigured to allow for continuous operations in the event of a ring failure.

The ADM must be able to terminate (accommodate) both OC-n connections as well as conventional electrical connections. The ADM can accept traffic from an incoming OC-n signal and insert it onto an outgoing OC-n signal. ADMs can also provide groom-and-fill operations, although this capability is not defined in the current Bellcore standards.

ADM multiplexers are required to convey the DSn signals as they are received, without alteration. They operate bidirectionally, which means they can add or drop DS1, E1, or other signals from either direction. The ADM uses both electrical-to-optical (E/O) interfaces, which are specified in great detail in the ITU-T and ANSI/Bellcore documents.

It is conceivable that ADMs will evolve into protocol converters as the technology matures. This means that instead of only providing simple multiplexing and bridging functions, ADMs may also be designed to perform protocol conversion functions by internetworking SONET with LANs, SMDS, frame relay, and other systems.

Recall from Chapter 1 that SONET uses synchronous clocks for timing, and BITS is the U.S. implementation for this operation. (BITS is examined in Chapter 3.) Timing is distributed to the network elements with BITS, which is used at these elements to synchronize the output onto the lines.

The topology for the ring can take several forms. We refer to Figure 5–12 again, which shows a simple arrangement, known as a unidirectional self-healing ring (SHR). Two fibers are used in this example: One is a working fiber, and the other is a protection fiber. In the event of a failure on a fiber or at an interface to a node (shown here as an ADM), the ring will take corrective action (self-heal) and cut out the problem area. An example of this operation is provided shortly.

Although not shown in Figure 5–12, the topology can also be established to include four fibers and operate with a second arrangement,

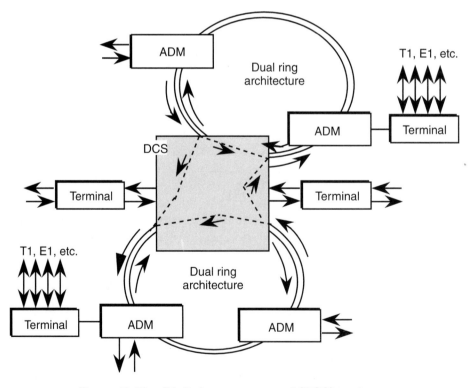

Figure 5–13   Digital cross-connect (DCS) systems.

known as bidirectional SHR, in which case traffic shares the working and protection fibers between two nodes and traffic is routed over the shortest path between nodes.

The digital cross-connect systems (DCSs) are used to cross-connect virtual tributaries (see Figure 5–13). One of their principal jobs is to process certain of the transport and path overhead signals and map various types of virtual tributaries to others. In essence, DCS is a switch that provides a central point for the grooming and consolidation of user payload between two ring systems. The DCS is also tasked with trouble isolation, loopback testing, and diagnostic requirements. It must respond to alarms and failure notifications. The DCS performs switching at the VT level, and the tributaries are accessible without demultiplexing. It can segregate high-bandwidth traffic from low-bandwidth traffic and send these signals out to different ports.

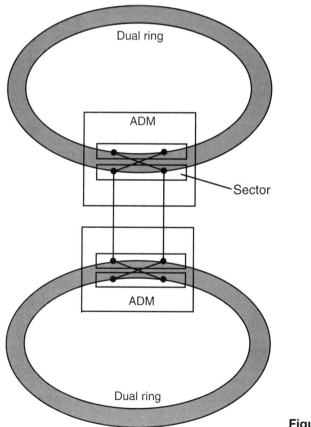

Figure 5–14   Multiple rings.

For some applications, it may be necessary to provide extra capacity in the system. For others, it may be necessary to ensure survivability of the network in the event of problems. In either case, path protection switching (PPS), and self-healing rings (SHRs) are employed, and in some instances multiple PPS rings may be employed. An SHR is a collection of nodes joined together by a duplex channel. This arrangement is quite flexible. For an example see Figure 5–14. The rings are connected together, but they are independent of each other and can operate at different speeds. The rings also can be expanded by adding other ADMs, DCSs, or PPS rings to the existing topology. The ADMs are called serving nodes. Any traffic that is passed between the rings is protected from a failure in either of the serving nodes. The small boxes within the ADM in Figure 5–14 depict selectors that can pass the signals onto the same ring or to the other ring.

SUMMARY

This chapter has expanded on the SONET concepts introduced in Chapter 1 and introduced how the DSn payloads introduced in Chapter 4 can be carried in the SONET payload. The remaining chapters of this book now delve into greater detail about these operations.

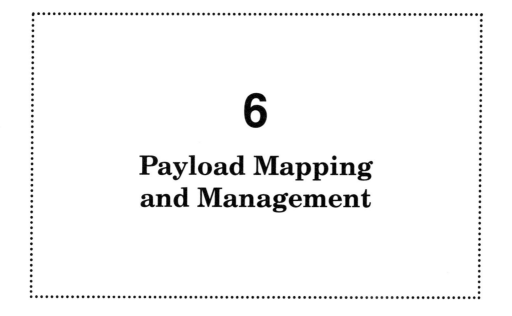

6

Payload Mapping and Management

This chapter examines in more detail how SONET performs payload mapping operations. The virtual tributary (VT) concept is examined, as well as SONET multiplexing and demultiplexing. A typical SONET configuration is also explained with the AT&T DDM-2000 equipment.

During this analysis, keep in mind that the purpose of payload mapping is to place the asynchronous DSn and CEPTn payloads into the SONET synchronous envelope in an organized manner.

A BRIEF REVIEW

Chapter 4 introduced the traditional asynchronous multiplexing DS1–DS3 levels in the North American digital hierarchy. We also covered the frame formats and the standards that are set by Bellcore and ANSI for DS1, DS1C, DS2, and DS3 signals.

We learned that the MX3 (with DS1, DS1C, and DS2 as the inputs and DS3 as the output) multiplexers create their output signals through stages of multiplexing from one or any combination of these three inputs.

We have also learned that problems exist with the asynchronous multiplexing technique. First, the bit-interleaving process does not provide a reliable way of ascertaining where a particular DS0 or DS1 falls within a DS3 bit stream. Without a known location within the DS3 frame, it is difficult to extract a single DS0 or DS1 signal. Second, when demultiplexing takes place and the overhead bits and the random stuff bits are discarded, a continuous state may not exist, which creates timing problems.

With accurate clock sources (the building integrated timing supply) now available, it is possible to synchronize the inputs. This makes the stuffing bits always the same, and C-bits (which previously controlled the stuffing) are therefore available for other functions. AT&T is in the process of converting to the C-bit parity service for an end-to-end parity check capability, discontinuing the older M13 and unformatted services. This process of combining 28 DS1s into a DS3 is referred to as M28.

As discussed in earlier chapters, the basic SONET building block is the 51.84 Mbit/s optical carrier-1 (OC-1). It is made up of one DS3, or multiple DS1s, and the SONET headers. Just as the asynchronous DS3 signal was used in multiples for higher-level multiplexing in the asynchronous digital hierarchy, the DS3 signal is also used for multiples in the OC hierarchy. The OC-1 (one DS3) is the lowest level optical signal to be used at equipment and network interfaces. STS-1 (51.84 Mbit/s) is the electrical component of the OC-1 and is currently defined as the internal signal.

The STS-1 is converted from electrical pulses to optical pulses to form the OC-1 signal. Three STS-1 signals can be multiplexed together to create the STS-3 signal. The STS-3 (155.52 Mbit/s) signal is the electrical component of the OC-3 signal, and likewise is scrambled and converted from electrical-to-optical format to form the OC-3 signal. The OC-9 is comprised of nine DS3s, the OC-12 is comprised of 12 DS3s, and so on. Table 6–1 shows the optical transmission hierarchy and the equipment

Table 6–1   Optical transmission and relationship to telecommunications.

Electrical	Optical Hierarchy	Transmission Line Rate (Mbit/s)	DS-3 Equiv.(#)	DS-1 Equiv.(#)	DS-0 Equiv. (#)
STS-1	OC-1	51.840	1	28	672
STS-3	OC-3	155.520	3	84	2,016
	OC-9	466.560	9	252	6,048
	OC-12	622.080	12	336	8,064
	OC-18	933.120	18	504	12,096
	OC-24	1244.160	24	672	16,128
	OC-36	1866.240	36	1008	24,192
	OC-48	2488.320	48	1344	32,256
	OC-192	9953.280	192	5376	129,024

number of DS3s, DS1s, or DS0s contained within each optical carrier level.

SONET STS-1 Envelope

Figure 6–1 is a redrawing of material in Chapter 5 and depicts the SONET STS-1 envelope. It consists of 90 columns and nine rows of 8-bit octets, and carries 810 octets or 6480 bits. SONET transmits at 8000 frames/sec. Therefore, the frame length is 125 microseconds (μsec). This approach translates into a transfer rate of 51.840 Mbit/s (6480 × 8000 = 51,840,000).

As previously noted, the first three columns of the frame contain transport overhead, which is divided into 27 octets, with nine octets allocated for section overhead and 18 octets allocated for line overhead. The other 87 columns comprise the payload or STS-1 SPE (although the first column of the envelope capacity is reserved for STS path overhead). The

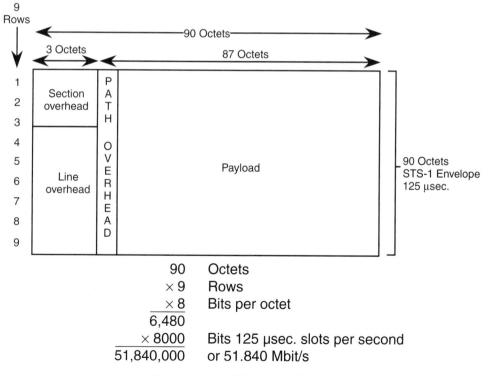

Figure 6–1   STS-1 envelope.

section overhead in this envelope is also known as region overhead in certain parts of the world and the line overhead is also known as the multiplex section. The frame consists of two distinct parts: the user SPE part and the transport part.

Since the user payload consists of 86 columns, or 774 octets, it operates at 49.536 Mbit/s (774×8 bits per octet $\times 8000 = 49{,}536{,}000$). Therefore, the user payload can support VTs up to the DS3 rate (44.736 Mbit/s).

An SDH envelope begins at STS-3, which is also used in SONET. It consists of three STS-1 envelopes and operates at a bit rate of 155.52 Mbit/s ($51.840 \times 3 = 155.52$ Mbit/s). The STS-3 SPE has sufficient capacity to carry a broadband ISDN H4 channel.

The original SONET standard published by Bellcore did not provide for the European rate of 140 Mbit/s. Moreover, it dealt inefficiently with the European 2.048 Mbit/s system. Bellcore and the T1 committee accommodated European requests and accepted the basic rate for SDH at 155.52 Mbit/s, and other higher multiplexing rates were also approved. All parties worked closely to accommodate the different needs of the various administrations and countries, which resulted in a worldwide multiplexing structure that operates with North American, European, and Japanese carrier systems.

THE SONET STS-3C FRAME STRUCTURE

The designation of a "c" in the frame name refers to concatenation. This term describes a payload in which multiple STS-1 frames (or OC-1 frames to create OC-3c envelopes) are concatenated (joined) together. The idea of concatenation is to allow a rate greater than the STS-1 rate of 51.84 Mbit/s, notably the STS-3c rate of 155.52 Mbit/s. In addition, STS-3c provides an unchannelized link. This term means the 155.52 Mbit/s frame is not channelized into three separate STS-1 "chunks." Instead these three STS-1s are joined or concatenated together. This concatenation is thought of as one payload; that is, it is simply a raw bandwidth of 155.52 Mbit/s. This concept is similar to the well-known unchannelized T1, in which the 24 8-bit DS0s are not so identified; rather, each T1 frame is a frame of 192 contiguous bits.

It is certainly possible to achieve a 155.52 Mbit/s rate by sending three separate STS-1s. But this approach (called channelized or nonconcatenated frames) treats each STS-1 as a separate entity. Indeed, each STS-1 has its own set of payload pointers, as well as the other section and line overhead bytes.

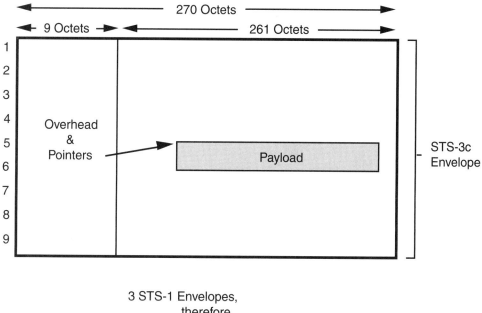

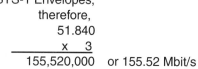

Figure 6–2   The STS-3c envelope.

The STS-1c Envelope

Figure 6–2 shows the general structure of the STS-3c frame. As noted in previous discussions (see Chapter 5, the section titled, "The SONET OAM Headers"), some of the bytes in the STS-N overhead area of the frame are not used; that is, they are used only in the first STS-1 of the STS-N frame. The specific uses of the bytes in the STS-1c envelope are discussed later in this chapter.

AT&T DDM-2000 OC-3 SHELF

Let us look at the AT&T/Lucent DDM-2000 shelf (shown in Figure 6–3), which will aid us in explaining DS1 and DS3 mapping signals into VT 1.5 and STS-1 signals as they relate to physical hardware. The inputs into these multiplexers interface with the low-speed cards and are referred to as low-speed signals; the multiplexed signals interface with the high-

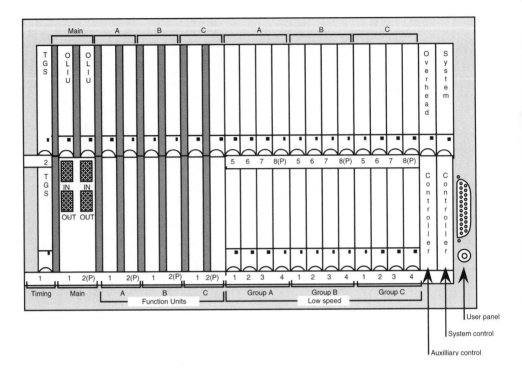

Figure 6–3   DDM-2000 C-3 multiplexer shelf-front view.
Notes:
(a) Functional units can be one of the following: MXRVO,
     DS3, STS-1E, or OLIU (optical line interface unit).
(b) Low speeds are DS1 cards.

speed cards and are referred to as high-speed signals. Therefore, the terms low- and high-speed signals are used in relation to the multiplexer being addressed.

The three main cards residing in the DDM-2000 are the control, synchronization, and transmission/receive circuit packs. The functions for each circuit pack are listed below:

Control Circuit Pack
The system controller card (SYSCTL) provides:

1. Fault detection
2. Automatic power-up and reset
3. Protection switching
4. Circuit pack inventory

The overhead controller card provides:

1. Interface to OLIU (optical line interface unit) cards with SONET overhead channel
2. Remote operations center with alarms and status information, parallel telemetry, TBOS (telemetry byte-oriented serial), and TL1/X.25
3. Environment alarm (open door, smoke, temperature indicator)

Synchronous circuit pack
- External timing mode, loop timing mode, or free-running mode

Transmission / receive circuit pack
Please refer to Figures 6–4 and 6–5 during this discussion:

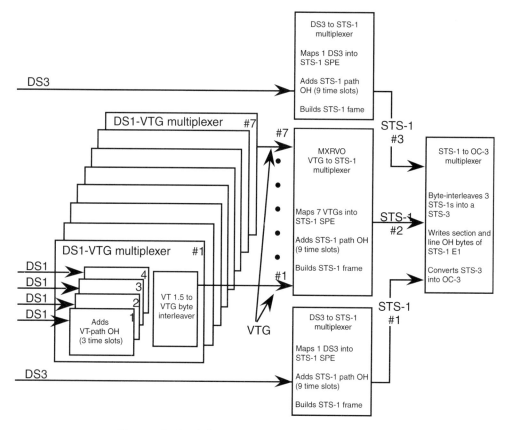

Figure 6–4   SONET multiplexing procedure.

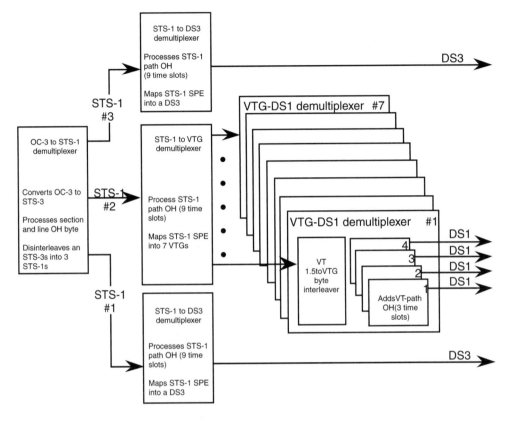

Figure 6–5   SONET demultiplexing procedure.

For a DS1 low-speed interface, the pack:

1. Receives four DS1 signals from DSX-1, AMI, or B8ZS
2. From each DS1 signal recovers clock information
3. Synchronizes each DS1 signal and maps it into VT 1.5 payload (SPE)
4. Adds VT path overheads
5. Multiplexes (with byte-interleaving four) VT 1.5 SPEs onto a VT-G signal
6. Provides the VT-G to a MXRVO card
   • The receive transmission circuit pack deals with the same signals only in reverse order

The multiplexer provides for four functional units. If installed, they operate as follows. MXRVO (multiple transmit/receive virtual overhead) VT-to-STS-1 multiplexer accepts seven VT-G signals from the low-speed cards and multiplexes them into one STS-1 SPE. It adds STS-1 path overhead and provides the STS-1 signal to the main OLIU cards. Its receive function is the same as the transmit function, only in reverse.

STS1E (synchronous transport signal-1 electrical) accepts the high-speed VT-Gs from the DS1 cards, multiplexes the VT-Gs into a SPE and adds STS-1 path overhead. Then, SONET transport overhead is added, B3ZS encoding is performed and the traffic is sent to the STS-1. For the low-speed mode, it receives the EC-1 (electrical carrier-1) from the STS-1, decodes the B3ZS and removes the transport overheads. It then processes the STS-1 pointers, synchronizes the signal, and sends it to the OLIU card. The receive function is the same as the transmit function, only in reverse.

The OLIU accepts the signals from the functional slots (STS-1 inputs from MXRVO, STS-1E, DS3, or OLIU). Next, it provides STS-1/VT 1.5 signal cross-connections, and adds SONET transport overheads for STS-1 and path overheads for VT 1.5. Then, it byte-interleaves the three STS-1 signals into one STS-3 signal and changes the STS-3 electrical signal into the standard SONET OC-3 signal for transport. The receive function is the same as the transmit function only in reverse (see Figure 6–5).

The DS3 low-speed interface receives the B3ZS signal from the DSX-3 and recovers the DS3 clocking. It then inserts the STS-1 path overhead and synchronizes the STS-1 signal rate before providing the signal to the OLIU card. The receive function is the same as the send function only in reverse.

User Panel

The user panel on the DDM-2000 provides a serial ASCII terminal interface using the 25-pin female connector. Most common terminals or personal computers can be used because the interface is an EIA-232-E connector. The terminal parameters must be set to full duplex, eight data bits, no parity, no flow control, one start bit and one stop bit. The signaling rate can be 300, 1200, 2400, 4800, 9600, or 19,200 bit/s as long as this rate is also supported by the system controller. This terminal gives the user the ability to do software provisioning, protection switching, add-and-drop mapping, and system performance verification and other testing capabilities.

The DDM-2000 has been developed in various stages (releases). Each release brings with it various applications and enhancements for interfacing with SONET equipment. Each release specifies different configurations of cards for the various applications. Later in this chapter, we explain how VT 1.5, VT2, VT3, and VT6 signals are created through the low-speed cards.

Shelf Layout

The DDM-2000 OC-3 accepts only asynchronous DS1 and DS3 signals for multiplexing into SONET payloads. This system will also accept various SONET signals.

Four DS1s are changed into VT 1.5 (which is 1.728 Mbit/s) and then multiplexed into a VT-G. The DS1 cards perform this function. The MXRVO card and the STS-1E card are responsible for creating the STS-1 signal from the seven VT-Gs. Later in this chapter, we will show an example view of how the frame is constructed.

Signal Flow

The DDM-2000 contains three muldems (multiplex and demultiplex) groups of low-speed cards in the shelf. They are designated as groups A, B, and C. Each group is made up of seven low-speed cards. The eighth card is for protection in case one of the seven cards on the line within that group fails. Each low-speed card can accept up to four DS1s as inputs. Within the DS1 low-speed card, the DS1 signals are converted to 1.728 bit/s (which is the VT 1.5 level) by adding section, line, and path overhead. The four VT 1.5s are then multiplexed in a VT-G (virtual tributary group) with a rate of 6.912 Mbit/s. The VT-G rate from the seven low-speed cards goes to the MXRVO card in the functional slot for its respective group. Next, the MXRVO creates the STS-1 electrical (51.84 Mbit/s rate) signal from the seven incoming VT-Gs. The MXRVOs for groups A, B, and C send their STS-1s to the OLIU (optical line interface unit) in the main slot, and the OLIU multiplexes the three STS-1s into one STS-3 (electrical 155.52 Mbit/s rate) signal. Then, another circuit in the OLIU changes the STS-3 signal to an OC-3 (optical carrier 3) signal, which is still a 155.52 Mbit/s signal.

The asynchronous DS3 signals can be cross-connected as input to DS3 cards, and are considered low-speed in this configuration. The DS3 cards can also reside in the function units slots. The DS3 (44.736 Mbit/s) signal is cross-connected to the DS3 card with a coaxial cable. The DS3

Table 6–2 DS1 to VT 1.5 mapping.

DS1 Address	VT 1.5 within STS-1	VT-G within STS-1	STS-1 within STS-1	DS1 Address	VT 1.5 within STS-1	VT-G within STS-1	STS-1 within STS-1	DS1 Address	VT 1.5 within STS-1	VT-G within STS-1	STS-1 within STS-1
a-1-1	1	1	1	b-1-1	1	1	2	c-1-1	1	1	3
a-1-2	8	1	1	b-1-2	8	1	2	c-1-2	8	1	3
a-1-3	15	1	1	b-1-3	15	1	2	c-1-3	15	1	3
a-1-4	22	1	1	b-1-4	22	1	2	c-1-4	22	1	3
a-2-1	2	2	1	b-2-1	2	2	2	c-2-1	2	2	3
a-2-2	9	2	1	b-2-2	9	2	2	c-2-2	9	2	3
a-2-3	16	2	1	b-2-3	16	2	2	c-2-3	16	2	3
a-2-4	23	2	1	b-2-4	23	2	2	c-2-4	23	2	3
a-3-1	3	3	1	b-3-1	3	3	2	c-3-1	3	3	3
a-3-2	10	3	1	b-3-2	10	3	2	c-3-2	10	3	3
a-3-3	17	3	1	b-3-3	17	3	2	c-3-3	17	3	3
a-3-4	24	3	1	b-3-4	24	3	2	c-3-4	24	3	3
a-4-1	4	4	1	b-4-1	4	4	2	c-4-1	4	4	3
a-4-2	11	4	1	b-4-2	11	4	2	c-4-2	11	4	3
a-4-3	21	4	1	b-4-3	21	4	2	c-4-3	21	4	3
a-4-4	25	4	1	b-4-4	25	4	2	c-4-4	25	4	3
a-5-1	5	5	1	b-5-1	5	5	2	c-5-1	5	5	3
a-5-2	12	5	1	b-5-2	12	5	2	c-5-2	12	5	3
a-5-3	19	5	1	b-5-3	19	5	2	c-5-3	19	5	3
a-5-4	26	5	1	b-5-4	26	5	2	c-5-4	26	5	3
a-6-1	6	6	1	b-6-1	6	6	2	c-6-1	6	6	3
a-6-2	13	6	1	b-6-2	13	6	2	c-6-2	13	6	3
a-6-3	20	6	1	b-6-3	20	6	2	c-6-3	20	6	3
a-6-4	27	6	1	b-6-4	27	6	2	c-6-4	27	6	3
a-7-1	7	7	1	b-7-1	7	7	2	c-7-1	7	7	3
a-7-2	14	7	1	b-7-2	14	7	2	c-7-2	14	7	3
a-7-3	21	7	1	b-7-3	21	7	2	c-7-3	21	7	3
a-7-4	28	7	1	b-7-4	28	7	2	c-7-4	28	7	3

card builds the 51.84 Mbit/s frame by adding the section, line, and path overheads. The STS frame then is sent to the OLIU.

The functional slots can also accept STS-1 signals from a cross-connect to interface with STS-1E cards. The purpose of this option is to pass this signal on to the OLIU card in the MAIN slots when it is functioning as a low-speed card. These slots can be "optioned" as a high-speed card. With this arrangement, it accepts the seven VT-G signals from the low-speed DS1 cards and creates one STS-1 signal. The STS-1 signal then leaves the backplane. Using coaxial cable to the STSX-1 (STS cross-connect level 1), it is cross-connected to a higher level OC multiplexer.

Now that we are familiar with the OC-3 shelf and the basic function of the cards, let us look at the STS-1 frame and how the various input signals are mapped. The four VT types and how many VTs are within each type in a group are shown in Table 6–2. It will be helpful to refer to this table during the following discussion.

MAPPING AND MULTIPLEXING OPERATIONS

This section provides more examples of the SONET mapping and multiplexing functions. One idea should be kept in mind when reading this section: A principal function of these operations is to create a payload format and syntax that is the same for any input (DS1, CEPT1, etc.) after the initial multiplexing and pointer processing is completed. Therefore, the DS1 and CEPT1 rates of 1.544 Mbit/s (and the 3.152, 6.312, and 2.048 Mbit/s rates) are mapped and multiplexed into a 6.912 Mbit/s frame. Then, these signals are multiplexed further into higher levels.

Another View of the Multiplexing and Mapping Hierarchy

Figure 6–6 presents another view of the SONET multiplexing and mapping hierarchy. This figure is used in several of the SONET specifications, and its scheme is also used in SDH (and explained in Chapter 10). The convention is to show the flow of operations from the right side of the page to the left side. The boxes on the right-most side indicate the user payloads that are multiplexed and mapped into the higher levels of VTs, VT groups, and STS-n signals. The notation xN indicates the level of multiplexing—that is, how many lower level signals are multiplexed into the next higher level signal.

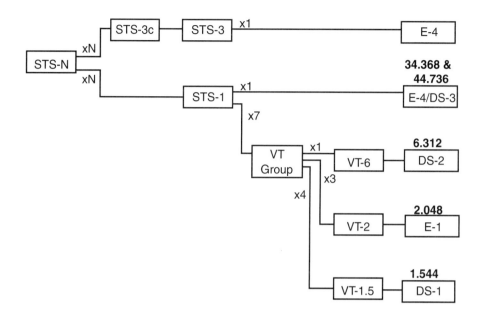

Figure 6–6 SONET multiplexing and mapping hierarchy.

VT 1.5

This section shows all the mapping and multiplexing possibilities, but concentrates on the VT 1.5, which multiplexes four DS1 systems as shown in Figure 6–7. First, the bipolar code is converted to unipolar code. Each 1.544 Mbit/s DS1 signal is converted to a 1.728 Mbit/s virtual tributary. The additional bits are created to provide flags, buffering bits, conversion bits, and VT headers.

The four DS1s are multiplexed together to equal a 6.912 Mbit/s VT-G output. Then the 6.912 Mbit/s output is input into additional multiplexing functions in which seven VT-Gs have path, line, and section overhead bits added to them. In addition, pointer bits are added to align the VT-G payloads in the SONET envelope. The result of all these operations is a 51.84 Mbit/s STS-1 signal.

Even though bit stuffing is usually associated with asynchronous systems in which the bits compensate for speed differences between the input and output, SONET also uses the technique. The intent is to create a constant output stream of 6.912 Mbit/s, which requires insertion of the stuffed bits, since the input streams of 1.544 Mibit/s and 2.048 Mbit/s differ.

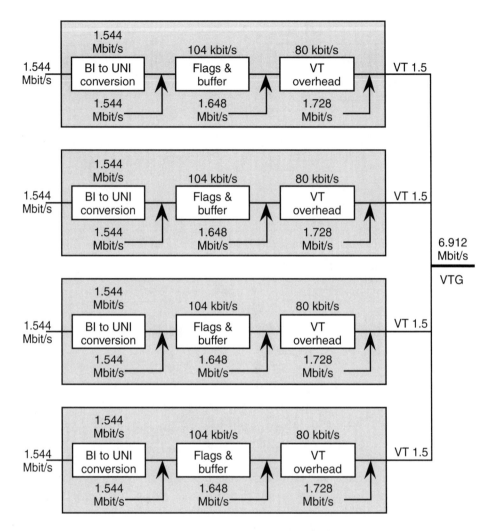

Figure 6–7   Virtual tributary (VT) 1.5.

VT2

The European CEPT1 is converted to a VT 2 signal of 6.912 Mbit/s (see Figure 6–8). It can be seen that the approach of the multiplexing scheme is to provide a preliminary payload of 6.912 Mbit/s for all input streams.

For the CEPT conversion, 3 CEPT transmissions of 2.048 Mbit/s are input into the SDH conversion operation. The operation adds flags, buffering bits, and VT overhead bits that equal 256 kbit/s. Therefore, each CEPT signal is converted to a 2.304 signal. Three CEPT signals at 2.304 equal the desired 6.912 Mbit/s output stream.

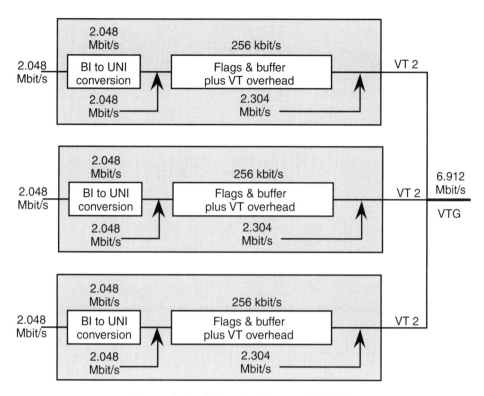

Figure 6–8   Virtual tributary 2 (VT 2).

VT3

For the asynchronous DS1C conversion, the bipolar code is converted to unipolar and then the 3.152 Mbit/s must be demultiplexed back into its constituent DS1s (see Figure 6–9). Then the same process, used for DS1 conversion, takes place and overhead is added. However, the four 1.728 Mbit/s are referred to as VT3 because that was the original input (3.152 Mbit/s). The output again is 6.912 Mbit/s, the VTG level.

VT6

For the DS2 rate conversion (see Figure 6–10), the initial process is identical to the DS1C operation. The system converts from bipolar to unipolar and demultiplexes the DS2 signal down to the constituent DS1s. After the overheads are added, the four signals are referred to as VT6. Finally, the VTG of 6.912 Mbit/s is derived by multiplexing the four VT6 signals together.

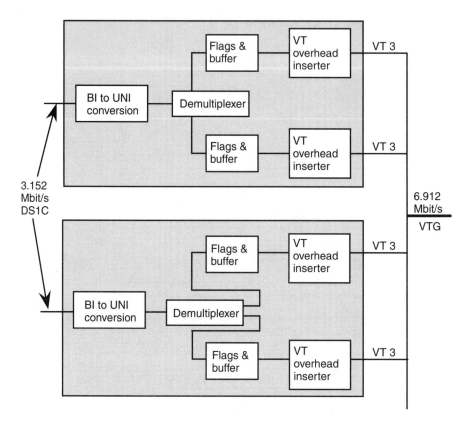

Figure 6–9   DS1C conversion to VT-G.

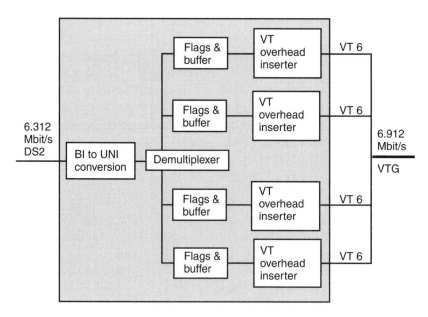

Figure 6–10   DS2 conversion to VT-G.

The VT 1.5 Group Envelope

Figure 6–11 shows the envelope of a VT 1.5 group. The signal occupies three columns and nine rows. The user traffic consists of 24 octets in accordance with a T1 24 slot frame. The remaining three octets are used for SONET control. A VT 1.5 group supports four VT 1.5 transmissions to

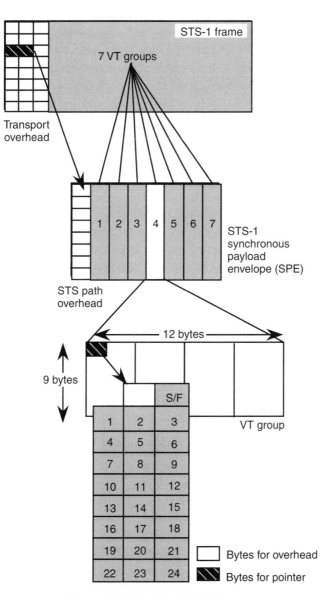

Figure 6–11   The VT 1.5 group.

occupy the full 12 columns of the VT structure. The VT is organized as a masterframe structure and spread over multiple frames. Each frame contains VT payload pointers, which locate the payload in the envelope, as well as specify the size of the VT. The pointers also have error-checking capabilities as well as some bits that provide for path status information. These bits will be discussed later.

The bit rate of each VT 1.5 in the group is 1.728 Mbit/s. Although the full rate of a T1 is 1.544 Mbit/s (24 octets $\times$ 8 bits $\times$ 8000 = 1,536,000 + 8000 occurrences of the 193rd bit = 1,544,000). The 193rd bit is not conveyed in the VT. Therefore, the VT 1.5 rate of 1.728 Mbit/s is derived from: 1,536,00 + 192,000 = 1,728,000 (the 3 overhead octets $\times$ 8 bits $\times$ 8000 = 192,000).

The header octets are used to indicate the offset of the SPE payload from the second header byte. Like the STS SPE these headers also allow frequency justification of the VT SPE. They also have bits that indicate the size of the VT (VT 1.5, VT 2, VT 3, and VT 6).

Summary of the VT Types

The four VT types (and how many VTs of that type make up a group) are shown in Table 6–3. Also shown is the standard signal and the megabit rates for their signal. The fifth column shows the number of bytes for that VT in an STS-1 frame, and in parentheses are the number of columns in the STS-1 frame that will be needed to map the signals.

ROWS AND COLUMNS OF THE VTS

Figure 6–12 gives us another insight into SONET mapping by showing the rows and columns for each of the four types of VTs. Figure 6–13 amplifies this information with a conceptual view of the nine rows and 10 of

Table 6–3   Submultiplexing via the VT group in an STS frame.

VT Type	Number in a VT Group	Signal Standard	Signal Rate (in Mbit/s)	Number Bytes (Columns)
1.5	4	DS-1	1.544	27 (3)
2	3	CEPT-1	2.048	36 (4)
3	2	DS-1C	3.152	54 (6)
6	1	DS-2	6.312	108 (120)

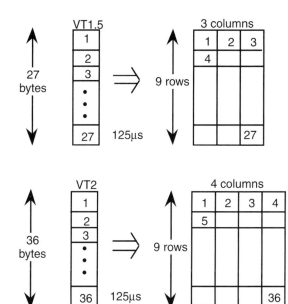

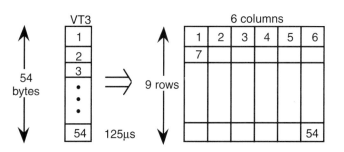

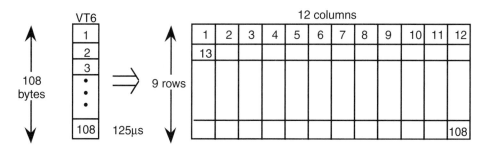

Figure 6–12   VT sizes.

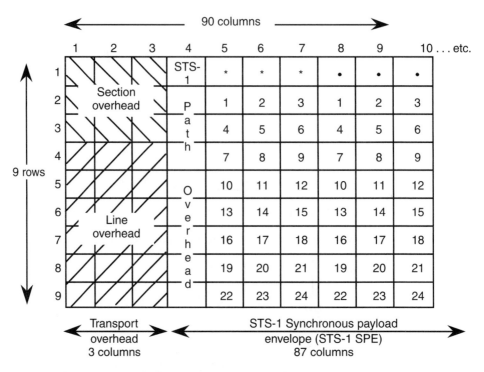

Figure 6–13   STS-1 frame format.
Notes:
(a) Row 1 columns 5, 6, and 7 are a three 8-bit bytes for DS1 #1 identification.
(b) Row 1 columns 8, 9, and 10 are a three 8-bit bytes for DS1 #2 identification.

the 90 columns. This view gives us an idea of what is taking place in the mapping operations. Row 1, columns 5, 6, and 7 are the VT's three bytes of identification for the DS1 mapped from rows 2 through 9. As you can see, first channel 1, then 2 and 3 occupy row 2. Row 3 contains channels 4, 5, 6, and so on. Finally, row 9 has channels 22, 23, and 24.

Columns 8, 9, and 10 contain the second VT and the identifications are in row 1 columns 8, 9, and 10. Channels 1, 2, and 3 are mapped in row 2 and channels 4, 5, and 6 in row 3, and so on. The actual columns assigned for mapping will be explained later in the chapter.

There are 90 columns to an STS-1 frame. The first three are used for section and line overhead and the fourth is for path overhead. Columns 30 and 59 are reserved for future applications. Therefore, each of the 28 DS1s requires three columns, which equals a total of 84 columns. Then two columns are added for reserve to a total of 86 columns. Then four columns are added for SONET overhead, which brings the total to 90 columns.

CONSTRUCTION OF THE ENTIRE SPE

STS-1, SPE for all VT 1.5

Figure 6–14 shows how the payloads of the VTs are mapped into a STS-1 envelope. Table 6–4 should also be studied during this discussion. The 28 VT 1.5s are byte interleaved such that (for example) VT 1 of VT

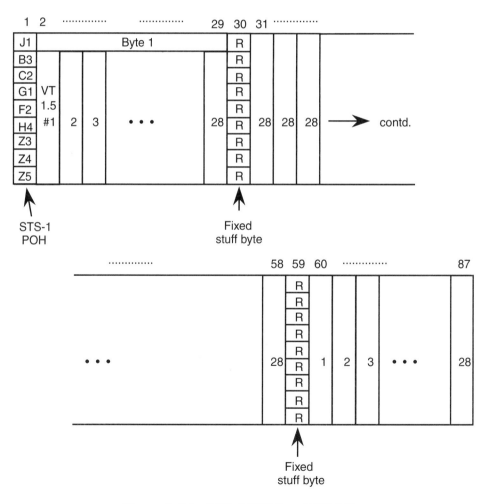

Figure 6–14   STS-1 SPE for all VT 1.5s.

Table 6–4   VT 1.5 locations in the STS-1 SPE.

VT 1.5#	Group #, VT #	Column #s
1	1,1	2,31,60
2	2,1	3,32,61
3	3,1	4,33,62
4	4,1	5,34,63
5	5,1	6,35,64
6	6,1	7,36,65
7	7,1	8,37,66
8	1,2	9,38,67
9	2,2	10,39,68
10	3,2	11,40,69
11	4,2	12,41,70
12	5,2	13,42,71
13	6,2	14,43,72
14	7,2	15,44,73
15	1,3	16,45,74
16	2,3	17,46,75
17	3,3	18,47,76
18	4,3	19,48,77
19	5,3	20,49,78
20	6,3	21,50,79
21	7,3	22,51,80
22	1,4	23,52,81
23	2,4	24,53,82
24	3,4	25,54,83
25	4,4	26,55,84
26	5,4	27,56,85
27	6,4	28,57,86
28	7,4	29,58,87

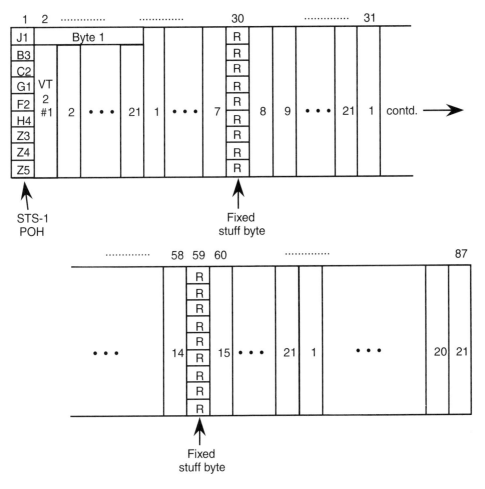

Figure 6–15   STS-1 SPE for all VT2.

group 1 occupies columns 2, 31, and 60 of the envelope. Note that column four of STS-1 frame is referenced here as column one because it is the first column of the STS-1 envelope for the payload.

STS-1 SPE, for all VT 2

Figure 6–15 shows how the payloads of the VT 2s are mapped into an STS-1 envelope. The 21 VT 2s are byte interleaved such that (for example) VT 1 of VT group 1 occupies columns 2, 23, 45, and 67 of the envelope, as shown in Table 6–5.

Table 6–5   VT 2 locations in the STS-1 SPE.

VT 1.5#	Group #, VT #	Column #s
1	1,1	2,23,45,67
2	2,1	3,24,46,68
3	3,1	4,25,47,69
4	4,1	5,26,48,70
5	5,1	6,27,49,71
6	6,1	7,28,50,72
7	7,1	8,29,51,73
8	1,2	9,31,52,74
9	2,2	10,32,53,75
10	3,2	11,33,54,76
11	4,2	12,34,55,77
12	5,2	13,35,56,78
13	6,2	14,36,57,79
14	7,2	15,37,58,80
15	1,3	16,38,60,81
16	2,3	17,39,61,82
17	3,3	18,40,62,83
18	4,3	19,41,63,84
19	5,3	20,42,64,85
20	6,3	21,43,65,86
21	7,3	22,44,66,87

STS-1 SPE, for all VT 3

Figure 6–16 shows how the payloads of the VT 3s are mapped into an STS-1 envelope. The 14 VT 3s are byte interleaved such that (for example) VT 1 of the VT group 1 occupies columns 2, 16, 31, 45, 60, and 74 of the envelope, as shown in Table 6–6.

STS-1 SPE, for all VT 6

Figure 6–17 shows how the payloads of the VT 6s are mapped into an STS-1 envelope. The seven VT 6s are byte interleaved such that (for example) VT 1 of VT group 1 occupies columns 2, 9, 16, 23, 31, 38, 45, 52, 60, 67, 74, and 81 of the envelope, as shown in Table 6–7.

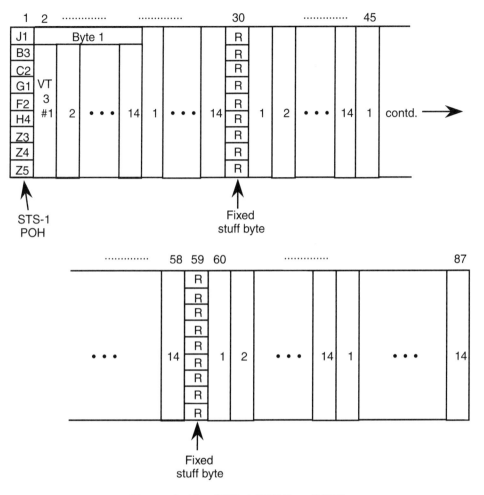

Figure 6–16   STS-1 SPE for all VT3.

Table 6–6   VT3 locations in the STS-1 SPE.

VT 3#	Group #, VT #	Column #s
1	1,1	2,16,31,45,60,74
2	2,1	3,17,32,46,61,75
3	3,1	4,18,33,47,62,76
4	4,1	5,19,34,48,63,77
5	5,1	6,20,35,49,64,78
6	6,1	7,21,36,50,65,79
7	7,1	8,22,37,51,66,80
8	1,2	9,23,38,52,67,81
9	2,2	10,24,39,53,68,82
10	3,2	11,25,40,54,69,83
11	4,2	12,26,41,55,70,84
12	5,2	13,27,42,56,71,85
13	6,2	14,28,43,57,72,86
14	7,2	15,29,44,58,73,87

Composite Mapping

Finally, Figure 6–18 shows all four VT mappings. For ease of reading, the VTs are identified as:

ABCD:	VT group 1.5
XYZ:	VT group 2
MN:	VT group 3
O	VT group 0

Label	*VTx #*	*Group #, VT #*
A	1,1	1,1
B	VT 1.5 #8	1,2
C	VT 1.5 #15	1,3
D	VT 1.5 #22	1,4
X	VT 2 #2	2,1
Y	VT 2 #9	2,2
Z	VT 2 #16	2,3
M	VT 3 #3	3,1
N	VT 3 #10	3,2
O	VT 6 #4	4,1

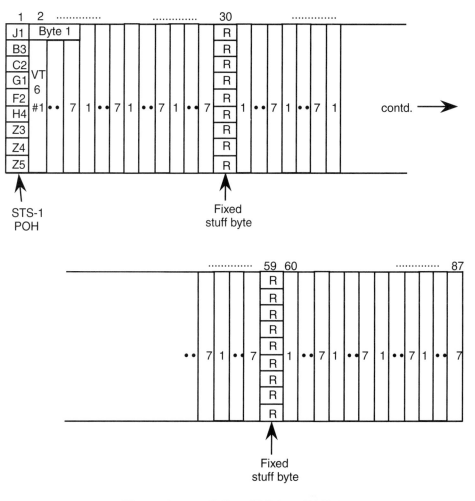

Figure 6–17 STS-1 SPE for all VT 6.

Table 6–7 VT6 locations in the STS-1 SPE.

VT 6#	Group #, VT #	Column #s
1	1,1	2,9,16,23,31,38,45,52,60,67,74,81
2	2,1	3,10,17,24,32,39,46,53,61,68,75,82
3	3,1	4,11,18,25,33,40,47,54,62,69,76,83
4	4,1	5,12,19,26,34,41,48,55,63,70,77,84
5	5,1	6,13,20,27,35,42,49,56,64,71,78,85
6	6,1	7,14,21,28,36,43,50,57,65,72,79,86
7	7,1	8,15,22,29,37,44,51,58,66,73,80,87

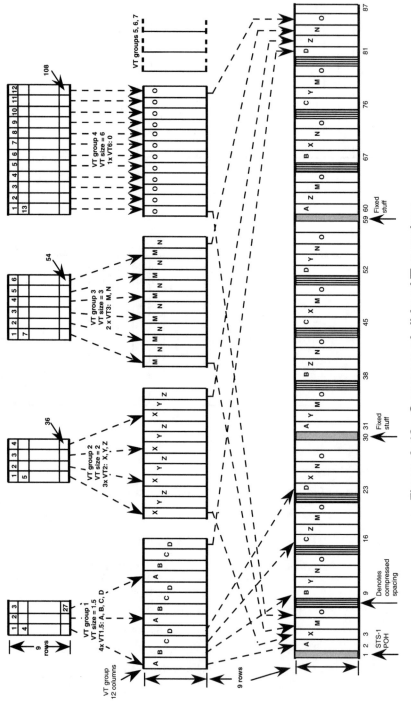

Figure 6–18 Summary of all four VT mappings.

A FINAL LOOK AT ANOTHER MAPPING OPERATION

Figure 6–19 shows (a) how 28 DS1s are mapped into the DS1 payload and (b) how a DS3 transmission is mapped into the STS-1 payload. The two mappings are taken from two separate operations on two separate input streams. They are shown together to illustrate how both input streams are mapped first to 48.384 Mbit/s, second to 50.112 Mbit/s, and finally to 51.840 Mbit/s.

The purpose of the initial multiplexing and mapping is to create an intermediate stream of 48.384 Mbit/s; thereafter, both DS1, CEPT, and DS3 transmissions are treated the same. All these transmissions have path, line, and section overhead bits added as well as the STS-1 pointer.

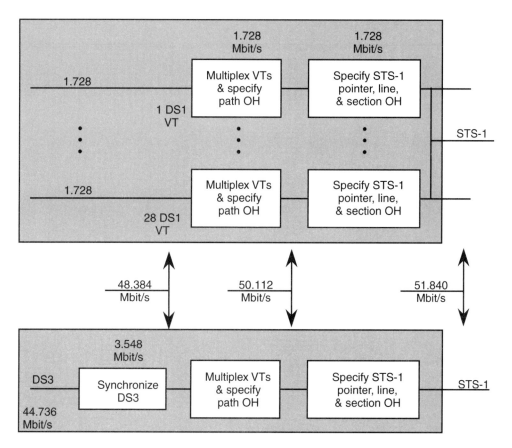

Figure 6–19   The STS-1 payload.

The result is shown on the right-hand side of the figure as the 51.840 Mbit/s STS-1 envelope.

SUMMARY

The SONET specification contains many pages on how asynchronous payloads are mapped into the SONET envelope. The idea is to map all VT and VC payloads into a common rate of 6.912 Mbit/s. The VTs and VCs are then used to keep the payload organized in the synchronous payload envelope.

7

Topologies and Configurations

This chapter provides a more detailed explanation of SONET topologies and configurations, with the emphasis on SONET rings. Protection switching is examined as well. Newer systems, such as SONET, permit remote provisioning of add/drop multiplexers (ADMs) and digital cross-connect systems (DCSs) through software. In this chapter, we show examples of how the ADMs and DCSs can be provisioned to add, drop, or cross-connect payload on the ring.

TYPICAL TOPOLOGIES

Figure 7–1(a) shows a topology for a SONET ring called a bidirectional ring [KRAU94]. This ring uses two fibers, each one sending traffic in one direction opposite from each other. As seen in Figure 7–1(b), in the event of a failure at node interface or a cut in the fiber, the ring is still intact, and all nodes can be reached from any other node.

You are likely thinking, "Figures 7–1(a) and 7–1(b) are identical!" If so, you are correct, except for the big X in Figure 7–1(b) that represents a link or link interface failure. Now, using Figure 7–1(b), you can see that the cross-connects in nodes A and D keep the ring operational.

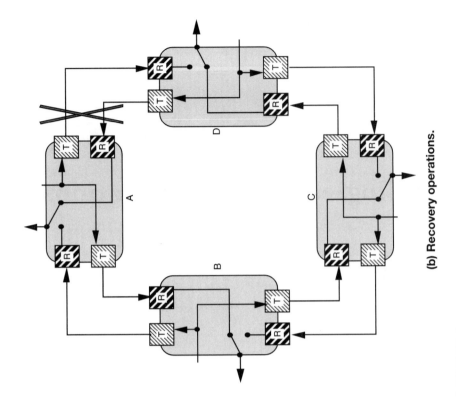

(b) Recovery operations.

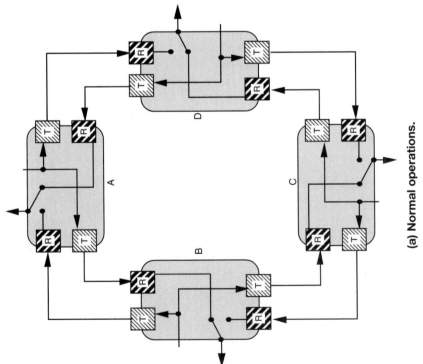

(a) Normal operations.

Figure 7–1   A SONET ring.

PROTECTION SWITCHING IN MORE DETAIL

Figure 7–2 shows another SONET ring topology, and is only one of several configurations possible. This topology is called a bidirectional line-switched self-healing ring (BLSR). Notice that some of the fiber is acting as stand-by, in the event that the working fiber (or a node) fails. The protection copy becomes working copy, and traffic is diverted around the problem. This approach makes for a very robust system and provides very high reliability.

Since optical fiber has such a large information-carrying capacity and supports many simultaneous connections, the loss of the fiber can be quite serious and disruptive. Several approaches are used to reduce the chances of disruptions.

One approach is called line protection switching, or 1:1 switching (see Figure 7–3(a)). This configuration consists of two point-to-point fiber pairs between each network element. If the working fiber is lost or the signal degraded, the protection pair assumes the job of carrying the traffic between the network elements.

Another approach is called 1+1 protection switching. In it, the switching takes place at a low-speed or STS-1 input into the network element (see Figure 7–3(b)). With this arrangement, the traffic is sent on both the working and protection fibers. The two copies of the traffic are

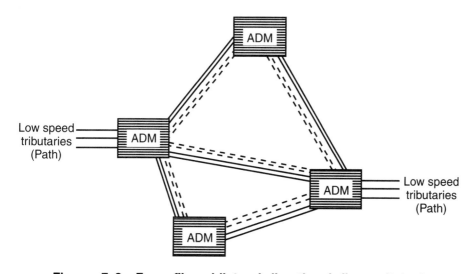

Figure 7–2 Four fiber bilateral-directional line-switched rings (BLSR). Note: Solid lines indicate working fiber, dashed lines indicate protection fiber.

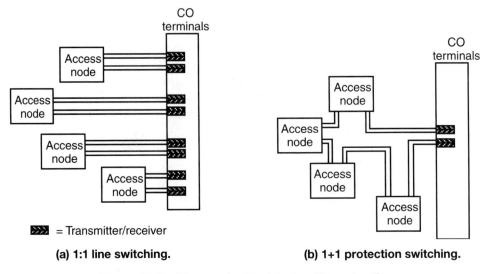

(a) 1:1 line switching.   **(b) 1+1 protection switching.**

Figure 7–3   Line protection and path protection.

received at the receiving network element. Here, they are compared, and only the better copy is used.

For example, a fiber might carry 48 STS-1s, with channels 1–24 used to carry traffic and channels 25–48 used for protection. In the event one of the working channels is faulty, the receiving network element will replace it with the other copy on the protection fiber. This approach is quite fast and does not result in any loss of traffic. Problem restoration is quite efficient, and the other 23 STS1s are not affected.

Using Figure 7–3(b) of the previous illustration as a reference point, Figure 7–4 shows how a shared protection ring can reconfigure and recover from a node or fiber failure. In Figure 7–4(a), all is well; the working path and nodes that connect this path are up (operational). In Figure 7–4(b) a node is down so the signal is diverted to an alternate path by the upstream node (relative to the failed node). In Figure 7–4(c), a path is down, so the signal is diverted by the downstream node (relative to the failed path).

THE BLSR

Figure 7–5 shows another example of a ring. It is also called a four fiber bidirectional line-switched ring (four fiber BLSR). Once again, there are four fibers in the ring, set up as two pairs. One pair is the working pair, and the other is the protection pair. One fiber of the pair transmits

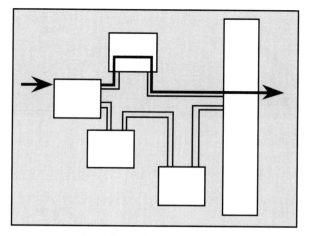

(a) Path and nodes are up.

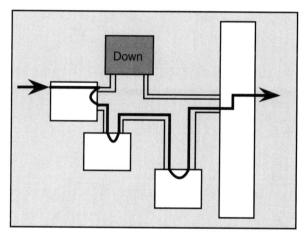

(b) Node is down.

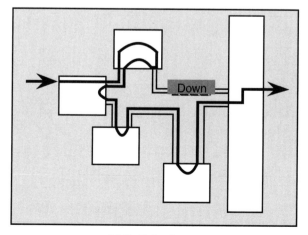

(c) Path is down.

Figure 7–4   Restoration alternatives.

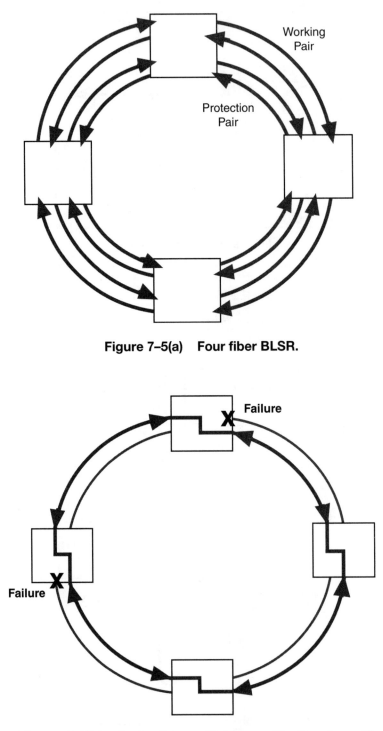

Figure 7–5(a)   Four fiber BLSR.

Figure 7–5(b) Protection switching with the four fiber BLSR.

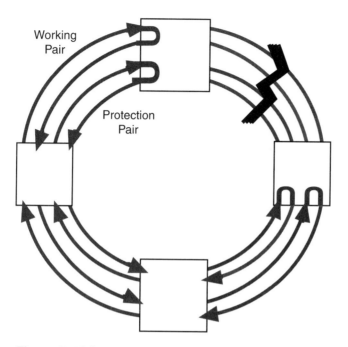

Figure 7–5(c)   Another option with four fiber BLSR.

in one direction, and the other fiber transmits in the other direction. The topology is used because it obviously provides for more capacity, and if the entire installation is performed at the same time, the benefit of the extra fibers and interfaces outweigh the costs to provide them.

The four fiber BLSR gives the network provider considerable flexibility in using the fibers and in recovering from problems. Figure 7–5(b) shows one example.

The arrangement does not restrict the working copy fiber segments to be used with the only other working copy fiber segments. The optical cross-connect node can "mix and match" the segments, based on the operational capability of the topology.

For example, in Figure 7–5(b), two problems have occurred, noted by the black Xs. The problems could be the failure of the fiber itself (perhaps a cut), or the failure of the node interface that supports the fiber. Whatever the case, the optical cross connect uses both the working pair and the protection pair to provide for protection switching for the traffic, as indicated by the bold lines.

Figure 7–5(c) is another example of protection switching with a four fiber BLSR. In this situation, an entire segment has been taken out of commission, either due to problems, or perhaps preventative maintenance.

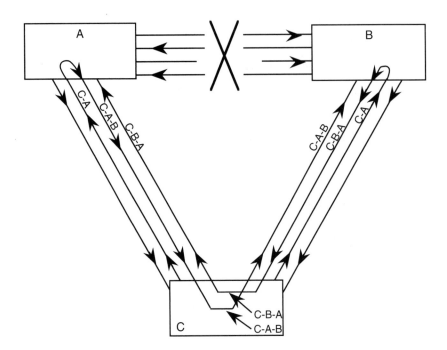

Figure 7–6   Four fiber BLSR line switching.

Whatever the case, the two optical cross-connects notice the problem (or it can be configured by the network operator) and route the traffic back across the partner fiber pair for both the working and protection copies.

If traffic has been running on the "other" fiber of the fiber pair, it must of course be removed from the transmissions. This approach will work just fine if the network operator has placed, say, low-priority traffic on these links.

Placing the working fiber on a diverse route is the best way to achieve robustness. Indeed, protection switching is useless if the working and protection copies are placed together and are both lost.

In the example in Figure 7–6, ring switching is used to loop traffic back from the failed fiber onto the working copy. The path between nodes A and B is not available, so the traffic for these nodes is diverted through node C. The loop-around arrows at nodes A and B show that the traffic to/from A/B is looped through node C. How these operations are achieved is explained in the next section of this chapter.

A Common Approach

All major SONET vendors provide shared protection in their products. With this operation, protection channels are shared, which reduces the number of protection channels required, and which also increases the number of working channels available for user payload. Of course, this approach reduces the costs for the system.

In Figure 7–7, the nodes are connected with two fibers. The STS-1s (carrying DS3 traffic) numbered 1–24 carry traffic, and the STS-1s numbered 25–48 are used for protection. The use of two fibers in this arrangement is called a bidirectional shared protection ring.

In the event of a node or link failure, a bidirectional shared ring recovers by the operations depicted in Figure 7–8. In the top figure, node A fails. This failure affects STS-1 #1 between nodes A and B, so this channel is remapped into the protection channel STS-1 #25. Traffic is diverted through the ring through nodes C, D, and B. At node B, the traffic is mapped from the protection channel STS-1 #25 back to the channel on the interface card that was receiving the traffic before the failure occurred. Traffic going from node B to node C is handled in a similar manner. This operation takes place in less than 50 ms and requires no external control.

The bottom part of Figure 7–8 is an example of self-healing operations that occur in the event of a link failure. It is similar to the opera-

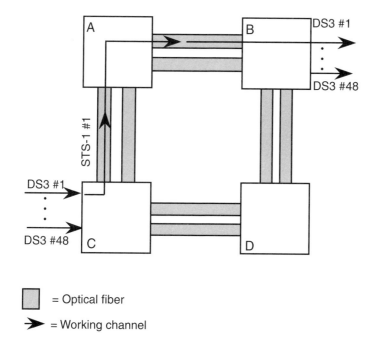

Figure 7–7   Example of a normal operation on a ring.

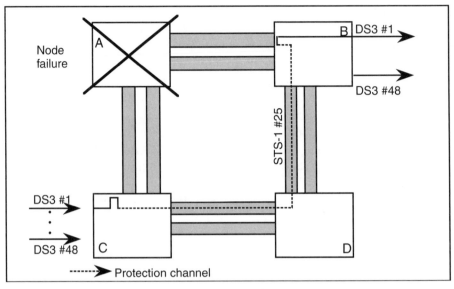

(a) Normal operations.

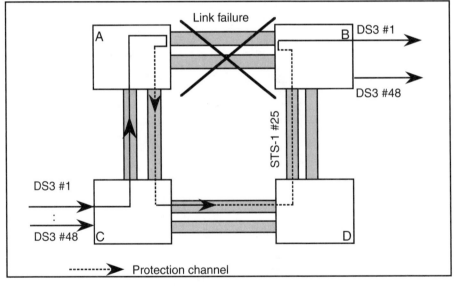

(b) Ring recovery operations.

Figure 7–8   Reovery from node or link failures.

tions that take place for node failures, except that (in this example) all nodes process the traffic, including node A.

ADD-DROP AND CROSS-CONNECTS ON RING OR POINT-TO-POINT TOPOLOGIES

One-Way Cross-Connections

Figure 7–9 shows a cross-connection example of a typical SONET machine.[1] Sixteen tributaries are available on an OC-n at interfaces 1W (west) and 1E (east). With this topology, STS-3 tributaries 1–8 are service tributaries and tributaries 9–16 are protection tributaries. The low-

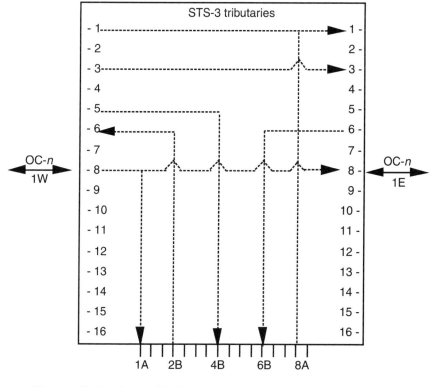

Figure 7–9 An add-drop, cross-connect ring network element.

---

[1]This specific example is based on the AT&T/Lucent 2000 node, but other vendors offer a similar crafting capability.

speed interface slots are used to add, drop, or cross-connect payload. This example is a one-way cross-connection that provides the following connections:

- Add cross-connections: Any low-speed interface slot is made to any high-speed 1W or 1E tributary. In Figure 7–9, the low-speed 2B slot is cross-connected to outgoing STS-3 tributary 6 on OC-n line 1W.
- Drop cross-connections: These connections are the opposite of the add cross-connections. Any incoming STS-3 tributary on lines 1W and 1E can be dropped off to a low-speed slot. In Figure 7–9, STS-3 on the 1W tributary 5 is dropped off to the low-speed interface slot 4B.
- Through cross-connections: This connection is a straight pass-through the machine. An STS-3 tributary on either line 1W or 1E is connected to the same-numbered tributary on the opposite line. In Figure 7–9, the OC-n tributary 3 on line 1W is connected to OC-n tributary 3 on line 1E.
- Bridge cross-connections: A bridge cross-connection is both a drop cross-connection and a through cross-connection from the same STS-3 source. This connection allows payload to be dropped-off and also passed downstream. In Figure 7–9, the tributary 8 on line 1W (as the source) is dropped-off to low speed slot 1A, and through cross-connected to tributary 8 on line 1E.

For a two fiber bidirectional ring, when an STS-3 payload is dropped off at either line 1W or 1E, payload can be added to the same-numbered STS-3 tributary on the other line. In Figure 7–9, tributary 6 on incoming line 1E is dropped to low-speed slot 6B. This dropped cross-connection permits the adding of the low-speed 2B slot to tributary 6 on line 1W.

One-Way DRI Cross-Connections

Figure 7–10 depicts a dual ring interworking architecture (DRI). This configuration connects two ring networks with a common node. The DRI allows a circuit with a termination in one ring and another termination in the other ring to recover from a loss of signal at the shared node.

Some vendors provide the capability for the one-way DRI cross-connection to be shared by two sources. Any low-speed slot can be added to any outgoing tributary. In effect, this configuration is an added cross-connection and a through cross-connection.

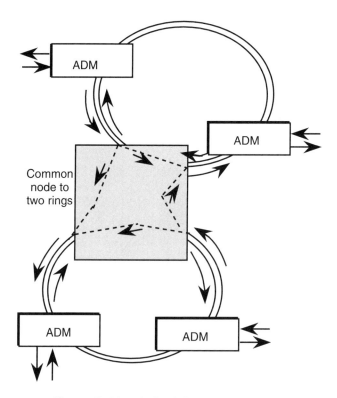

Figure 7–10   A dual ring architecture.

Two-Way Cross-Connections

Figure 7–11 shows examples of an add/drop terminal supporting two-way cross-connections. This example is common to most offerings, which allows add-drop cross-connections between any low-speed interface slot and any STS-3 tributary of OC-48 1E or 1W. This figure also shows two-way through cross-connections on tributaries 3 and 14. When an STS-3 tributary on 1E or 1W is cross-connected to a low-speed interface slot, another low-speed interface slot can be cross-connected to the same numbered tributary. In Figure 7–11, low-speed slots 2B and 6B and tributary 6 show this option.

The SONET ADM allows extra traffic to be placed on protection tributaries, but the traffic is pre-empted if ring protection switching occurs. In Figure 7–11, protection tributaries 10 and 14 are being used for extra traffic.

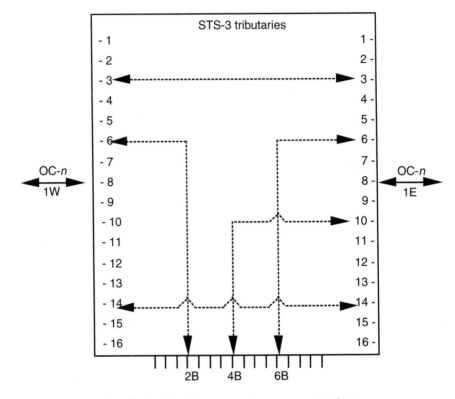

Figure 7–11   Two-way cross-connections.

PROVISIONING SONET MACHINES FOR ADD-DROP AND CROSS-CONNECT OPERATIONS

How do SONET machines determine how payload is to be added, dropped off, or cross-connected at the various machines in the network? The answer is that these capabilities are provisioned locally at each machine through a direct interface port into the machine, a dial-up link into the machine, or remotely from a data communications channel (DCC), which are all fields residing in the SONET overhead headers. In most systems, the SONET machine can be accessed through an X.25/TL1 interface. We will use the term craft interface terminal (CIT) to describe the terminal that is used for provisioning.

The craft operations are provided to the terminal user (the provisioner) with menu-driven screens and user-friendly prompts. For example, to set up cross-connections in a multiplexer or cross-connect device, a prompt of "CONFIGURATION-Enter-Cross-connection-STS3" enables the provisioner to enter (1) the source slot of the traffic, (2) the destination line on the source machine, (3) the destination tributary on destination line, and (4) the destination node's identification.

One-Way and Two-Way Cross-Connections

Figure 7–12 shows a four node, two fiber bidirectional ring. The dashed lines and arrows indicate how the traffic is to be cross-connected, added, or dropped off. To provision this ring, the terminal command "CONFIGURATION-Enter-Cross-connection-STS3" is used, and the parameters are specified as shown next. Be aware that these terminal parameters have been generalized for ease of reading.

For node 0, the provisioner enters these parameters:

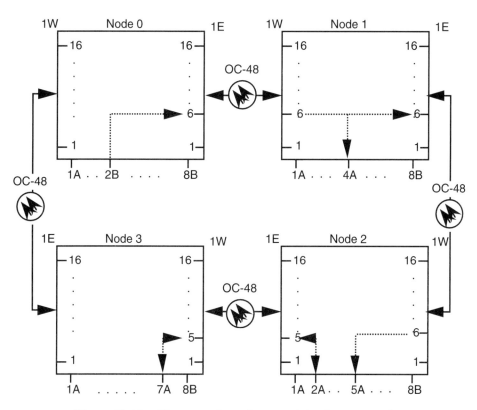

Figure 7–12   Ring topology for provisioning example.

- Source (slot)
- Source low-speed interface slot (slot 2B)
- Destination line (line 1E)
- Destination STS-3 tributary (tributary 6)
- Destination node TID (node 2 TID)

For node 1, the provisioner enters these parameters to set up a one-way through cross-connection:

- Source (tributary)
- Source line (line 1W)
- Source STS-3 tributary (tributary 6)
- Source node TID (node 0 TID)
- Destination (tributary)
- Destination node TID (node 2 TID)

For node 1, the provisioner enters these parameters to set up a one-way drop cross-connection:

- Source (tributary)
- Source line (line 1W)
- Source STS-3 tributary (tributary 6)
- Source node TID (node 0 TID)
- Destination (slot)
- Destination low-speed interface slot (slot 4A)

For node 2, the provisioner enters these parameters to set up to set up a one-way drop cross-connection:

- Source (tributary)
- Source line (line 1W)
- Source STS-3 tributary (tributary 6)
- Source node TID (node 0 TID)
- Destination (slot)
- Destination low-speed interface slot (slot 5A)

For node 2, the provisioner enters these parameters to set up a two-way add-drop cross-connection:

- Source (slot)
- Source low-speed interface slot (slot 2A)
- Destination line (line 1E)
- Destination STS-3 tributary (tributary 5)
- Destination node TID (node 3 TID)

For node 3, the provisioner enters these parameters to set up a two-way add-drop cross-connection:

- Source (tributary)
- Source line (line 1W)
- Source STS-3 tributary (tributary 5)
- Source node TID (node 2 TID)
- Destination (slot)
- Destination low-speed interface slot (slot 7A)

One-Way Cross-Connections

Figure 7–13 shows a one-way connection on a two-fiber bidirectional ring. This topology is part of a dual ring interworking system. One-way and one-way DRI cross-connections are used at the primary and secondary nodes. The craft command to establish this configuration is "CONFIGURATION-Enter-Cross connection-STS-3." For node 2 (primary node), the provisioner enters these parameters to set up a one-way DRI cross-connection:

- Source low-speed interface slot (slot 5A)
- Destination line (line 1W)
- Destination STS-3 tributary (tributary 6)
- Destination node TID (node 0 TID)
- Secondary node TID (node 3 TID)

For node 3 (secondary node), the provisioner enters these parameters to set up a one-way ADD cross-connection by specifying:

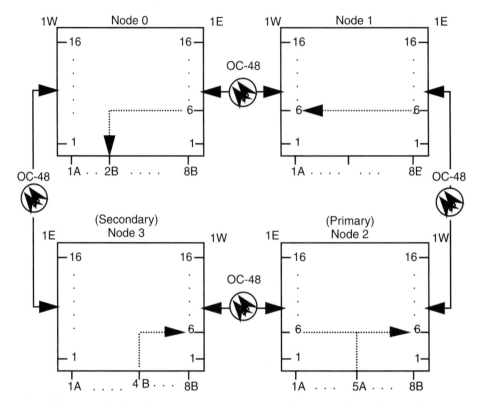

Figure 7–13   One-way cross-connections in two-fiber bi-directional ring.

- Source (slot)
- Source low-speed interface slot (slot 4B)
- Destination line (line 1W)
- Destination STS-3 tributary (tributary 6)
- Destination node TID (node 0 TID)

Rolling Cross-Connections

Figure 7–14 shows a rolling cross-connection configuration on a two-fiber bidirectional ring. The rolling cross-connection "rolls" traffic from an existing source to a new source for a one way circuit.

For node 0 the provisioner enters these parameters to set up traffic:

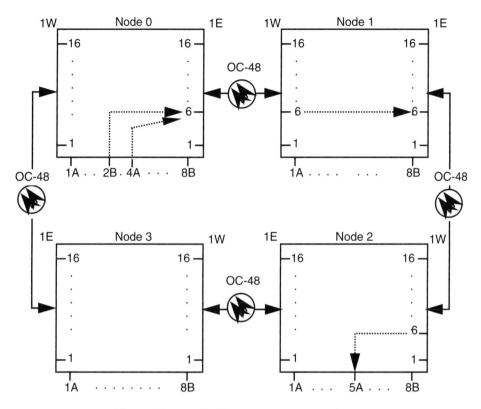

Figure 7–14   Rolling cross-connections.

- Source (slot)
- Source low-speed interface slot (slot 2B)
- Destination line (line 1E)
- Destination STS-3 tributary (tributary 6)
- New cross-connection type (one-way)
- New source (slot 4A)

Deleting Cross-Connections

Cross-connections are deleted with the "CONFIGURATION-Delete-Cross connection-STS3" command. Refer to Figure 7–12 for this example.

For node 0, the provisioner enters these parameters to delete the one-way add cross-connection:

- Source (slot)
- Source low-speed interface slot (slot 2B)
- Destination line (line 1E)
- Destination STS-3 tributary (tributary 6)

For node 1, the provisioner enters these parameters to delete the one-way through cross-connection:

- Source (tributary)
- Source line (line 1W)
- Source STS-3 tributary (tributary 6)
- Destination (tributary)

For node 1, the provisioner enters these parameters to delete the one-way drop cross-connection:

- Source (tributary)
- Source line (line 1W)
- Source STS-3 tributary (tributary 6)
- Destination (slot)
- Destination low-speed interface slot (slot 4A)

For node 2, the provisioner enters these parameters to delete the one-way drop cross-connection:

- Source (tributary)
- Source line (line 1W)
- Source STS-3 tributary (tributary 6)
- Destination (slot)
- Destination low-speed interface slot (slot 5A)

For node 2, the provisioner enters these parameters to delete the two-way add-drop cross-connection:

- Source (slot)
- Source low-speed interface slot (slot 2A)
- Destination line (line 1E)
- Destination STS-3 tributary (tributary 5)

For node 3, the provisioner enters these parameters to delete the two-way add-drop cross-connection:

- Source (tributary)
- Source line (line 1W)
- Source STS-3 tributary (tributary 5)
- Destination (slot)
- Destination low-speed interface slot (slot 7A)

EXAMPLE OF PROTECTION SWITCHING ON A TWO FIBER BIDIRECTIONAL RING

In this section, we continue our discussion of two fiber bidirectional rings and show an example of how automatic ring protection switching handles a signal degradation or a signal failure on an incoming tributary.

Figure 7–15 illustrates a ring topology under normal conditions. Tributaries 1–8 are service tributaries, and tributaries 9–16 are protection tributaries. The following connections have been established:

- Tributary 6 carries: Service traffic between slot 4A at node 0 and slot 5A at node 2.
- Tributary 3 carries: Service traffic between slot 3A at node 1 and slot 2A at node 3.
- Tributary 14 carries: Extra traffic between slot 2B at node 0 and slot 4B at node 3.

Figure 7–16 shows the altered configuration when a fiber failure occurs between nodes 0 and 1. Dashed lines indicate traffic flow before the failure. Solid lines indicate flow after protection switching occurs.

The failure is detected by the node 0, 1E, and node 1, 1W circuit packs. The 1W node 1 sends a switch request to the other nodes using the automatic protection switch (APS) channel. All nodes preempt extra traffic, which means tributary 14 is used to assist in the recovery. At nodes 2 and 3, through cross-connections are established on tributaries 11 and 14. Otherwise, nodes 2 and 3 are intermediate nodes in this recovery and are not actively involved in the protection switching.

At node 1, the following alterations have occured:

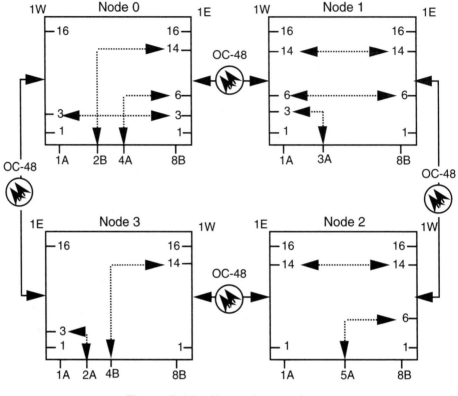

Figure 7–15   Normal operations.

- The low-speed and high-speed circuit packs switch traffic to the protection tributaries on line 1E.
- An add-drop connection is established between slot 3A and cross-connected to protection tributary 11 on line 1E.
- Traffic transmitted toward the failure is looped back to the protection tributaries. Tributary 6 is looped back to protection tributary 14.
- Node 1 returns a switch confirmation to node 0 on the APS channel on line 1E.
- At node 0, the following alterations have occurred:
- The low-speed and high-speed circuit packs switch traffic to the protection tributaries on line 1W.
- An add-drop connection is established between slot 4A and cross-connected to protection tributary 14 on line 1W.

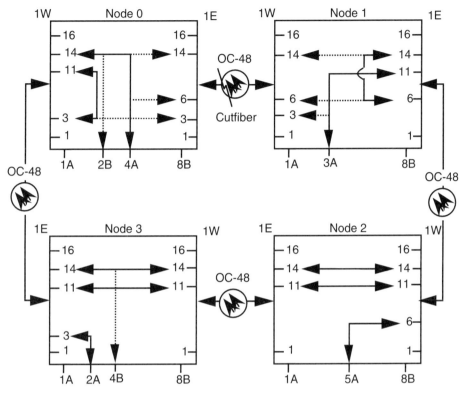

Figure 7–16   Results of protection switching.

- Traffic transmitted toward the failure is looped back to the protection tributaries. Tributary 3 is looped back to protection tributary 11 on line 1W.

CASCADING THE TIMING ON MULTIPLE RINGS

To conclude this chapter, we return to the subject of timing and synchronization, and show a typical example of how the clocks are provided in a more complex topology. Figure 7–17 shows two types of timing on a SONET ring:

1. A free-running and through-timed configuration.
2. A source-clocked and through-timed configuration.

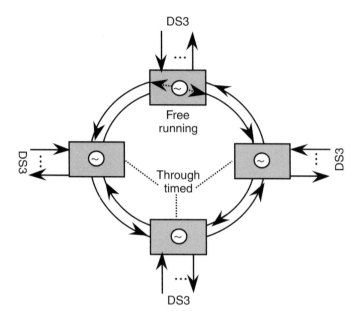

(a) Free running and through-timed configuration.

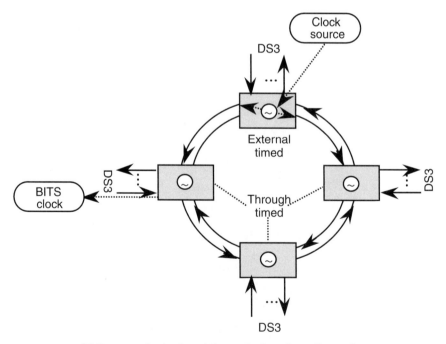

(b) Source clocked and through-timed configuration.

Figure 7–17   Cascading timing on rings.

In Figure 7–17(a), one of the nodes is free running the others are through-timed. In Figure 7–17(b), external clocks are used.

The topologies explained in this chapter can use the combinations of free-running and through-timed clocking mechanisms. For example, the ring topology in Figure 7–12 could have some nodes using one method, and the other nodes using the other method. The authors recommend you try to avoid free-running clocks on your topologies. If possible, the best approach is to use one clocking source, which is usually attainable in local and metropolitan networks. If multiple clocks are used, the use of synchronization messages (explained in earlier chapters) between the nodes is very important. Multiple clocking sources may be the only alternative in wide area networks in which the rings of one service provider are connected to the rings of another service provider.

SUMMARY

SONET provides powerful mechanisms for setting up a linear or ring topology, and the SONET equipment vendors provide software-based craft systems to configure the topology for addressing, cross-connect, and pass-through operations. This approach allows the user to provision remote SONET network elements through crafting commands that are entered into the SONET DCC bytes or into the payload area of the SONET envelope.

8

Operations, Administration, and Maintenance

SONET uses about 4 percent of its available bandwidth for a wide variety of control, network management, and signaling purposes which are referred to as operations, administration, and maintenance (OAM), or simply network management. These operations are explained in this chapter, as well as the SONET headers that are used to provide signaling control, alarm generation, alarm surveillance, equipment type, framing operations, and error checking operations. The latter part of the chapter introduces two network management protocols, the common management information protocol (CMIP) and the simple network management protocol (SNMP).

NEED FOR RIGOROUS TESTING

While testing in any network is important and must be performed to ensure proper functioning of all components, it is vital in a network such as SONET, because SONET is able to carry enormous amounts of traffic from many users. The loss or malfunction of SONET equipment can cause severe disruption of services, as well as a significant loss of revenue to a SONET service provider and the provider's customers. Moreover, with previous systems, many carrier networks' equipment was supplied by the same vendor that implemented proprietary OAM protocols. As a consequence, testing in these networks was simpler because different vendors' components were not interworking. Of course, since one of the purposes of SONET is to provide standard interfaces between different vendors' equipment, a new dimension is added for testing. This testing must be performed under rigorous rules to ensure proper interfaces between equipment from different vendors.

ALARM SURVEILLANCE

One of the principal activities of SONET OAM is alarm surveillance. This activity entails the detection of specific problems in the network and the reporting of those problems. The condition that is reported is called a "state." The network element (NE), such as a switch or multiplexer, enters a state upon detecting the occurrence of an event and exits the state when the occurrence of the event is no longer detected. The change of the state may also lead to an "indication," which represents the presence of a condition. SONET equipment must support the alarm surveillance operations listed in Table 8–1. The terms state, indication, and condition are explained in more detail later in this chapter in the section titled "Maintenance Signals and Layers."

Table 8–1   Failure states and alarm surveillance operations.

Failures invoke alarm indication signals (AIS)

- *Loss of Signal (LOS):* All zeros pattern for 10 μsec or longer. Restored when two consecutive valid frame alignment procedures are encountered.

- *Loss of Frame (LOF):* Four consecutive frames with errored framing patterns encountered. Restored when two consecutive A1 and A2 bytes successfully encountered.

- *Loss of Pointer (LOP):* Eight consecutive frames encountered with invalid STS or VT pointers. Restored when three consecutive valid pointers encountered.

- *Equipment failure:* A variety of failures encountered. Classified as service affecting (SA), non-service affecting (NSA), critical (CR), major (MJ), or minor (MN).

- *Loss of synchronization:* Detection of the loss of timing source when transient exceeds 300 nsec between periods of 100–1000 seconds.

CATEGORIES OF TESTS

Figure 8–1 shows an arrangement we shall use in this section of the chapter to discuss testing operations of the SONET transport capability. As the figure shows, the testing operations are organized into four parts. These categories of tests and their underlying methodology are based on approaches taken by Hewlett Packard [HEWL92].

We limit discussion on the specific SONET OAM fields (OAM headers) in this section, since they have not been explained in detail but are covered later in this chapter under the title "The SONET OAM Headers." Testing and OAM headers are inter-related, and obviously one must be discussed before the other. So, for the occasional citation of an OAM field, the reader may wish to look forward for the description of that field.

Returning to Figure 8–1, transport capability tests include bit error rate (BER) testing, as well as mapping and demapping testing. As a whole, these tests are used to make certain the payload is carried correctly through various parts of the SONET network.

Payload pointer tests, as the name implies, include tests such as determining timing offset and payload output jitter. These tests verify that SONET accommodates to any type of asynchronous variation in the network. Their purpose is to ensure that ongoing SONET equipment does not interfere with the operation of other non-SONET equipment operating in other networks and interworking with SONET.

The embedded overhead tests include operations such as performance monitoring and alarm functions. This category also includes protocol testing. These tests insure that SONET equipment will react in a predictable manner under several unusual conditions that could affect network performance.

Finally, the line interface tests category includes tests to analyze and monitor the capabilities of the physical SONET line interfaces.

Using the Hewlett Packard model, Figure 8–2 shows an "entity under test" configuration that serves as the basis for our examination of

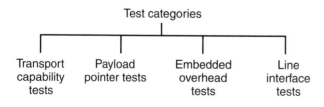

Test categories

Transport capability tests

Payload pointer tests

Embedded overhead tests

Line interface tests

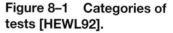

Figure 8–1   Categories of tests [HEWL92].

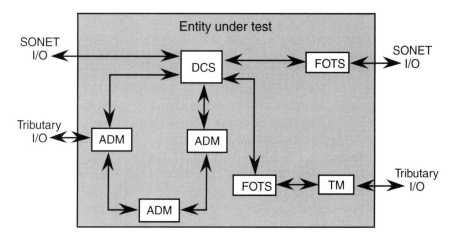

Figure 8–2 Model for testing operations.

the SONET test categories. The entity under test is a link or interface for a full SONET signal or a tributary. The input and output (I/O) interfaces that exist in a SONET network are the same for all interfaces at all network elements. Therefore, common operations can be established for the following tests:

1. SONET input to SONET output
2. SONET input to tributary output
3. Tributary input to SONET output
4. Tributary input to tributary output

This approach allows a network to establish a common range of tests to verify the performance of the SONET equipment, for both SONET and tributary interfaces for add-drop multiplexers, digital cross-connects, terminals, and of course the fiber optic transmission system. With these thoughts in mind, we now examine each of the test categories depicted in Figure 8–1.

Transport Capability Tests

Mapping and Demapping Testing. Mapping testing is performed by a tributary tester that creates a DSn signal and sends this signal to the entity under test. The tributary tester is actually simulating a DS3 or DS1 signal. The bit rate of the tributary test can be altered to test the synchronization capabilities in the entity under test. As depicted in

Figure 8–3(a), the entity under test accepts the DSn, maps it into the synchronous payload envelope (SPE), which is called a mapping test response, and sends it to a SONET tester. This device recovers the signal for analysis. The tests are verified by the SONET tester through a bit error rate (BER) test. While this figure shows the SONET tester performing the analysis, the SONET tester could also pass the signal back to a different receive tributary tester to perform the tests.

The opposite tests are demapping testing, as shown in Figure 8–3(b). In this situation, the SONET tester creates a tributary signal (demapping test stimulus) and maps it into a SONET envelope. The entity under test demaps the tributary signal and sends the resulting DSn signal to the tributary tester. The tributary tester then measures the level of jitter on the signal and performs a bit error check to verify how accurately the entity under test is performing.

Bit Error Rate (BER) Testing. Bit error rate (BER) testing verifies that the entity under test is processing the SONET traffic correctly from an input port to an output port. As shown in Figure 8–4, two SONET testers are involved in this test, one on the transmit side and one on the receive side of the entity under test. On the transmit side, the SONET tester sends a simulated SPE (the test stimulus) to the entity under test. Then, the entity under test processes the SPE and relays the test response through an output port to the receive SONET tester. The test response is demultiplexed and verified through a conventional BER operation at the receive SONET tester.

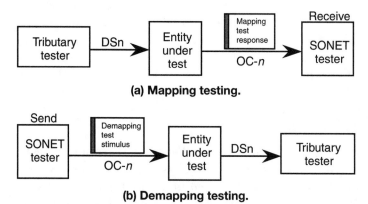

(a) Mapping testing.

(b) Demapping testing.

Figure 8–3   Mapping and demapping testing.

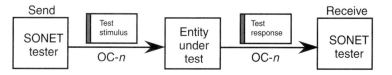

Figure 8–4   BER testing.

This test is called a BER test because a BER is measured. In the case shown in the figure, the test does not measure line-related errors. It is testing how accurately the entity under test is receiving, processing, and sending the SONET frames.

Payload Pointer Testing

Payload Output Jitter Testing.   SPE pointer movements create tributary jitter because a pointer adjustment (with each adjustment) means that a byte in the payload is moved. When this occurs, 8-bit timing discontinuities are introduced into the signal. For this reason, payload pointer adjustments should not be done often.

It is desirable to keep tributary jitter to a minimum. Payload output jitter testing is one method used to measure the amount of jitter introduced during a pointer-adjustment operation (see Figure 8–5(a)). The purpose is to test jitter at an entity under test to determine if the jitter is occurring within acceptable limits. As shown in Figure 8–5(a), two SONET testers are involved. A send SONET tester produces the test as a

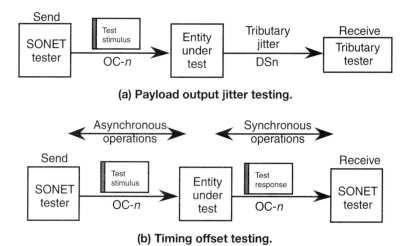

(a) Payload output jitter testing.

(b) Timing offset testing.

Figure 8–5   Payload pointer testing.

stimulus SPE. The send SONET tester also adds pointer adjustments to the test stimulus SPE, which will require the entity under test to demap the traffic by using the pointer and send the resulting DS1 signals to a receive tributary tester. Next, the receive tributary tester verifies the integrity of the payload and determines the degree of jitter introduced at the entity under test. The measurement is performed with a BER check.

Timing Offset Testing. Figure 8–5(b) shows the arrangement for verifying the operation of pointer processing by an entity under test. With this test, the sending SONET tester creates a test stimulus SPE, but the line signal is not synchronized to the entity under test. The sending SONET tester is operating asynchronously with the entity under test. Therefore, the test is used to determine the pointer processing capabilities within the entity under test.

The timing differences between the sending SONET tester and the entity under test require the payload pointer of the tested SPE to be adjusted to synchronize the incoming test stimulus SPE with the outgoing test response SPE. The entity under test performs its required operations and sends a test response to the receive SONET tester.

In this situation, the entity under test and the receive SONET tester are operating synchronously. The receive SONET tester processes the payload pointer and recovers the test response SPE. The integrity of the operation is verified through a BER test. This test is also used to measure timing offsets at different points in the network and the number of pointer adjustments that have been made during a measured period of time.

Embedded Overhead Tests

SONET defines several events for the detection of problems and failures. Additionally, SONET provides information on how the detection of these problems is signaled to various parts of the SONET system. Figure 8–6 shows how the detection of certain events can trigger alarm signals. There are six failure conditions shown in this figure. Some of these conditions are also described in Table 8–1. The others are explained next.

1. Loss of signal (LOS)
2. Loss of frame (LOF)
3. Loss of pointer (LOP)
4. Alarm indication signal (AIS)

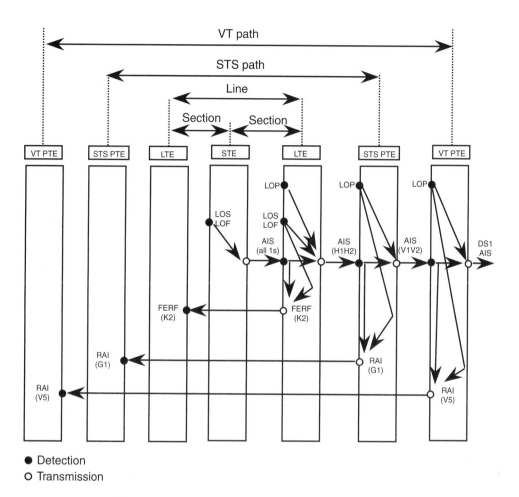

Figure 8–6   In service testing and alarm events.

5. Far end receive failure (FERF)

6. Remote alarm indication (RAI)

The AIS is an alarm that is sent downstream in reaction to a LOS, LOF, or LOP. The FERF is sent upstream in reaction to a LOS, LOF, or LOP. The RAI is sent end to end in reaction to a LOS, LOF, or LOP.

The detection of LOS, LOF, or LOP at the section terminating equipment (STE) or line terminating equipment (LTE) causes the generation of alarms on that device's output port to the downstream network element. For example, if an STE detects a LOS or LOF, its output port generates an AIS of all 1s to the downstream[1] LTE, which in turn generates an AIS with H1, H2 to the path terminating equipment (PTE), which in turn generates and AIS with V1, V2 to the virtual tributary (VT) PTE. The VT PTE might then generate a DSn AIS on the tributary.

These events also invoke upstream signals. The LTE sends a FERF, using a K2 signal, to its associated LTE upstream. Likewise, the STS PTE sends an RAI (G1) to its associated upstream STS PTE, and the VT PTE sends an RAI (V5) to its peer VT PTE.

Alarm Testing. We just learned that alarm conditions, such as loss of signal (LOS), loss of pointer (LOP), and loss of frame (LOF), will cause the alarm indication signal to be sent downstream. In turn, the far end receive failure (FERF) will be sent upstream in the line overhead if line AIS, LOS, or LOF has been detected. Figure 8–6 also shows that the remote alarm indication (RAI; also known as the yellow alarm) is sent upstream in both STS path and VT path overheads, after path AIS or LOP has been detected in the STS path or VT path, respectively.

Given these various conditions, the purpose of alarm testing is to ensure that monitoring for these alarms is occurring correctly and that the entity under test is sending the correct signals both upstream and downstream. The operations for alarm testing are depicted in Figure 8–7. In this situation, the SONET testers are used to verify that the entity under test is correctly generating OAM signals both downstream and upstream.

Performance Monitoring Testing. Performance monitoring uses the bit interleave parity (BIP-8) check calculated on a frame-by-frame basis. These checks are inserted on the overhead associated with either the section, line, or path headers and their associated spans. Performance monitoring also can check for STS path or VT path failures and will produce a far end block failure based on errors detected on the STS path and VT path bits, respectively. As illustrated in Figure 8–8, the test response signal is sent from the entity under test to the upstream originating component.

Protocol Testing. The upcoming section titled "The SONET OAM Headers" explains the use of the two data communications channels (DCCs). One channel operates on the section overhead at 192 kbit/s and

---

[1]In this example (Figure 8–6), upstream-to-downstream is the flow of the traffic from left to right. Downstream-to-upstream is the flow of traffic from right to left.

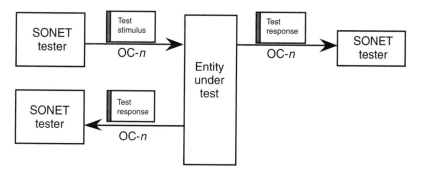

Figure 8–7   Alarm testing.

the other operates on the line overhead at 576 kbit/s. To explain briefly, the DCCs are used to carry a network management message between various elements and the operations support system. Typically, message-based information is transferred by means of a typical OSI stack operating with the common management information protocol (CMIP), or the simple network management protocol (SNMP) at the applications layer.

The purpose of the protocol test is to verify that the entity under test is detecting the test stimulus frames and generating appropriate DCC management information, according to the type of error encountered. Therefore, a SONET tester, as shown in Figure 8–9, can send a bit error, an alarm error, or any type of test stimulus (that is embedded into the SONET signal) to check the entity's ability to (1) respond to the error and (2) generate the proper DCC network management message. This message is analyzed by an attached protocol analyzer.

Protection Testing.   This test determines if an entity under test is properly reacting to continued or disrupted signals by switching to a

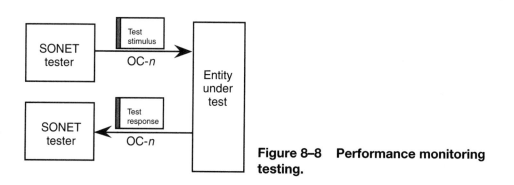

Figure 8–8   Performance monitoring testing.

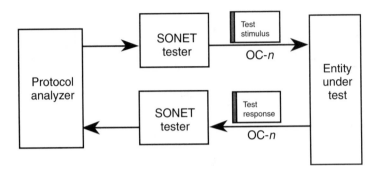

Figure 8–9   Protocol testing.

standby line when an error rate reaches a preset threshold. This operation is shown in Figure 8–10. An optical attenuator is placed before the
working line input, and the tributary tester attached to the network entity under test determines if this entity has properly switched to the
standby link. The tributary tester monitors the error rate. The operation
provides an accurate estimate of the error rate that is detected by the entity under test. It also tests the ability of the entity under test to monitor
the circuits.

Line Interface Tests

The last testing example in this section deals with parametric testing on the line for either optical or electrical signals. These tests include
the measurements of the signal, such as noise, attenuation, spectral or

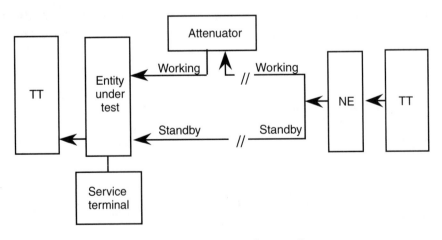

Figure 8–10   Protection testing.

chromatic dispersion, and other aspects of non-fiber, or fiber transmissions, which are explained in Appendix A.

With this background information in mind, let us return to the SONET layers and analyze how they are used in OAM operations. We also introduce ATM OAM here, since the ITU-T Recommendations tie together the OAM of both SONET and ATM.

OAM AND THE SONET LAYERS

The OAM operations are classified as information levels, and are associated with the hierarchical, layered design of SONET, as well as the asynchronous transfer mode (ATM). Figure 8–11 shows the five OAM levels and their corresponding OAM operations, which are labeled F1, F2, F3, F4, and F5. The F1, F2, and F3 functions reside at the physical layer and pertain to SONET OAM. The F4 and F5 functions reside at the ATM layer. The Fn tags depict where the OAM information flows (i.e., moves) between two points.

The five OAM information flows occur as follows. Refer to Figure 8–12 during this explanation. Please note that these OAM flows are examples and not all-inclusive.

F5 OAM information flows between network elements performing ATM virtual channel (VC) functions. From the perspective of a B-ISDN configuration, F5 OAM operations are conducted between B-NT2/B-NT1 end points (the far end B-NT2/B-NT1 is not shown in this figure). F5 deals with degraded VC performance, such as late arriving cells, lost cells, cell insertion problems, etc.

F4 OAM information flows between network elements performing virtual path (VP) functions. From the perspective of a B-ISDN configuration, F4 OAM flows between B-NT2 and ET. F4 OAM reports on an unavailable path or a VP that cannot be guaranteed.

F3 OAM information flows between elements that perform the assembling and disassembling of payload, header error control operations, and cell delineation. From the perspective of a B-ISDN configuration, F3 OAM flows between B-NT2, VP cross connect, and ET.

F2 OAM information flows between elements that terminate section end points. It detects and reports on loss of frame synchronization and degraded error performance. From the perspective of a B-ISDN configuration, F2 OAM flows between B-NT2, B-NT1, and LT.

F1 OAM information flows between regenerator sections. It detects and reports on loss of frame and degraded error performance. From the perspective of a B-ISDN, F1 OAM flows between the LTs and regenerators.

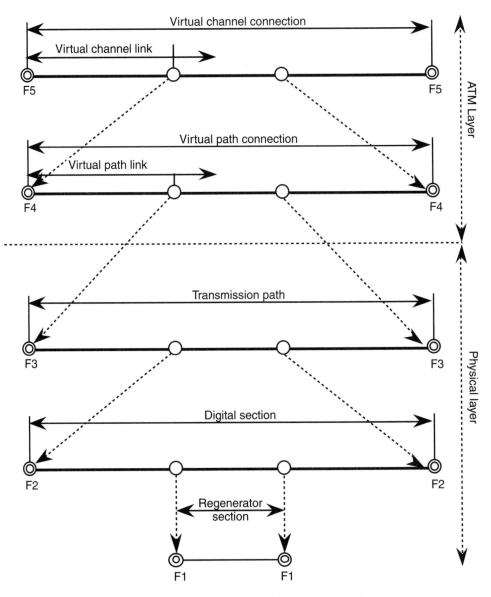

Figure 8–11   ATM & SDH/SONET OAM structure [ITU=T .311].

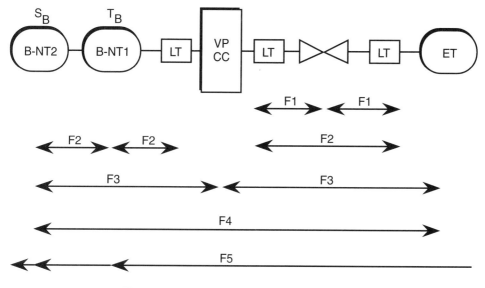

Figure 8–12   The Fn information flows.

THE SONET OAM HEADERS

Figure 8–13 shows the structure and abbreviated names of the three OAM headers and the bytes within the headers. The reader may recall that each of the three major components (and its associated layer) is responsible for creating a header at the transmitting network element and processing the header at the receiving network element. Notice the use of four columns of the SONET frame for the OAM bytes. Also notice the position of the three headers.

Section Overhead

Figure 8–14 illustrates and describes the section overhead fields. The A1 and A2 bytes are called the *framing* bytes, and they are flags used by a receiving machine to synchronize onto the SONET signal; they identify the start of an STS-1 frame. They are coded as 1111–0110 and 0010–1000. These bits must appear in every STS-1 signal in a composite (higher multiplexed) signal. They are not scrambled in order to make their detection easier.

The J0 byte is called the *section trace* and is used for STS-1 identification. It is a unique number that is assigned to each STS-1 of an STS-n

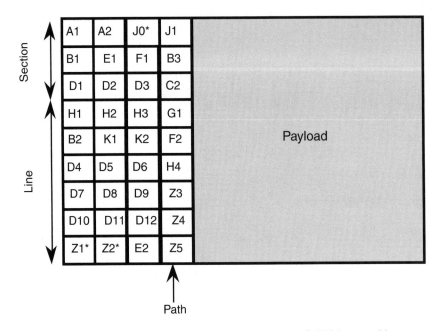

Figure 8–13   Abbreviated names for the OAM bytes. Note:
For J0*, Z1*, Z*, see text for additional byte designations.

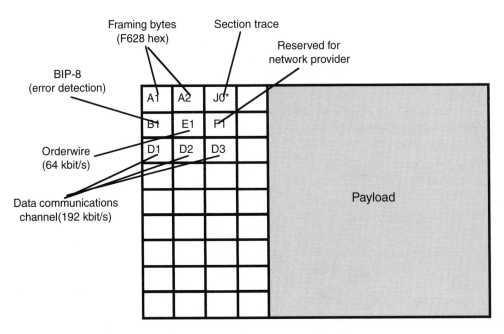

Figure 8–14   Section overhead.

signal. The J0 byte in the STS-1 can be set to a number that corresponds to its order in the STS-n frame, although the SONET standards have not defined its exact use. Notwithstanding, it is assigned to each STS-1 signal before the signal is byte-interleaved into an STS-n frame. The idea of this byte is to be able to trace the origin of any STS-1 frame, which is a good idea, since many frames may be multiplexed from many sources.

The J0 byte is defined only for the first STS-1 in an STS-n from the same source. Earlier implementations of SONET simply incremented a value in this field by one for each succeeding STS-1 frame. This older practice will be abandoned as fiber speeds increase and the eight-bit byte will be insufficient to act as an incremental counter. Currently, this byte is designated as Z0 for its entry in any STS-1 frames beyond the first frame in the STS-n signal.

The B1 byte is the *bit interleaved parity* byte, and usually called *BIP-8*. SONET performs a parity check on the previously sent STS-1 frame and places the answer (the parity) in the current frame. The BIP-8 byte checks for transmission errors over a section. It is defined only for the first STS-1 of the STS-n signal.

The E1 byte is an *orderwire* byte. It is a 64 kbit/s voice path that can be used for maintenance communications between terminals, hubs, and regenerators. This byte is somewhat of an historical relic, based on copper-based orderwire used by crafting personnel in older networks.

The F1 *user* byte is set aside for the network provider to use in any manner deemed appropriate, but it is used at the STE within a line. Some vendors use F1 for OAM.

The D1, D2, and D3 bytes are called the *data communications channel* bits and are used for data communications channels. They are part of 192 kbit/s operations that are used for signaling control, administrative alarms, and other OAM. Later discussions in this book show examples of the use of these bytes.

Line Overhead

The line overhead fields are shown in Figure 8–15. The bytes occupy the bottom six octets of the first three columns in the SONET frame. Line overhead is processed by all equipment except for the regenerators.

The first two bytes (labeled H1 and H2) are *pointer* bytes that indicate the offset in bytes between the pointer and the first byte of the SPE. This pointer allows the SPE to be located anywhere within the SONET envelope, as long as capacity is available. These bytes also are coded to indicate whether any new data are residing in the envelope.

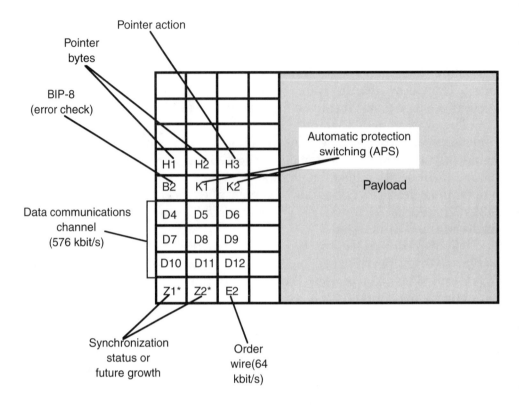

Figure 8–15 Line overhead.

The *pointer action* (H3) byte is used to frequency justify the SPE—that is, to allow for possible slight timing differences that may exist between SONET nodes. In the event that the arriving payload exceeds the outgoing transmission rate (a timing difference of a full byte is required), the pointer action byte is used to carry this byte.

To illustrate how this byte operates, let's assume that an incoming SPE of 783 bytes (90 columns −3 columns for the section and line overhead = 87 columns × 9 rows = 783) has experienced timing differences in the downstream nodes. So, an extra byte (the 784th byte) has arrived and is in the receiving buffer. This byte is stored in the H3 byte, a process called negative timing justification.

Other parts of this book explain the use of the H bytes in more detail. If you wish to delve into this information, see Chapter 3, "Floating Payload and SONET Pointers."

The B2 byte is a *BIP-8* parity code that is calculated for all bits of the line overhead. Its use is identical to the BIP-8 byte found in the section header, except this byte pertains only to the line header.

Bytes K1 and K2 are the *automatic protection switching* (APS) bytes. They are used for (1) detecting problems with the line terminating equipment for bidirectional traffic, (2) alarms and signaling failures, and (3) network recovery.

All the *data communications channel* bytes (D4–D12) are used for line communication and are part of a 576 kbit/s message that is used for maintenance control, monitoring, alarms, etc. Originally, the Common Management Information Protocol (CMIP) was defined for use in the bytes, and some vendors (for example, Nortel Networks) still use CMIP. Others use the Transaction Language 1 (TL 1) in these bytes, or in the F1 byte.

The Z1 and Z2 bytes originally were reserved for future growth and are now partially defined. The Z1 byte is also designated as the S1 byte. It is used to convey synchronization information about the SPE and allows the SONET node to make decisions about potential clocking sources. Bits 5–8 are used for this purpose, with bits 1–4 reserved for future use. Chapter 3 provides information on the S1 byte (see "Synchronization Status Messages (SSMs) and Timing Loops").

The Z2 byte is also designated as byte M0 or byte M1. Its use is to convey information about error conditions back to the source of the SPE. The specific use of the byte is somewhat involved, but we can summarize the idea of M0 or M1 by stating that the values reveal if the payload is a simple STS-1 or a more involved STS-n structure. Thus, the FERF notification (also called a line level remote error, or REI-L) operation uses bits 5–8 of M0 to send back the STS-1 error count back to the source. The M1 byte is used for the same purpose: to convey this information about STS-n payloads. Once again, the rules for these bytes are more involved than this overview (for example, their uses are slightly different at the STS-48 level and above), so we encourage you to delve into the SONET specifications if you need more information.

Finally, the E2 byte is an orderwire byte, which was explained in a previous part of this chapter.

Path Overhead

Figure 8–16 illustrates the path overhead. The path overhead remains with the payload until the payload is demultiplexed at the far-end SONET node (the STS-1 terminating equipment). This processing might be, and usually is, at the customer premises equipment (CPE). SONET

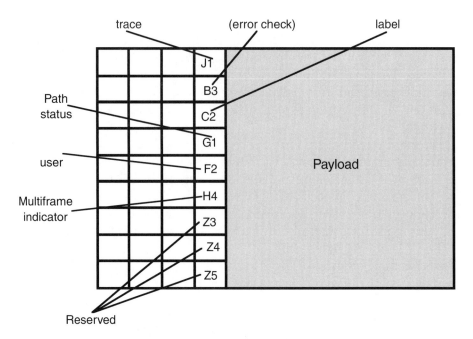

Figure 8–16   Path overhead.

defines four classes provided by path overhead. The classes are summarized as follows:

Class A   Payload independent functions (required)

Class B   Mapping dependent functions (not required for all payload types)

Class C   User specific overhead functions

Class D   Future use functions

All path terminating equipment must process class A functions. Specific and appropriate equipment also processes classes B and C functions.

For class A functions, the *path trace* byte (J1) is used to repetitively transmit a 64-byte fixed length string in order for the recipient path terminating equipment to verify a connection to the sending device. J1 is typically used by the SONET network operator, and typical entries are the Common Language Location Identifier (CLLI) of a telephony end office, an ISDN address (E.164), or even an IP address. It is operator-specific.

The *BIP-8* (B3) is an error-check byte. Its function is the same as that of the line and section BIP-8 fields, except that it performs a BIP-8 parity check calculated on all bits in the path overhead.

The *path signal label* (C2) is used to indicate the construction of the STS payload envelope. The path signal label can be used to inform the network that different types of systems are being used, such as ATM, FDDI, etc.—something like a protocol identifier for upper layer protocols. It can be coded to indicate if path terminating equipment is not sending traffic—that is to say, that the originating equipment is intentionally not generating any SPEs. This signal prevents the receiving equipment from generating alarms.

The *path status* byte (G1) carries maintenance and diagnostic signals, such as an indication for block errors, etc., for class A functions. For class B functions, a multiframe indicator byte (H4) allows certain payloads to be identified within the frame. It is used, for example, for VTs to signal the beginning of frames. It also can be used to show a DS0 signaling bit, or as a pointer to an ATM cell.

For class C functions, the one-byte F2 is used by the network provider. For class D functions, the future growth bytes of SONET Z3 are to be used for DQDB mapping; Z4 for SONET and SDH is still growth byte, and Z5 for both SONET and SDH is for Tandem Monitor. Bits 1–4 are used for incoming error monitoring. Bits 5–8 are used as a communication channel.

MORE INFORMATION ON THE D BYTES

All vendors use the section D1–D3 (192 kbit/s) and line D4–D12 (576 kbit/s) bytes. The actual contents of the bytes can be configured by the network operator. Some vendors run CMIP or SNMP in these bytes, and others use proprietary schemes. Another example is being defined by the Open Domain Service Interconnect Coalition (ODSI). This body specifies the use of the line DCC for a control channel to request bandwidth on demand from the SONET network [ODSI01].

STS-3c FRAMES AND OVERHEAD

Let's take a more detailed look at the STS-3c (or OC-3c) frame. Recall that it is possible to concatenate three STS-1s into one STS-3c frame. This operation is common when payload, such as ATM or IP, is transported, and a channelized structure is not needed. Figure 8–17 shows the STS-3c format. Since only one payload exists, there is no need for three sets of pointer fields. Also, many of the overhead bytes are not needed, and are shown in Figure 8–17 with an X.

Note also that the H1 bytes in the second and third columns would be used for parts of the second and third set of pointers for a nonconcatenated frame. However, they are not needed for this purpose, so they are used as concatenation indicators; that is, they show that the frame is in a concatenated format.

As explained in Chapter 6, SONET performs byte interleaving of the user payload. For STS-3c, the multiplexing of the three STS-1s has the effect of interleaving one STS-1 column, then the next, and then the next. The result of this operation can be seen in Figure 8–17, where the A1 bytes (and others) are interleaved into the overhead area. So, the first column is occupied by STS-1, the second column by STS-2, the third column by STS-3, and so on.

The conventional H1/H2 pointer of 10 bits is not long enough to identify where the payload is located within the payload area, since this field identifies values of 0–782, and the payload can be located within the payload area in byte positions 0–2348. The potential problem is easily solved by using the first two H1/H2 bytes' values (columns 1 and 4) and multiplying by 3. So, an H1/H2 offset of 1 actually means 3, an offset of 606 actually means 1818, etc.

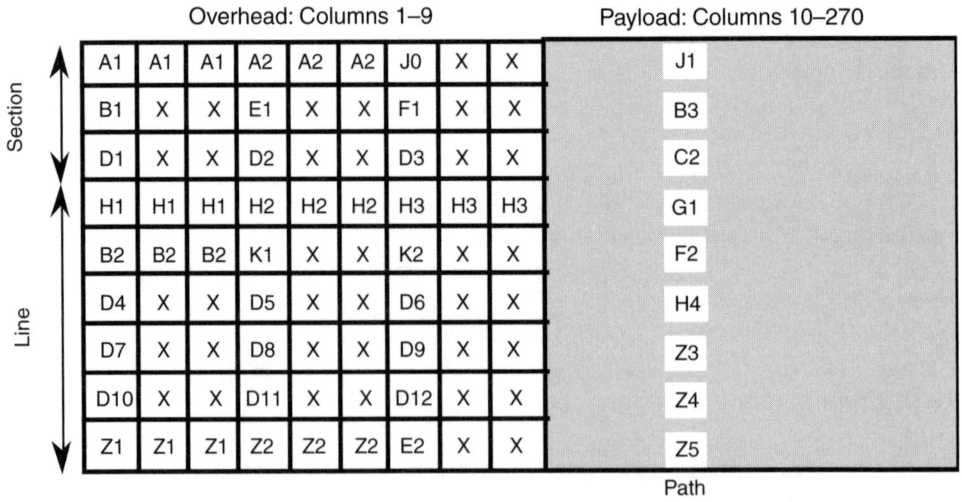

	Overhead: Columns 1–9								Payload: Columns 10–270
A1	A1	A1	A2	A2	A2	J0	X	X	J1
B1	X	X	E1	X	X	F1	X	X	B3
D1	X	X	D2	X	X	D3	X	X	C2
H1	H1	H1	H2	H2	H2	H3	H3	H3	G1
B2	B2	B2	K1	X	X	K2	X	X	F2
D4	X	X	D5	X	X	D6	X	X	H4
D7	X	X	D8	X	X	D9	X	X	Z3
D10	X	X	D11	X	X	D12	X	X	Z4
Z1	Z1	Z1	Z2	Z2	Z2	E2	X	X	Z5

Section / Line / Path

Figure 8–17   The STS-3c frame and overhead.

MAINTENANCE SIGNALS AND LAYERS

SONET maintenance functions include trouble detection, repair, and restoration. To support these functions, SONET is designed with a number of alarm surveillance operations to detect a problem or a potential problem. Before the surveillance operations are explained, the terms state, indication, and condition must be defined.

The term state describes an occurrence in the network that must be detected. A network element (NE) enters a state when the occurrence is detected and leaves the state when the occurrence is no longer detected. The detection of an occurrence may lead to an alarm being emitted by the NE, which is called an indication. An indication represents the presence of a condition.

Indications sometimes are not reported, but are available for later retrieval by an operating system (OS). Others may be reported immediately as an alarm or a nonalarm indication.

The purpose of the alarm indication signal (AIS) is to alert downstream equipment that a problem at an upstream NE has been detected. Different types of AISs are reported for the various layers. Figure 8–18 shows the relationships between the layers and the AIS.

Figure 8–18 also shows two aspects of OAM. (It also may be helpful to refer to Figure 8–6 during review of this section.) To address the first aspect, on the left of the figure are vertical arrows and their associated OAM indications. Their purpose is to inform the downstream entity of a failure.

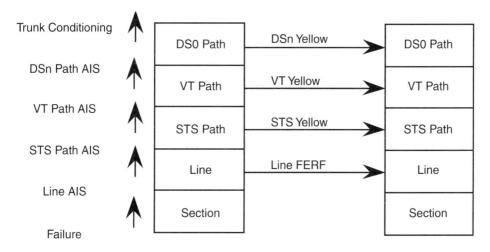

Figure 8–18   Maintenance signals and layers.

The position of the vertical arrows is meant to convey the following events (note once again that the AIS OAM flow is upstream to downstream):

1. An upstream section terminating equipment (STE) informs a downstream line terminating equipment (LTE) of a failure (a line AIS).

2. An upstream STE informs a downstream path terminating equipment (PTE) of a failure (an STS path AIS).

3. Upon detection of a failure (a line AIS) or an STS path AIS, an upstream STS PTE informs a downstream STS PTE of the failure (a VT path AIS, DS3 AIS, or DS0 AIS, depending on the specific STS SPE).

4. If DSn signals are being transported, a NE informs a downstream NE of the failure or a termination of the DSn path (DSn AIS).

OAM Actions

The far end receive failure (FERF) is a SONET line layer maintenance signal, and yellow signals are STS and VT path layer signals. Yellow signals can be used for trunk conditioning or by a downstream terminal to inform an upstream terminal to initiate trunk conditioning on the failed circuit. These signals are used for troubleshooting and trouble sectionalization [BELL89a].

The position of the horizontal arrows in Figure 8–18 is meant to convey the following events (note this OAM flow is the opposite of the AIS OAM flow; it is downstream to upstream):

1. A downstream LTE informs an upstream LTE about a failure along the downstream line (line FERF).

2. A downstream PTE informs an upstream PTE that a downstream failure indication has been declared along the STS path (STS path yellow).

3. A downstream VT PTE informs an upstream VT PTE that a failure indication has been detected along the downstream VT path (VT path yellow).

4. DSn yellow signals are generated due to failures or for DSn paths that are terminated (DSn yellow).

A number of factors lead to the use of DSn yellow signals, but that is beyond our general descriptions for this chapter. The interested reader should consult Bellcore TR-TSY-000499 for more information.

Figure 8–19 provides an example of how NEs react to a failure. This example shows only a few actions among the wide array of actions that are possible. Obviously, the various types of AIS, FERF, and yellow signals sent between the NEs will vary, depending upon the nature of the failure.

Two parts of this figure have not been explained: the red alarm and the performance monitoring parameters. The red alarm is generated if a NE detects a failure state that persists for 2.5 seconds, or if the NE is subject to continuous, intermittent failures. The collection of performance monitoring parameters is suspended during the handling of a failure state; after all, there is no meaningful performance on which to report.

EXAMPLES OF OAM OPERATIONS

Figures 8–19 and 8–21 also show examples of several OAM flows in relation to user equipment. The layer titled ATE means ATM terminating equipment. ATM alarms are not shown in this figure. The OAM octets shown in this figure perform the following services:

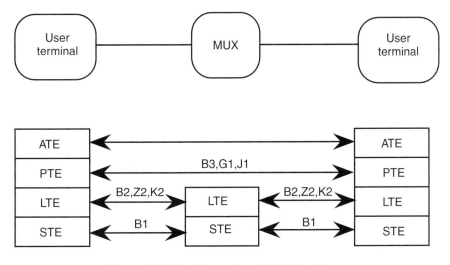

Figure 8–19   Example of OAM actions.

J1:   Verifies a continued connection between the two ATM switches (contents = user defined)

G1:   Indicates an STS yellow signal (contents = the value 1 in bit 5)

B3:   A BIP-8 calculation results on the previous STS SPE (contents = even parity calculation)

B2:   A BIP-8 calculation results on the previous line overhead and STS-1 envelope (contents = even parity calculation)

Z2:   Conveys back to the originator (as an FEBE, far end block error) the error counts from the B2 calculations (contents = count in the Z2 octet of third STS-1)

K2:   Indicates a line FERF and that the LTE is entering a LOS or LOF state (contents = 100 in bits 6, 7, and 8)

B1:   A BIP-8 calculation results on all bits of the previous STS-n frame (contents = even parity calculation)

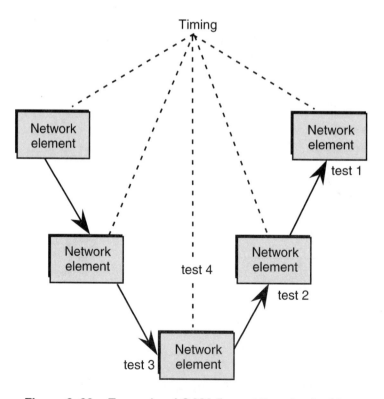

Figure 8–20   Example of OAM flow at the physical layer.

Troubleshooting Timing Problems

If timing problems occur, the network manager looks for two possible sources: (1) the NE or (2) the timing feed. As depicted in Figure 8–20, tests can be conducted with test sets to determine where pointer adjustments are being made. By working back toward the upstream NEs (test 1, test 2, and test 3), the tests reveal a point where pointer adjustments are not being made; the NE will exhibit pointer adjustments on the output side, but not the input side (test 2 and test 3). The next task is to determine if the clock recovery board in the NE is faulty, or if the BITS timing has been isolated from the NE (test 4).

ATM AND SONET OAM OPERATIONS

This section shows some examples of ATM OAM operations. The examples are not exhaustive, but will give you an idea of how ATM OAM is related to SONET OAM.

As shown in Figure 8–21, the physical layer SONET OAM alarms (F1, F2, and F3) can trigger ATM layer OAM alarms. This relationship can be demonstrated by reviewing this figure. The physical layer informs the ATM layer about a problem, which permits the ATM to issue

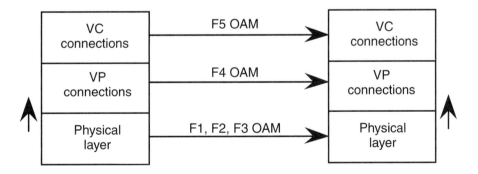

Figure 8–21   Troubleshooting timing problems.

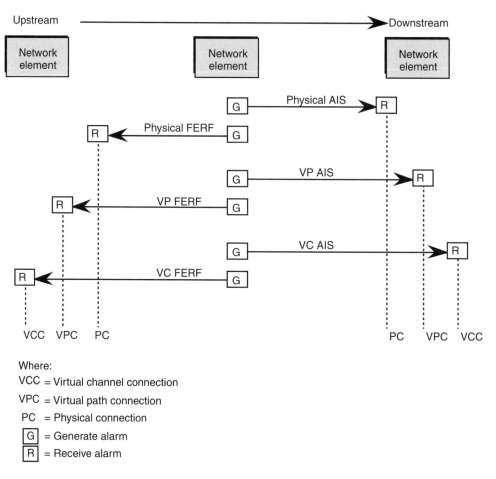

Figure 8–22   SONET and ATM OAM relationships.

AIS/FERF cells, labeled F4 OAM[3] and F5 OAM in the figure. In this situation, the ATM alarms would identify a physical problem.

Figure 8–22 shows the relationships of the physical, VP, and VC AIS and FERF operations. Be aware that this example represents only one combination of how these OAM operations are implemented. Moreover,

---

[3]ATM is divided into a virtual path and virtual channel layers. These two layers are used to create two types of connections: virtual paths and virtual channels. This approach allows virtual channel corrections to be bundled (multiplexed) inside virtual path connections.

physical layer OAM actions do not necessarily have to invoke ATM layer actions. Likewise, certain ATM actions can be generated independently of the physical layer actions. For this example, ATM VPC and VCC layers should generate AIS and FERF operations, due to the physical layer defect.

SONET AND NETWORK MANAGEMENT PROTOCOLS

The ISO and ITU-T have been working on the development of several Open Systems Interconnection (OSI) network management standards for a number of years. These standards revolve around the Common Management Information Protocol (CMIP), and Common Management Information Service Element (CMISE).

Another major thrust into network management standards has been through Internet activities. These initial efforts were organized through the ARPANET research project that originated in the United States. In 1971, the Defense Advanced Project Research Agency (DARPA) assumed the work of this earlier organization. DARPA's work in the early 1970s led to the development of the Transmission Control Protocol/Internet Protocol (TCP/IP). In the last few years, the Internet Engineering Task Force (IETF) itself has assumed the lead in setting standards for the Internet, and has published the Simple Network Management Protocol (SNMP).

The key goal of these network management standards is to develop an integrated set of procedures and standards that apply equally well across different vendors and networks. SONET fosters this concept with its definitions of the three OAM headers discussed earlier. CMIP and SNMP offer enhanced services beyond the SONET OAM. For example, CMIP or SNMP can run inside the DCC bytes (D1–D12).

One other component is vital to a network management system. It is called the management information base (MIB). The MIB defines the contents and structure of a database that is shared between the network nodes to provide information about the managed network elements.

THE NETWORK MANAGEMENT MODEL

Figure 8–23 provides a general view of the network management model, with emphasis on the OSI Model. The managing system (the agent) is responsible for directing the actions of the managed system (i.e., a SONET node). The managed system consists of a remote manager as well as the

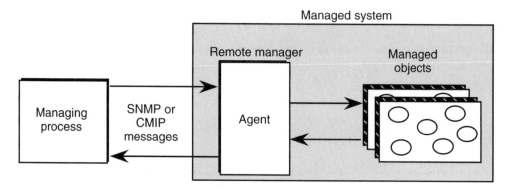

Figure 8–23   Relationships of alarms.

managed objects. This remote manager is comprised of a local representative called an agent. The agent is responsible for receiving network management messages from the managing process and ensuring that proper access control measures are taken regarding the managed objects. It also is responsible for providing and controlling local logging operations and, through the use of an event forwarding discriminator, it makes decisions about whether or not messages are to be returned to the managing process.

While Figure 8–23 shows a one-to-one relationship between a managing process and a managed system, the managing process can also act as an agent (managed) process. No restriction exists on the roles that these two entities play. Indeed, the roles may be exchanged.

It also is useful to note that, while the OSI Model in this figure has the managed object as part of the managed system, in the real world that need not be the case, because the managed system need not control the managed objects. Once again, it is important to understand that OSI merely represents how messages are emitted between the systems and how the managed objects are viewed. It is quite permissible for other systems to have a view of the same resource, and that view could be different. As an example, the existence of a SONET node among other nodes in a network may or may not be recognized, depending on a particular state of that node in a given time. Therefore, this managed object could be viewed differently by other systems.

Network Management Layers

OSI.   The OSI network management model is consistent with the overall OSI application layer architecture (see Figure 8–24). The systems management application service element (SMASE) creates and uses the protocol data units transferred between the management processes of the two machines. These data units are called management application data units (MAPDUs). As shown in Figure 8–25, SMASE messages pertain to fault, performance, configuration, accounting, and security operations. CMIP supports these messages through the use of a common set of procedures (Get, Set, Create, etc.).

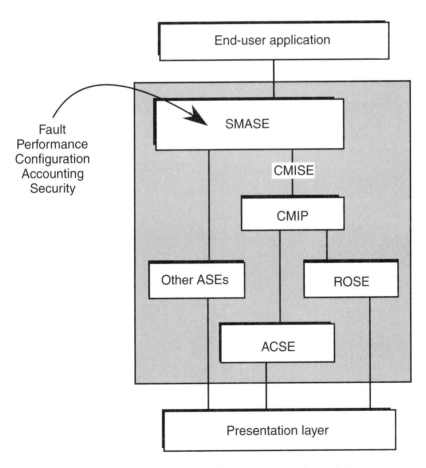

Figure 8–24   The network management model.

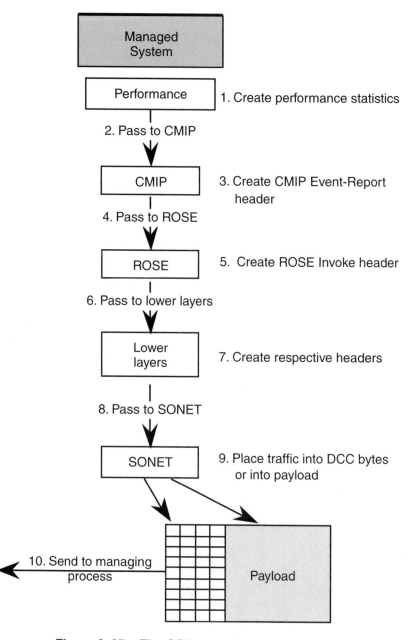

Figure 8–25   The OSI network management model.

The SMASE may use the communications services of application services elements (ASEs) or the common management information service element (CMISE). As depicted in Figure 8–24, the use of CMISE implies the use of CMIP with either ROSE or ACSE.

In accordance with OSI conventions, two management applications in two open systems exchange management information after they have established an application context. The application context uses a name that identifies the service elements needed to support the association. ISO-10040 states that the application context for OSI management associations implies the use of ACSE, ROSE, CMISE, and SMASE. The purpose of ACSE is to set up an association (session) between the managing process and the agent. Once this association has been established, ROSE is used by the SMASE and CMIP to invoke operations between the managing process and the agent.

For example, in Figure 8–25 a managed system (or agent in a SONET node) chooses to send some performance statistics to the OS at the managing system (event 1). These statistics are application-dependent (i.e., report on traffic conditions at the node or whatever). In event 2, these statistics are passed to CMIP, which creates a header (event 3) to indicate what type of network management message is being conveyed to the CMIP residing at the OS. This header also instructs CMIP how to process the traffic—that is, what type of message CMIP is to generate. In this example, it is an Event-Report type message.

In event 4, the performance information and the CMIP header are passed to ROSE, which in event 5 creates an Invoke header and appends this header to the other traffic that emanated from the upper layers (the performance data and the CMIP header). This header is used by ROSE at the OS to govern its actions (whether it is to report back to the node about the success or failure of the operation at the OS or some other possible actions).

In events 6 and 7, all this traffic is passed down through the lower OSI layers of the SONET node. In event 8, the SONET layer receives the traffic, and event 9 places these bytes into the DCC bytes of the SONET header or into the payload of the SONET envelope. (The former operation is preferable in order to keep the payload area available for user traffic.) Finally, in event 10, this information is sent to the OS (managing process).

At this machine, the process is reversed; the various headers and data are passed up through the layers to reach the performance entity, which processes the data in accordance with an application-specific requirement.

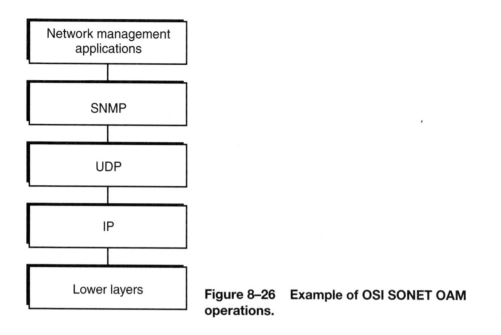

Figure 8–26   Example of OSI SONET OAM operations.

Internet.   The layering for the Internet suite is simpler than the OSI suite (see Figure 8–26). The simple network management protocol (SNMP) forms the foundation for the Internet architecture. The network management applications (the OSI SMASE) are not defined in the Internet specifications. These applications consist of vendor specific network management modules, such as fault management, log control, security and audit trails, etc. As illustrated in the figure, SNMP rests over the User Datagram Protocol (UDP). UDP in turn rests on top of IP, which then rests upon the lower layers (the data link layer and the physical layer). UDP's job (along with other software) is to keep track of the ongoing SNMP operations across the two machines (with SNMP ports). IP's job is to identify the traffic being exchanged between the two machines (in this case, UDP traffic).

Figure 8–26 shows "network management applications" running on top of SNMP. This relationship may or may not exist, and it is not defined in the Internet standards.

The interactions of these layers with SONET are quite similar to OSI (see Figure 8–25). SONET maps the SNMP traffic into the DCC fields or the payload area for transmittal to another machine.

SUMMARY

SONET provides a rich variety of OAM functions through the use of the path, line, and section headers. SNMP, CMIP, and MIBs enhance these services further. Using both tools, vendors have implemented a wide variety of diagnostic tools for detecting loss of signal, loss of frame, loss of pointer, and other failures/problems that might occur in the network.

9

Manufacturers' and Vendors' Systems

INTRODUCTION

There are many manufacturers and vendors with products that interface with SONET networks. The SONET machines support a wide range of local loop, interoffice, public backbone, and private network applications.

The examples in this chapter are based on several of the leading manufacturers of SONET equipment and their applications. Also, we examine several deployed systems to give you an idea of how SONET is being used by customers and service providers.

SONET RELEASES

SONET was released in phases. Manufacturers and vendors had to be aware of this "schedule" in their research and development, as well as for the planning and implementation of their products.

The hardware requirements and physical parameters are laid out in the phase 1 portion of the SONET standards process. Phase 1 products do not permit the passage of control information or network management between different vendors' equipment. Issues were addressed in the phase 1 standard for the section data communication channels (bytes D1, D2, and D3), so the network management can be fully integrated into the equipment. These three bytes are now considered as one 193 kbit/s message base channel for control, administration, monitor, alarms, maintenance, and other communication needs between section terminating equipment (STE). This channel can be accessed for manufacturers' internally generated and externally generated messages.

Phase 2 defines the protocol used on data communications channels D1 to D3, but not the full message set. The way SONET equipment constructs the data messages is defined in phase 2. How the objects should interact on the SONET network creates a need for an information model, which is being developed by ANSI Committee T1M1 subcommittee. This model will serve as the foundation for the network management aspects of operations, administration, maintenance, and provisioning. Phase 2 encourages the different vendors to make equipment capable of communicating with each other and with the operating system support (OSS) that manages the public network. Phase 2 also includes the development of:

- A short optical link called the intraoffice optical interface (interconnecting equipment in the central office environment of less than 20 miles)
- Tightening the jitter on DSX-3 ports
- Refining STS-1 interfaces so they will support 112 and 450 foot cable lengths within the central office

Phase 3 defines the D1 through D3 message sets that support the application interfaces and the line data communications channels (D4 through D12). These nine bytes are considered one 576 kbit/s message-based channel for alarms, maintenance, control, monitor, administration, and other communication needs. These bytes are defined only for the first STS-1 of an STS-n signal.

Phase 3 also includes:

- User channels F1 and F2
- Growth channels Z1 through Z5

Phase 3 finishes the definition of message sets that are exchanged between the SONET network elements to provide such things as security, performance monitoring, and alarm detection.

All phases are complete. The major changes that have occurred since the conclusion of phase 3 deal principally with further definitions of the overhead bytes, refining the definition and use of fixed and floating payloads, expansion to support IP, ATM, and Ethernet payloads, and clarifying several OAM&P procedures.

THE MAJOR VENDORS

In the first edition of this book, we listed the five major manufacturers competing in the SONET market as:

- Nortel
- Fujitsu Network Transmission Systems
- Alcatel Network Systems
- AT&T Network Systems
- NEC

The list has not changed much. The major manufacturers today (as of this writing, the industry is going through a shake-out due to the down turn in the economy) are:

- Nortel Networks
- Fujitsu Network Transmission Systems
- Alcatel Network Systems
- Lucent Technologies
- NEC

The major players have not changed, except that Lucent Technologies represents the former AT&T Network Systems. In addition, there are scores of vendors that offer SONET products, and we do not mean to ignore these companies. But this book is about SONET, and is not intended as a market survey. Space limits the number and detail of discussions about SONET vendors. These companies are chosen because the authors have more experience with their products; it is not meant as a slight to the other companies. Also, each vendor has a specific way of constructing its hardware and bay layouts; they are variations on the same theme. So, we show several examples instead of delving into details about scores of product offerings.

First some general comments are in order about these vendors. There are similarities, as well as differences, between these products, and a potential purchaser of SONET/SDH networks will have to do a lot of "sorting out" of information in order to learn what is the best fit for the purchaser's needs. All these vendors have extensive offerings in WDM, DWDM, automatic backup and recovery, crafting/provisioning capabilities, and OAM&P. All of them support ATM. The more recent announcements pertain to (a) use of MPLS, (b) support of IP, (c) support of Ethernet, (d) use of DiffServ/RSVP, and (e) migration to the new ITU-T Optical Transport Network (OTN).

Let's now take a general look at some of the principal features of these vendors' optical network products.

EXAMPLES OF NORTEL NETWORKS' PRODUCTS

Nortel Networks' SONET products were originally called FiberWorld. They are now known by several names, the most notable of which is OPTera. This product is similar to those of the other SONET vendors listed above, in that it provides a family or portfolio of products. Like OPTera, all the vendors have incorporated WDM into their products.

Here is a brief summary of the OPTera portfolio. After this summary, we will take a look at some of the components in the portfolio.

- Long Haul 1600 Optical Line System: A 1.6 Tbit/s system operating on a single optical fiber. The product is modular in that the following components can be added if needed: (a) wavelength translators, (b) wavelength combiners, (c) optical amplifiers, (d) regenerators, (e) ADMs, and (f) ring protection switching.
- Long Haul 5000 Optical Line System: Similar to OPTera 1600, except the total capacity is 6.4 Tbit/s. In addition, the links can span 1000 kilometers without the use of regenerators
- Metro 3000 Series Multiservice Platform: This product line offers several specific SONET nodes (ranging from the OPTera Metro 3000 to the OPTera Metro 3500) that are targeted for metropolitan area customers. The system supports various combinations of DS1, DS3, and OC-3 to OC-48 signals.
- Metro 2400 Open Air System: This wireless product is designed for metropolitan traffic to compete with the local loops (access network). This product supports full duplex traffic at 622 Mbit/s, with plans to scale the system to OC-48/STM-16. The wireless towers are placed from 100 to 500 meters apart, depending on the terrain, buildings, and foliage.
- Packet Core: The OPTera Packet Core is an optical switch/router that supports MPLS and IP routing, as well as route and bandwidth

management. It can be scaled to 19.2 Tbit/s. It also supports ATM and Frame Relay, and of course it is based on SONET/SDH.

EXAMPLE OF AN OPTera NODE

Figure 9–1 shows an example of the OPTera SONET node. This is one of the machines in the Long Haul 1600 product line [NORT01].

The unit shows the placement of the OC line cards, the wavelength translators (regeneration, reshaping, retiming), and other components.

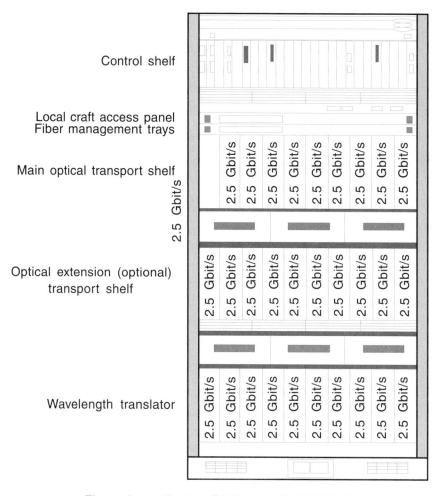

Figure 9–1   Typical OPTera node [NORT01].

The optional extension shelf can also hold repeaters (not shown). Also not shown is the option of installing a wavelength combiner bay in any of the areas where OC line cards reside. The combiner allows the aggregation of multiple independent lower speed channels into an aggregate higher speed channel.

The components on this node support the following features:

- Orderwires for a PSTN or an Ethernet wayside port
- Office alarms and user-defined alarms
- Operations system software: TL-1 over X.25, supporting 32 switched virtual circuits
- Operations system software: TL-1 over TCP/IP (via Telnet)
- Central office LAN support
- Three Ethernet ports for bridging to other units
- Security features, such as passwords, login logs, and intrusion detection

EXAMPLES OF FUJITSU'S PRODUCTS

In 1996 Fujitsu Network Communications introduced its "next generation" of products named FLASHWAVE, beginning with the FLASH OC-192, a SONET-based broadband transport network element for interoffice and long-haul networks. Over the next four years, the OC-192 was enhanced through system upgrades to offer a variety of 10-gigabit architectures with the choice of different tributary interfaces to provide the following options:

- OC-192 1+1 Terminal
- OC-192 0:2 Terminal
- OC-192 Regenerator
- OC-192 Unidirectional Path-Switched Rings
- OC-192 Two Fiber BLSR
- OC-192 Four Fiber BLSR

As shown in Figure 9–2, the FLASH OC-192 consists of three main shelves: a High Speed Shelf comprised of Transport and management sections, and optional Routing and Optical Tributary shelves. The FLM 2400 could be considered as an additional optional tributary shelf. The

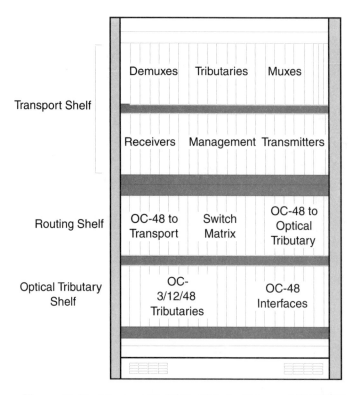

Figure 9–2   Typical FLASH-192 shelf layout [FUJI01]

combination of these main shelves supports interfaces from DS3, EC-1, OC-3/3c, OC-12/12c, and OC48/48c.

The OC-192 offers 47 different ITU-compliant, narrowband wavelengths for direct connection with dense wavelength division multiplexers (DWDM), such as FLASHWAVE™ 320G and FLASHWAVE™ Metro systems. This allows the network manager to connect up to 32 FLASH-192s to the FLASHWAVE™ 320G to create full 320-gigabit spans for maximum fiber utilization.

Fujitsu Network Communications has gone beyond the offering of individual narrowband transmitters by providing a set of 12 tunable transmitter modules that can each be set to one of four wavelengths.

NEW FLASH PRODUCT

In 2000 Fujitsu Network Communications began the introduction of their new FLASH products which are as follows.

The FLASH 150 ADX supports the following traffic types:

- Traditional telephone traffic: DS1, DS3, EC-1, and OC-3 interfaces
- Data traffic: 10/100 Ethernet™ and DS1 frame relay interfaces
- DS3 UNI and OC-3/OC-12 UNI/PNNI ATM interfaces
- SONET networks: OC-3 and OC-12 line rates; point-to-point and UPSR architectures

The FLASH 150 ADX operations include these features:

- TL1 protocol over X.25, OSI/LCN, or IP/LCN SNMP protocol
- Software download and remote memory backup
- Bellcore OSMINE compliant

The FLASH 600 ADX supports the following traffic types:

- Traditional telephone traffic: DS1, DS3, EC-1, OC-3, and OC-12 interfaces
- Data traffic: 10/100 Ethernet; DS3 UNI and OC-3/OC-12 UNI/PNNI ATM interfaces
- SONET networks: OC-3, OC-12, and OC-48 line rates; point-to-point, linear ADM, plus UPSR, and BLSR ring architectures

The FLASH 2400 ADX supports the following traffic types and network features:

- OC-48 and OC-192 line optics (plus STM-16 and STM-64)
- DS3, EC-1, OC-3/3c, OC-12/12c, and OC-48/48c tributary connections (plus STM1, STM4, and STM16)
- Full 864 x 864 STS1 nonblocking switch matrix for ring interconnections, hairpinning, TSI, broadcast, and multiple ring support
- Unrestricted mix and match of OC-3, OC-12, and OC-48 UPSR subtending rings
- Ability to protect or not protect STS-1s
- Extra switch module slots for future data switch fabric
- Narrowband tunable OC-48 and OC-192 optics for direct connection to DWDM systems

The FLASHWAVE 320G supports the following traffic types and network features:

- A complete end-to-end DWDM system
- Up to 64-to-2 direct fiber consolidation
- Up to 256-to-2 fiber consolidation for up to 128 OC-48 networks with FLASH OC-192 based muxponder front-ends
- A choice of 40 or 320-gigabit architectures in a single shelf
- Direct support of OC-48 and OC-192 connections from FLM-2400 ADM, FLASH 600 ADX, and FLASH OC-192
- 100Mbps up to 10 Gbit/s data, asynchronous, and multivendor SONET connections with FLASHWAVE transponder/regenerator subsystem
- Up to 600 km spans without regeneration
- Multiple channels for metro, interoffice, and long-haul applications
- 40-gigabit version: 1 to 16 channels
- 320-gigabit version: 1 to 32 channels

Other Products

Here is a brief description of other optical products from Fujitsu.

FLASHWAVE Metro is designed to allow the expansion of capacity without more fiber. As a small, passive WDM unit, the FLASHWAVE Metro system directly combines up to eight or 16 fibers worth of traffic onto a single fiber. The FLASHWAVE Metro system does not require electrical power or network management. It directly recovers up to 15 fibers. It can also recover up to 51 OC-48 based fibers using FLASH OC-192-based muxponder front-ends.

The FLASHWAVE OADX uses the solid combination of DWDM and optical add/drop multiplexing to give the network operator:

- High density capabilities of up to 176 channels for 1.76 Tbit/s throughput.
- Scalable, flexible network architectures with add/drop provisioning.
- Long distances of up to 4000 km without regeneration.

The FLASHWAVE TPR enhances DWDM-based systems with individual channel transponder, protection, and regeneration mechanisms. It provides low-cost regeneration services for separate OC-48 and OC-192s. One module is sufficient in a given traffic path to provide full retiming, reshaping, and regenerating (3R) functionality.

FWX Metro is the SDH version of the FLASHWAVE Metro. Its distinguishing features are:

- This small passive WDM unit combines up to 8 or 16 STM-16 fibers worth of traffic onto a single fiber.
- It allows minimization of cost by retaining existing FLX2500A STM-16 systems.
- If STM-16 tributary support is not enough capacity, the FWX Metro system will support STM-64 in the near future.

Fujitsu also offers several SDH products, which are briefly summarized here.

The FLX 150T is a dual STM1 terminal multiplexer which combines 2 Mbit/s and/or 34 Mbit/s tributaries into two STM1 lines and serves as tributary shelf for FLX 150/600, FLX600A, and FLX2500A add/drop multiplexers.

The FLASH MSX complements the FLASH/FBX series of products with:

- E1 to STM-64 interfaces
- 288 x 288 VC-4 switch fabric (10-gigbit capacity)
- 4032 x 4032 VC-12 switch fabric (10-gigabit capacity)
- Additional slots for data switch fabric
- STM-16 and STM-64 tunable, narrowband transmitters for direct DWDM applications

The FWX 40 Gbps allows up to 16 STM-16 channels with 40 Gbit/s in each direction and a maximum distance 600 km. It is upgradable to 320 Gbit/s.

The FWX 320 Gbps supports up to 32 STM-64 and / or STM-16 channels with 320 Gbit/s in each direction and a maximum distance of 600 km.

EXAMPLES OF ALCATEL'S PRODUCTS

Alacatel is a major player in the SONET and SDH market. Alcatel USA has a global product line, called the Alcatel Optinex™ product family. The following is a list of some of the products that Alcatel offers under their Terrestrial Networks [ALCA01].

- Optical: 1680 OGX, 1680 OGM, 1640 OADM, 1690 OADM, Cross Light, and Alcatel Core Node
- Transport: 1631 LMC, 1630 GSX, and 1603 SMX
- Network Management: 1353 GEM

Summary of Optinex Equipment

The following is a brief summary for the optical products in the Optinex generation of equipment.

The 1680 OGX provides gateway services between an optical layer of high bit rates (of managed wavelengths) and the lower-rate layer OC-3 rates and electrical DS3 and STS-1 rates. It supports both SONET and SDH payloads. Its scalable architecture supports from 80 to 2560 Mbit/s of traffic. It provides the path to manage traffic demands as they grow up to the multiterabit network level.

The 1680 OGM provides the following features:

- 10 Gbit/s ADM. Terminal MUX, Linear ADM, and interconnected rings
- Terminal MUX to Full ADM to 4FBLSR in service upgrades
- Interconnected, stacked, and subtended rings
- Add/Drop capabilities for OC-192 ADMs
- Transparent OC-48 Transport
- Transport Concatenated Payloads
- Forward Error Correction (FEC)
- Precision Transmitters for DWDM

The 1640 OADM provides the following features:

- 1510 nm Optical Supervisory Channel
- 240 Channel System
- 16 Channel Wavelength Add/Drop

- LAN Interfaces, Enhance PM, and Support for CMISE
- Forward Error Correction (OOB-FEC) Out-of-band FEC
- Two-stage next Generation Optical Amplifier

The 1690 OADM is designed for metropolitan or short-haul applications with the following features:

- Up to 32 channels on ITU 200 GHz spacing
- Bit Rate Compatibility: 100 Mb/s to 10 Gbit/s
- Range of interfaces up to 2.5 Gbit/s
- SNMP interface
- Fiber Route Diversity
- Optical Ring Support
- Wavelength Add/Drop

Cross Light is Alcatel's photonic cross-connect that is an optical switching matrix. The hardware eliminate the optical to electrical conversion. Some of the features are as follows:

- Bit Rate and Protocol Independent
- DWDM Integration
- Dynamic Bandwidth Allocation using MPLS
- SONET and SDH ports are software provisionable
- Automated routing of optical channels to congested routes
- One network management system used for provisioning voice or data circuits

The Alcatel Core Node is yet another Alcatel product. It has the following key features:

- Lambda management
- Bandwidth allocation
- G-MPLS
- OIF enabled interoperability
- Supports end-to-end IP Services (QoS, SLA, and VPN)
- Automated topology discovery

EXAMPLES OF LUCENT TECHNOLOGIES' PRODUCTS

In Chapter 6 the AT&T equipment was used to show examples of multiplexers. As noted, this equipment is considered rather old by today's standards, even though it is still being used. But to be fair to Lucent, and not dwell on older equipment, this section highlights the major features of Lucent's WaveStar™ product [ALEG99].

The flagship WaveStar product is the Bandwidth Manager (BWM). It is a DWDM add-drop multiplexer, as well as a digital cross-connect, supporting IP and ATM. Perhaps its most interesting capability is the ability to manage the optical bandwidth within the network nodes. It scales from 60 Gbit/s to 480 Gbit/s.

The BWM, like its competitors from the other vendors, is scalable and offers three basic configurations: (a) 1152 STS-1/384 STM-1, (b) 4608 STS-1/1536 STM-1, and (c) 9216 STS-1/3072 STM-1. All the systems support ADM and crossover operations. The upper end systems can support up to two four fiber OC-48/STM-16 rings, or up to four two fiber OC-48/STM-16 rings. Protection switching is completed within 50 ms. In addition, the WaveStar BWM has redundant switch fabrics, with each switch housed in a separate bay.

The WaveStar BWM is a significant technology advancement in comparison to its older AT&T ancestors. Among other features, it has been designed to provide a wide variety of services by consolidating heretofore multiple network elements into a single platform. Lucent states the use of this system can result in a 30 to 60 percent savings in equipment costs, a 70 to 86 percent reduction in floor space requirements, and a 60 to 80 percent improvement in transport reliability.

Ring Management

Figure 9–3 shows one BWM topology. The WaveStar BWM node provides a SONET/SDH gateway between a SONET ring on one side and an SDH ring on the other side. Each interface provides cross-connect capabilities, as well as pass-through and ADM services. These operations are on an STS-n/AU-m basis, where n can be 1, 3, 12, or 48, and m can be 3, 4, or 16.

Lucent has implemented a feature it calls hairpinning. The BWM node can support cross-connections between interfaces locally within a module without tying up bandwidth at the main STM switch fabric. Hairpinning has the following characteristics:

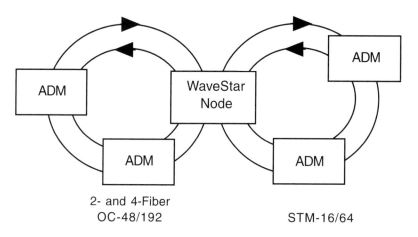

Figure 9–3   Lucent WaveStar BWM SONET/SDH ring inter-working.

- Customer can "oversubscribe" the STM cross-connect fabric without tying up the physical bandwidth of the switch fabric.
- Only connections requiring a cross connection to other modules traverse the STM switch fabric.
- Support is provided for ring-to-linear, or ring-to-ring connections in the same module or in different modules.

The STM switch fabric is STS-1 based, but it can support cross-connections of DS3, and AU-3/STS-1 signals. It can also support the following concatenated signals: 155 Mbit/s (AU4/STS-3c), 622 Mbit/s (STS-12c), 2.5 Gbit/s (AU-4–16c/STS-48c), or STM-64/OC-192.

Evolution of WaveStar BWM

Like Lucent's competitors, the WaveStar BWM is evolving into a system that implements a single platform to support IP-based protocols, such as VoIP, RTP, SMTP, and IPSec. These subjects are covered in Chapter 11.

EXAMPLES OF NEC'S PRODUCTS

Like the other vendors highlighted in this chapter, NEC also has a wide range of SONET/SDH products. This part of the chapter examines (a)

SpectralWave 160, (b) SpectralWave 32/16, (c) SpectralWave 40/80, and (d) SpectralWave Ring [NEC01].[5]

The SpectralWave 160 system uses ITU-defined 50 GHz wavelength spacing in both the C-band and L-band to transport up to 160 2.5G and/or 10 Gbit/s wavelengths on a single fiber, thus providing OC-48/OC-192 data transport capacity of 1.6 terabits per second (Tbit/s). The system can also support transmission of up to eighty (80) 40 Gbit/s channels, for a maximum transport capacity of 3.2 terabits per second (Tbit/s).

The SpectralWave 32/16 enables up to 32 fold (or up to 16 fold) use of a single fiber core with full utilization of the fiber bandwidth in a 1550 nm wavelength window.

In combination with STM-16 (2.5 Gbit/s) SDH transmission systems, it achieves up to an 80 Gbit/s (or up to a 40 Gbit/s) transmission capacity per fiber core.

The SpectralWave 40/80 supports up to 40 wavelengths in the C-band (expandable up to 80 channels using C/L-band) providing an open interface in any combination of STM-64, STM-16/4/1, Bit-Rate Free (100Mbit/s to 1.25Gbit/s), and so on. The universal slot function allows flexible combination of the above interfaces in the same subrack. Thus, the system can be flexibly changed in accordance with the requirements and scale of a telecommunication company. Expansion is facilitated by an in-service upgrade to 80 channels with C and L Band mixed configuration. The expanded system can multiplex up to 80 x STM-16 or 80 x STM-64; it achieves up to 800 Gbit/s of capacity.

The SpectralWave Ring is a key component of NEC's family of optical networking products. SpectralWave Ring provides optical ring reliability and survivability, enabling carriers to deploy and provision high-speed data applications, such as IP and ATM, with the quality of service and network survivability of proven optical ring technologies.

---

[5]Go to *www.cng.nec.com.*

10

The Synchronous
Digital Hierarchy

This chapter introduces the Synchronous Digital Hierarchy (SDH). We begin by providing a general comparison of SONET and SDH, principally in their operations of payload mapping. Next, a comparison is made between the section, line, and path overheads of SDH and SONET. We will learn that SONET and SDH are quite similar to each other, but there are also differences between them.

SDH SYSTEMS CONNECTING TO THE UNITED STATES

Figure 10–1 provides information on the transoceanic SDH systems that terminate in the United States or will terminate there by 2002 [GUDG01]. The anticipated total capacity for these systems alone is over 20 Tbit/s. Typical systems are exemplified by TAT-14. It suppports up to 8,192 unprotected or 4,096 protected STM-1s. It is estimated that this SDH termination capacity will continue to increase, and [GRUD01] cites a growth rate of 500 percent in 2002 alone, principally in Internet traffic. In many situations, the SDH signals (typically STM-1 at 155 Mbit/s) must be converted to their SONET counterparts (typically OC-3 at 155

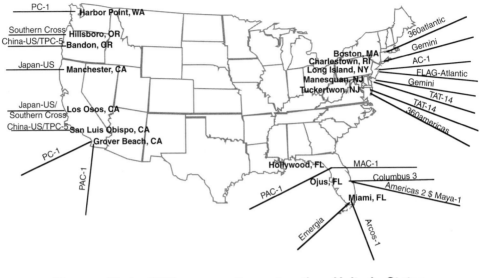

Figure 10–1 SDH connections to the United States [GUDG01].

Mbit/s) for the incoming traffic into the U.S., and a reverse operation must take place for the traffic leaving the the U.S. or another country. Thus, it is a good idea to know the operations of SDH.

COMPARISON OF SONET AND SDH

As noted in previous chapters, SONET is associated with the North American second-generation digital carrier hierarchy and SDH with the international counterpart, published by the ITU-T. Both are designed and intended for exactly the same purpose and uses. They realize the same benefits and are almost compatible.

The same five major vendors of SONET equipment are also manufacturing equipment for SDH applications. SDH is being offered by the vendors, either through new product offerings to interface with the European signals or by merely having an option for SONET or SDH application on their existing products. Where terrain prohibits the use of fibers on the lower bit rates, radios are being employed just as they are in the SONET arena. The topologies, protection switching schemes, and synchronization (timing) considerations are the same as they are for SONET.

Differences Between SONET and SDH

It has been said that SONET and SDH are the same and yet they are different. The major difference that creates confusion is the terminology that is used to describe the SONET and SDH signals and their tributary mapping scheme. Notwithstanding, there is a very close correlation between SONET and SDH signals and the tributary mapping. To address this issue, let's examine several SONET/SDH concepts. We can then understand their differences.

KEY TERMS

Table 10–1 provides some comparisons of SONET and SDH. Table 10–1 compares bit rates and associated terms, as well as service examples. We use this table and figure to help us compare the basic terminology used in the SONET and SDH multiplexing operations.

The key terms used throughout this chapter for the SDH signals are as follows: Container (C-n), Virtual Container (VC-n), Tributary Unit (TU-n), TU Group (TUG-n), Administrative Unit (AU-n), and AU Group (AUG). The "n" following the various designations represents an integer

Table 10–1   Comparison of SONET/SDH Rates and Services

SONET	SDH	Bit Rate in Mbit/s	Mux. Rate	Service Example
VT1.5		1.728	$4 \times 1.728 = 6.912$	Voice/data
	VT2	2.304	$3 \times 2.304 = 6.912$	Voice/data
VT3		3.456	$2 \times 3.456 = 6.912$	Voice/data
VT6		6.912	$1 \times 6.912 = 6.912$	Voice/data
STS-1	STM-0	51.84	7×6.912 or $1 \times 51.84 = 51.84$	Mx3 mux/DS3 clear channel = 44.736 Mbit/s + SOH = 51.84
STS-3	STM-1	155.52	$3 \times 51.84 = 155.52$	ATM, SMDS, FDDI, DQD, HDTV
STS-12	STM-4	622.08	$4 \times 155.52 = 622.08$	Uncompressed Extended Quality TV
STS-48	STM-16	2488.32	$4 \times 622.08 = 2488.32$	Uncompressed HDTV
STS-192	STM-64	9953.28	$4 \times 2488.32 = 9953.28$	Transport of the previous signals

number. The designations can have different numeric values following them. So "n" is substituted with a numerical value depending on what part of the SDH mapping hierarchy is being discussed.

Recall from earlier chapters that the proper way to express (say) M13 is to say Multiplex first level in and third level out, and not Multiplex thirteen. Furthermore, it is appropriate for M12 to refer to Multiplex first level in and second level out, and not Multiplex twelve. The numbers thirteen and twelve convey no meaning and, therefore, aren't useful.

This same idea is used in SDH when discussing tributary units, and the current SDH specifications define four basic signal rates. They are called Synchronous Transport Modules (STMs), and are: STM-1, STM-4, STM-16, and STM-64. This notion also applies to both the container (C) designations, and virtual container (VC) designations, as they can be represented with double digits. However, with the STM signals the decimal number following the letters STM represent its multiplexing level. As examples, STM-1 is the first level, STM-4 is four times that of STM-1, STM-16 is four times greater than STM-4, and STM-64 is four times greater than STM-16. This designation refers to bandwidth capacity, in that STM-4 has four times the bandwidth of STM-1. This idea is like the SONET STS signals using the basic building block of STS-3. STS-12 is four times the bandwidth of STS-3, STS-48 is four times the bandwidth of STS-12, and STS-192's bandwidth is four times greater than STS-12.

In SONET, STS-3 is comprised of three DS3s plus the SONET overheads, STS-12 has the bandwidth capabilities of 12 DS3s, STS-48 has 48 DS3s worth of bandwidth, and finally there are 192 DS3s equivalency of bandwidth in an STS-192 signal. Note that each jump in level is equal to four times; just as it is in the SDH STM hierarchy.

In previous chapters, it was noted that the higher multiplexing levels define the use the DS3 signals, because DS3 was the last level defined in the North American digital hierarchy during the time that the Bell standards were developed. It was further stated that because of this situation, all systems multiplexing above the DS3 level in the asynchronous multiplexing format must use the same vendor at both ends of point-to-point configuration.

Keep in mind that SONET deployment brought with it the ability to build (a) ring configurations for survivability and (b) midspan multivendor meet as well as other benefits previously mentioned. This same idea holds for SDH as well.

Table 10–2 Payloads (Tributary Signals) and Assoicated Terms

Payload	SONET	SDH
DS1	VT 1.5	TU-11
E1	VT-2	TU-12
DS1C	VT-3	—
DS2	VT-6	TU-2
E3	—	TU-3
DS3	STS-1	TU-3

TRANSPORTING E4, H4, AND DS1 SIGNALS

When SDH carries either an ITU-T E4 or an H4 signal inside an STM-1 envelope, this payload is called a C4 signal. This idea is exactly the same when SONET carries a DS1 inside the SONET frame, except that it is called a VT-1.5. If DS1 is carried inside the SDH frame, it is called C11.

So, as we said, most of the differences between SDH and SONET are ones of terminology. It is unfortunate that the two technologies are so closely aligned technically, but so far apart in how they are described. Perhaps we should just be happy that they are as closely aligned technically as they are.

Anyway, let us now take a look in more detail at SDH. Before we do, Table 10–2 should prove useful as you read the next section of this chapter. It shows the SONET and/or SDH payload and the corresponding SONET and/or SDH name for the payload. The payload is called the tibutary or tributary signal.

THE SDH MULITPLEXING HIERARCHY

Figure 10–2 shows the original SDH multiplexing hierarchy as published in the ITU-T G.707 and G.708 recommendations. The basic multiplexing scheme starts on the right side of the figure and progresses to the left side of the figure. This structure is quite similar to ANSI's SONET and the ETSI structure. At the lowest level, containers (C) are input to virtual containers (VC). The purpose of this function is to create a uniform VC payload envelope. Various containers (ranging from 1.544 Mbit/s to 139.264 Mbit/s) are covered by the SDH standard. Next, VCs are aligned

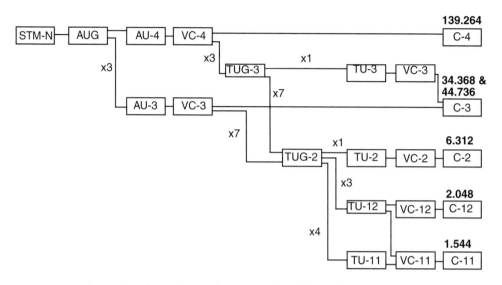

Figure 10–2   The SDH (original) multiplexing hierarchy.

with tributary units (TUs). This alignment entails bit stuffing to bring all inputs to a common bit transfer rate. Next, the VCs are aligned to TUs, where pointer processing operations are implemented.

These initial functions allow the payload to be multiplexed into TU groups (TUGs). As Figure 10–2 illustrates, the Xn indicates the multiplexing integer used to multiplex the TUs to the TUGs. The next step is the multiplexing of the TUGs to higher level VCs, and TUG 2 and 3 are multiplexed into VC-3 and VC-4. These VCs are aligned with bit stuffing for the administrative units (AUs), which are multiplexed into the AU group (AUG). This payload then is multiplexed with an even N integer into the synchronous transport module (STM).

SONET (1.544 MBIT/S) MAPPING AND MULTIPLEXING STRUCTURE

The SONET 1.544 DS1 multiplexing structure as recommended in ITU-T G.707 is also shown in Figure 10–2. For the purpose of transferring information, almost all digital signals of conventional asynchronous (North America) and PDH hierarchy can be employed. Figure 10–2 depicts the SDH terminology as it applies to the North American DS1 (1.544 Mbit/s) signal. This same approach is used to represent the DS1C (3.152 Mbit/s), DS2 (6.312 Mbit/s) and DS3 (44.736 Mbit/s) signal.

Each DS1 consists of 1.544 Mbit/s and is referred to as a Container (C). Each container (a C-11) becomes a Virtual Container (a VC-11) by the addition of Path Overhead (POH) bits and some stuffed bits in predefined positions. This procedure is called mapping.

The process referred to as aligning relates to the procedure of assembling the virtual container into a tributary unit (a TU-11), in which a pointer is added to indicate the position of the first byte of the virtual container in the tributary unit frame. The SONET term for TU-11 is VT1.5.

In SONET, four VT1.5s (that is, 4 TU-11s) are multiplexed together to create a VTG (Virtual Tributary Group of 6.912 Mbit/s). As Figure 10–2 shows, the SDH term for VTG is TUG-2 (Tributary Unit Group-2). Next, seven TUGs are multiplexed together to create an STS-1 in the SONET application. An STS-1 is equivalent to a TUG-3 in the SDH application. To accomplish this action, byte interleave is used.

Byte interleave multiplexing is also used when the three STS-1s (TUG-3s) are combined to form the VC-4. The STS-3 or VC-3 (150.336 Mbit/s) is assembled into administrative unit-3 (AU-3) by adding the AU-3 Pointer and becomes the STS-3 (155.52 Mbit/s), or STM-1 in SDH terminology. In Figure 10–2, we show this operation as the last stage of multiplexing. The STS-3 electrical signal passes through an electrical-to-optical converter thus becoming an optical signal referred to as OC-3 (155.52 Mbit/s), not shown in Figure 10–2.

Another point worth noting is that the SONET DS1 signals are byte interleaved during the mapping process, which allows the network operator to have direct access to the 64 kbit/s timeslots for troubleshooting and for checking quality of service.

SDH (2.048 MBIT/S) MAPPING AND MULTIPLEXING STRUCTURE

Let's now examine the E1 mapping and multiplexing structure. The SDH Multiplexing Structure as recommended in ITU-T G.707 is also shown in Figure 10–2.[2]

---

[2]For newly deployed networks, such as those being implemented in Central and Eastern Europe, multiplexing the 2 Mbit/s signals is an important type of SDH multiplexing, because these networks are often designed to bypass the intermediate level of multiplexing (which creates the plesiochronous hierarchy) and instead multiplex the 2 Mbit/s rate directly into the STM-1 level.

The POH assigned to each 2 Mbit/s signal consists of four bytes: namely, V5, J2, Z6, and Z7. More will be said about these bytes when the overhead bytes are discussed.

Unlike the byte interleaved mapping of the 139.264 Mbit/s and 34.368 Mbit/s signals, the 2 Mbit/s signal has three types of mapping. They are asynchronous, bit synchronous, and byte synchronous, and are explained shortly.

As noted, each E1 consists of 2.048 Mbit/s and is referred to as a Container (C). Each Container (a C-12) becomes a virtual container (VC-12) by the addition of POH and some stuffed bits in predefined positions. As before, this procedure is called mapping. Once again, aligning pertains to the procedure of assembling the virtual container into a tributary unit (TU-12), in which a pointer is added to indicate the position of the first byte of the VC in the TU frame.

Three TU-12s are multiplexed together to create a TUG-2 (Tributary Unit Group-2). Seven TUG-2s multiplexed together create a TUG-3. Thereafter, the multiplexing process proceeds in the same fashion that was descibed earlier in this chapter.

SONET (DS1C) MAPPING AND MULTIPLEXING STRUCTURE

To carry the SONET DS1C (which is not employed in many countries and not shown in Figure 10–2), the DS1C signal of 3.153 Mbit/s is simply multiplexed into TUG-2, to VC-3, and to AU-3 and so forth. There are other options for multiplexing DS1C. Which multiplexing structure is implemented is vendor specific and is likely based on the intended target network operator.

SONET (DS2) MAPPING AND MULTIPLEXING STRUCTURE

This section explains how SDH supports SONET/DS2 signals, as shown in Figure 10–2. Each DS2 consists of one 6.312 Mbit/s and is referred to as a Container (C-2). Each container becomes a Virtual Container (VC-2) by the addition of POH. Since there is only one circuit, there is no need for stuff bits to be added. Once again, aligning is the procedure of assembling the virtual container into a tributary unit (TU-2) in which a pointer is added to indicate the position of the first byte of the VC in the TU frame.

The SONET term for TU-2 is VT6. One VT6 with the POH added becomes 6.912 Mbit/s, which is equivalent to a VTG. The SDH term for VTG is TUG-2. The TUG-2 stage of multiplexing all the way to the AUG stage is exactly the same as it was for the DS1, DS2, and DS1C signals.

SONET 44.736 MBIT/S, SDH 34.368 MBIT/S, AND 139.264 MBIT/S MAPPING AND MULTIPLEXING STRUCTURE

The North American signal of 44.736 Mbit/s and European signal of 34.368 Mbit/s go through the same stages and structure for multiplexing and mapping. Each Container (C-3 for both signals) becomes a Virtual Container (VC-3) by the addition of POH. This procedure again is called mapping. The operations from the TU-3 stage all the way to the AUG stage are exactly the same as it is for the SDH 2.048 Mbit/s. Figure 10–2 illustrates the rest of the process for comparison.

The European signal of 139.264 is known as Container 4 (C-4). The POH bytes are added, raising the signal to 149.760 Mbit/s. Next, the signal goes to the next stage, known as VC-4. In VC-4, additional overheads raise the signal to 150.336 Mbit/s. Then it is on to the AU-4 where the signal finally becomes the 155.52 Mbit/s, which goes on to the final stage resulting in the AUG.

Vendors of these systems may choose to support only certain payloads, as well as certain multiplexing stages and mapping schemes, which would depend on their (target audience) customer base.

THREE TYPES OF MAPPING FOR THE VC-11, VC-12, OR VC-2 SIGNALS

Earlier, we stated that SDH supports three types of mapping. The example discussed here is for the SDH VC-2. However, it also applies to the VC-11 and VC-12 as well. In a nutshell, the mappings are distinguished by the following attributes: Asynchronous mapping lets SONET NEs see a stream of bits, bit-synchronous mapping lets the SDH NEs see a slightly different stream of bits, and byte-synchronous mapping lets SDH NEs see the DS0s. Any of the three mappings can be used in VT1.5. It all depends on how the SDH NE interfaces with the DS1s.

Asynchronous Mapping

The 2 Mbit/s signals that are not synchronized to the SDH signal are referred to as asynchronous mapped. The signal can be channelized (with framing) or unchannelized (without framing). However, direct access to the 64 kbit/s timeslots is not possible. Asynchronous mapping allows the E1 frame to be visible at the VT2 bit stream only. Asynchronous mapping allows an easy interface with existing PDH systems and is more common than byte synchronous mapping. In the case of 140 Mbit/s and 34 Mbit/s mapping, variable bit justification occurs as part of this type of 2 Mbit/s mapping.

Variable bit justification is similar to frequency justification. In the multiplexing of two signals, stuff bits must be used to make up for the unequal rates of the clocks doing the timing for each of the signals. As discussed previously, each signal must be raised to exactly the same bit rate and frequency as the other multiplexed signals. Consequently, the number of stuff bits will vary, depending on the bit rate or frequency of each of the signals being multiplexed together. These stuff bits may be merely "placeholders," or they can convey information depending on the vendor's preferences and the application of the customer.

Bit Synchronous Mapping

When the rate of the 2 Mbit/s signals is synchronized to the SDH signal, they are referred to as bit synchronous mapped. This technique uses the same VT2 structure as the asynchronous mapping, and in this case the framing (if any) of the 2 Mbit/s signal is not synchronized to the SDH signal. Unlike asynchronous mapping, the 2 Mbit/s signals to be mapped must already be synchronized to the SDH network, because there isn't any variable bit justification. As in the case of asynchronous mapping, direct access to the 64 Kbit/s timeslots is not possible.

Byte Synchronous Mapping

Both the bit rate and the framing of the 2 Mbit/s signal are synchronized to the SDH signal in byte synchronous mapping application. The 2 Mbit/s signal must meet the requirements of G.704 when using byte synchronous mapping. There is no bit justification performed on the 2 Mbit/s signals, so they must already be synchronized to the SDH network. This type of mapping does allow access to the 64 Kbit/s timeslots but has no advantage if unchannelized service demand prevails over channelized service.

REVISED SDH DIGITAL HIERARCHY

Figure 10–3 shows the revised SDH digital hierarchy. We have also included in this figure a legend that explains where the following operations take place: (a) mapping, (b) alignment, (c) pointer processing, and (d) multiplexing. This operations were defined in the original SDH recommendations, but to keep matters simple, they were not included in Figure 10–2. Note the STM-N frames on the left side of the figure. You might wish to compare this part of Figure 10–3 to the entires in Figure 10–2.

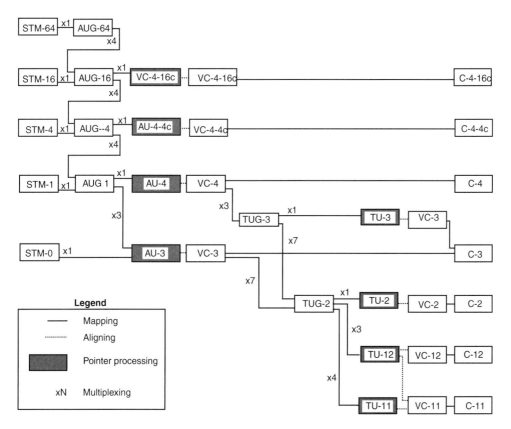

Figure 10–3   The revised SDH digtial hierarchy.

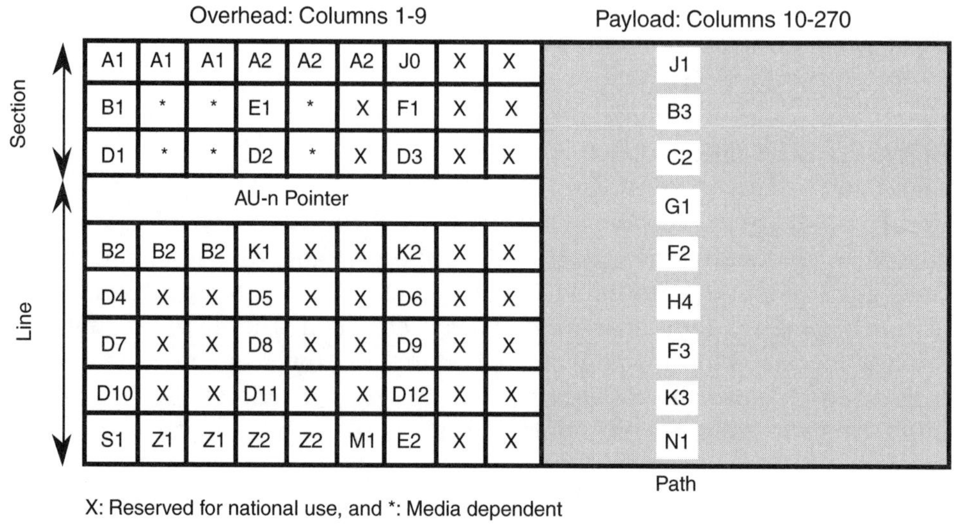

Overhead: Columns 1-9   Payload: Columns 10-270

A1	A1	A1	A2	A2	A2	J0	X	X	J1
B1	*	*	E1	*	X	F1	X	X	B3
D1	*	*	D2	*	X	D3	X	X	C2
AU-n Pointer									G1
B2	B2	B2	K1	X	X	K2	X	X	F2
D4	X	X	D5	X	X	D6	X	X	H4
D7	X	X	D8	X	X	D9	X	X	F3
D10	X	X	D11	X	X	D12	X	X	K3
S1	Z1	Z1	Z2	Z2	M1	E2	X	X	N1

Section · Line

Path

X: Reserved for national use, and *: Media dependent

Figure 10–4   The SDH STM-1 frame.

SDH OVERHEAD BYTES

There are three groups of overhead bytes for both SONET and SDH frame formats. As explained in Chapter 8, SONET refers to these overheads as Section, Line, and Path bytes. SDH refers to the same three categories as regenerator section overheads (RSOH), Multiplex Section Overheads (MSOH), and Path Overheads (POH) respectfully. In addition, SDH uses the term octet instead of byte.

Figure 10–4 shows the structure for the SDH STM-1 frame. If you compare it to the SONET STS-3c frame in Figure 8–17, you will see that the two are almost identical. The SDH overhead area does not show the bytes in row 4. Rather, the bytes are collectively called the AU-n pointer, and they can be used for either AU-3 or AU-4 pointers. They can be viewed as being part of the MSOH, and they are doing the same thing the SONET H1, H2, and H3 pointers are doing.

The Overhead Bytes and the SDH Link Components

Both SONET and SDH use these overhead bytes in a structured, modular fashion with regards to the optical link and the link components. You many wish to refer back to Figure 5–6 for a comparison to

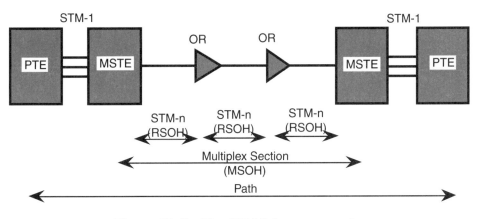

Figure 10–5   The SDH link components.

Figure 10–5. SDH further distinguishes differences in the path overheads. The first one is the Higher Order Path Overhead (HO-POH) and the second is the Lower Order Path Overhead (LO-POH). There is some difference in how they use these overhead octets are used. In the SONET arena, the overhead, are referred to as Section, Line, and Path overheads. There is no distinction of types of Path Overheads, unlike SDH with the aforementioned HO-POH and LO-POH. Furthermore, LO-POH distinction is only made in the SDH frame formats; they are not distinguished for the SONET frame.

Comparison of the Overhead Bytes

Tables 10–3, 10–4, and 10–5 show both the SONET and SDH overhead bytes. How each byte is used in these two networks is explained. The first row of the overhead is the same for SDH and SONET, except for the last two bytes/octets. They have not been assigned in the SONET specifications, and they are reserved for national use in the SDH specifications. For the second row, SDH sets aside octets 2, 3, and 5 to be used (and coded) based on the specific type of medium being employed. The last two bytes in the second row are assigned for national use. For SONET, these bytes are reserved for future use.

In the third row, SDH defines some media-dependent and national use octets. SONET simply reserves these same bytes for future use.

The pointer row (the fourth row) of SDH and SONET performs the same functions. Finally, the remaining bytes in rows 5–8 are the same, except some are reserved for national use (SDH) or reserved for future use (SONET).

Table 10–3   SDH RSOH Regenerator Section overhead (SONET Section Overhead)

Overhead Byte	A1	A2	J0	Z0	B1	E1	F1	D1-D3
Definition and Usage	Framing byte	Framing byte	Section trace	Spare	Section parity	Local orderwire	User bytes	DCC
SDH	Frame alignment	Frame alignment	Section trace	Reserved	Section monitoring	Local orderwire	Allocated for user's purposes	OAM&P
SONET	Framing	Framing	Trace STS-ID	Growth	Section monitoring	Local voice channel defined only for STS-1#1 of an STS-N	Optional for SONET. Defined only for STS-1#1 of an STS-N	Section DCC layer OSI stack using CMIP message format. Used for control operations

Table 10–4 SDH MSOH Multiplex Section OverHead (SONET Line Overhead)

Overhead Byte	H1-H3	B2	K1, K2	D4-D12	S1(Z1)	M0/M1 REI-L or Z2 Growth	E2
Definition and Usage	Payload pointer	Line parity	APS	Line DCC	Synchronization status	Far end block error	Express orderwire
SDH	AU-3 or AU-4 pointers	The BIP-n × 24, of an STM-n frame	Two bytes allocated for APS signaling for multiplex section protection	7 layer OSI stack CMISE message format for OAM&P between NEs and the OS/NMS	Synchronization status messages	Multiplex section remote error indication (MS REI)	For voice communications between multiplex section terminating equipment
SONET	H1 & H2 point to the start of the SPE. H3 used for pointer justification. In H1#1 bits 5–6 are undefined & H1#3 are set to "00" in STS-3c	Line BIP-8 Line error monitor in each STS-1 of an STS-N. Calculated from all line overhead bytes and payload bytes	Provides automatic protection switching signaling between line level entities. Defined only for STS-1#1 of an STS-N	Line DCC 7 layer OSI stack using CMIP message format for OAM&P between line terminating equipment. Defined only for STS-1#1 of an STS-N	Used for synchronization status messages (Bits 5–8)	M0/M1 is used for line remote error indication. Used for STS-3c and STS-12c. FEBE for B-ISDN	Optional express orderwire between line equipment. Defined only for STS1#1 of an STS-N
Notes			Formats are the same but SDH line switching definitions are not complete	Considered as one 576 kbit/s data communication channel between multiplex section termination equipment	SDH has renamed this byte from "Z1" to "S1"	SDH has renamed this byte from "Z2" to "M2"	SDH A-law to Mu-law conversion per ITU G.802

Table 10–5 SDH Path Overheads (SONET Path Overheads)

Overhead Byte	J1	B3	C2	G1	F2	H4	Z3/F3	Z4/K3	Z5/N1
Definition and usage	Path indication	Monitoring	Payload formats	Path status	User	Multiframe	See below	See below	See below
SDH	Path indication	Quality monitoring	Container format	Error ack	OAM	Protection switching	OAM	APS	Connection monitoring
SONET	Connect monitor	BIP-8	Tributary format	Status of PTE	End user use	Multiframe indicator	Growth	Growth	Growth

For the POH bytes/octets, one entry is different. N1 (also identified as Z3) is used in SONET for network management, SDH allows this octet to be used at the network operator's discretion.

ANSI has defined the Z5 byte for use as a tandem connection maintenance channel and a path DCC. A tandem is a switching office that switches between trunks and, therefore, has no CPE devices on the end of the links. This can be a problem with the SPE management, because no direct contact occurs with the originator of the SPE.

SUMMARY

At the risk of repeating ourselves, SONET and SDH are quite similar to each other. The major differences came about in the initial development of the two standards in order to accommodate specific North American and European legacy transport networks. The major network transport equipment vendors (described in Chapter 9) offer both SONET and SDH products, as well as facilities for interworking them together.

11

SONET and WDM, Optical Ethernet, ATM, IP, and MPLS

INTRODUCTION

This chapter takes us beyond the conventional SONET TDM/T1 operations. In so doing, we examine wave division multiplexing (WDM) and
explain how SONET operates in a WDM network. A relatively new technology that is gaining acceptance as an alternative to SONET is optical
Ethernet. This technology, along with passive optical networks (PONs),
is also analyzed, and its advantages and disadvantages are cited.

ATM has been designed as a partner to SONET, and several examples of ATM and SONET interworking are provided in Chapter 8. Yet
ATM over SONET is not universally accepted, and we will see why, while
at the same time examining operations in which an alternative to ATM is
being deployed: IP running over SONET.

We also provide information on recent efforts by the ITU-T and the
IETF to define a new model for optical networks. The chapter concludes
with a brief tutorial on label switching, with some examples of what
some people consider the next generation optical network: MPLS over
WDM.

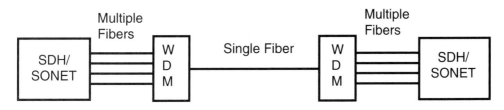

Figure 11–1   The WDM configuration.

INTRODUCTION TO WDM

A relatively new technology in the fiber arena is called wave division multiplexing (also called wavelength division multiplexing in some circles; both are known as WDM). A general WDM configuration is shown in Figure 11–1. WDM uses frequency division multiplexing (FDM) techniques by dividing the optical spectrum into multiple channels, called wavelengths and noted by the sign of (lambda) λ. These wavelengths are transported across one fiber. In contrast, conventional TDM optical links transport only one wavelength (one channel).

The technology uses an external coupling device that mixes different optical signals. Two forms of WDM are employed. Unidirectional WDM sends multiple wavelengths in one direction on the fiber, while bidirectional WDM allows these signals to pass in opposite directions.

CAPACITY OF WDM

The attractive aspect of WDM is its relatively low cost in relation to its transmission capacity. For example, WDM systems are available in which one fiber can operate at the terabit/s rate. This rate is 1,000,000,000,000, or 10^{12}, bit/s. To gain a sense of the capacity of this system, one WDM Tbit/s fiber can carry 35 million data connections, each operating at 28 kbit/s, or 17 million digital voice telephony channels, or 500,000 compressed TV channels, or any combinations thereof. Another system multiplexes 160 wavelengths of 10 Gbit/s each for a 1.6 Tbit/s rate. Some vendors are suggesting a system that supports 320 wavelengths in a single fiber, yielding a throughput of 3.2 Tbit/s per fiber.

It is not surprising that WDM is of keen interest to vendors, network operators, and network users.

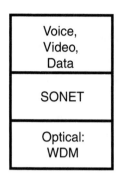

Figure 11–2   SONET over WDM.

RUNNING SONET OVER WDM

SONET is designed as a TDM architecture, since its original, basic job was/is to transport TDM signals, such as DS0, DS1, and DS3. However, it is quite common today to transport the SONET virtual tributaries over the WDM optical (photonic) layer. In this manner, the network manager has the bandwidth "power" of WDM and the network management features of SONET. This idea is shown in Figure 11–2. With this approach, each wavelength can carry SONET traffic. So, each wavelength is an instantiation of a SONET process. Certainly, this "multiprocessing" function requires substantial processing power at the SONET nodes, but the increased bandwidth more than compensates for the increased compexity.

TDM SONET AND WDM

Figure 11–3 shows the topology for a conventional optical TDM system and a WDM system. The WDM example is based on the Multiwavelength Optical NETworking (MONET) Consortium, funded partly by the Defense Advanced Research Projects Agency (DARPA) [JOHN99].

This example shows two layouts, each having a capacity of 40 Gbit/s. The terminals are OC-48 devices. In the TDM system, 16 fiber pairs operate at the OC-48 rate, each carrying one wavelength. In contrast, the WDM operates at the same capacity, using only a single fiber pair. The new system also needs fewer intermediate elements. For example,

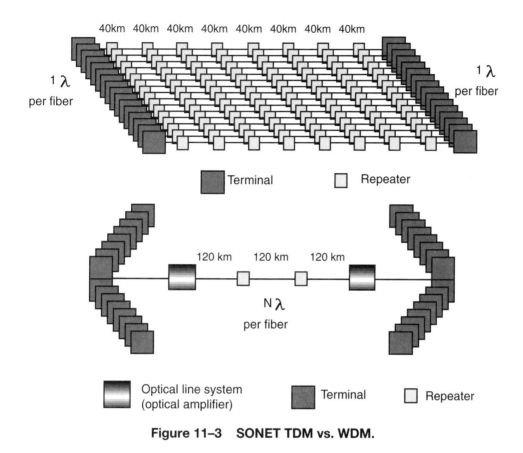

40km 40km 40km 40km 40km 40km 40km 40km

1 λ
per fiber

1 λ
per fiber

■ Terminal   □ Repeater

120 km   120 km   120 km

N λ
per fiber

Optical line system
(optical amplifier)   Terminal   □ Repeater

Figure 11–3   SONET TDM vs. WDM.

the number of optical repeaters and (obviously) the number of fibers is substantially reduced.

ERBIUM-DOPED FIBER (EDF)

With the advent of the erbium-doped fiber (EDF), the need for electronic circuitry in some of the optical components no longer exists. Moreover, EDF amplifiers (EDFAs) are transparent to a data rate. They also provide high gain and experience low noise. The major attraction is that all the optical signal channels can be amplified simultaneously at the EDFA in a single fiber. Of course, this approach is the essence of WDM.

Table 11–1   Role of Erbium-doped Fiber (EDF) in WDM Networks

- Has revolutionized optical communications
- Eliminates need for electronics in some parts of the network
- Transparent to data rate
- Transparent to data format
- Provides uniform gain across spectra, high power, low noise
- All WDM optical signals can be amplified simultaneously

EDFAs play a role in several parts of WDM optical networks. They can be found in amplifiers, optical cross connects, wavelength add/drop multiplexers (ADMs), and broadcast networks.

They are deployed as in-line amplifiers, in which they amplify an optical signal that has been attenuated by the fiber. They are used to boost optical power at the sending site as the signal enters the fiber (as well as at the receiver). They are found in optical cross-connects, and are used to compensate for signal loss, as well as in wavelength ADMs for the same function. Lastly, they are now employed in optical broadcast systems to boost the power for the distribution system. Table 11–1 provides a summary of the key attributes of EDF.

WDM AMPLIFERS

One of the key components of WDM optical networks is the optical fiber amplifier. In the past, optical networks used optoelectronic regenerators between optical terminals. These devices convert optical signals to electrical signals and then back to optical signals This approach requires expensive high-speed electronic circuitry and operates on one signal (one lightwave).

Figure 11–4 shows a typical schematic diagram for the use of optical amplifiers in a WDM transmission system. At the sending end, multiple optical channels are combined in an optical multiplexer. This combined signal is amplified before it is launched into the first fiber span. At the receiving end, the opposite operations occur. The incoming WDM signals are amplified by a "preamplifier," and then demuxed and sent to their respective receivers.

As mentioned earlier, the optical amplifier is deployed as an in-line amplifier; it amplifies the optical signal that has been attenuated by the

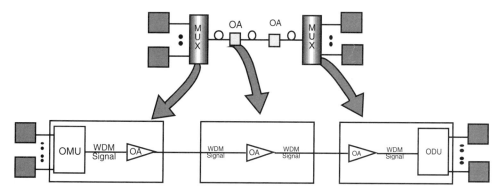

Figure 11–4   Optical amplifiers for WDM.

fiber. It also boosts optical power at the sending site (the optical multiplexing unit) and the receiving site (the optical demultiplexing unit).

The use of EDF for amplifiers in the late 1980s and early 1990s was a major milestone, leading to the development of a new generation of amplifiers. The erbium-doped fiber amplifiers (EDFAs) are significantly less expensive than the optoelectronic regenerators. They are oblivious to the bit rate or the data format on the link, so any upgrades do not affect them. In addition they can amplify multiple WDM wavelengths simultaneously.

WAVELENGTH WDMS

As the capacity of optical systems increases, opportunities are created for network service providers to provide more capacity to the systems' users. These users are located in many parts of a geographical region, including business sites, industrial parks, campuses, and stand-alone offices. These diverse sites require great flexibility in bandwidth management to meet the customers' requirements. In WDM networks, the service provider should be able to provision bandwidth in a fast, efficient, and cost-effective manner to these sites.

One on the key "tools" to support this environment is the wavelength add/drop multiplexer (WADM), shown in Figure 11–5. Based on earlier TDM ADMs, these devices support the management of fiber capacity by the selective adding, inserting, and removal of WDM channels at intermediate points in the network. A general example of these operations is shown in this figure.

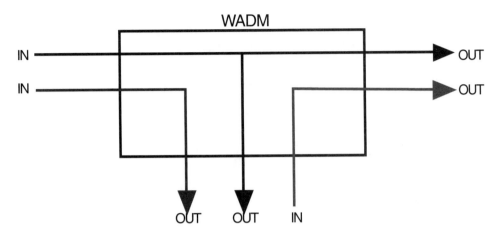

Figure 11–5   Wavelength add/drop multiplexers.

Metropolitan WDM networks are of keen interest in regards to WADM services. The requirements range from rearrangeable A/D of 1–8 channels, in a small business, to 40 or more channels in an interoffice ring.

Due to the diverse customer mix, each WADM channel should be capable of carrying a different data rate and channel mix. The emerging WADMs support all the requirements described in this section.

OPTICAL CROSS-CONNECTS (OXC) WITH WDM

The subject of cross-connects is explained in Chapter 5. Recall that one of their tasks is to switch the payloads, and map various types of virtual tributaries to others.

Figure 11–6 shows a functional diagram of an optical cross-connect (OXC). Four optical line systems (OLSs) are connected to the OXC [JACK99]. The WDM signals from two OLSs are demultiplexed and the resultant wavelengths are passed through wavelength converters. Each wavelength signal is cross-connected by the OXC, wavelength converted again, multiplexed, and sent out of a fiber interface.

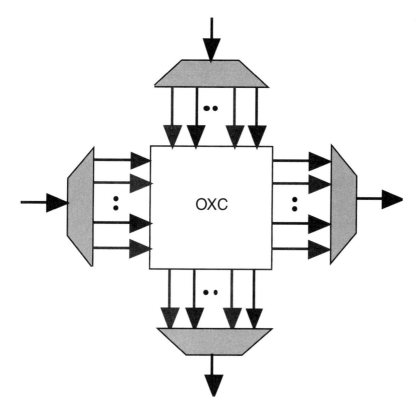

Figure 11–6   An optical cross-connect (OXC).

PASSIVE OPTICAL NETWORKS (PONS)

Passive optical networks (PONs) are really not passive. They are actively sending and receiving optical signals. They are called passive because the outside plant has no electronics to power or maintain the components. As a consequence, PONs eliminate expensive power-based amplifiers, rectifiers, and of course, batteries.

The active part of the PON is between the two ends. In most situations, these two ends are the service provider's node (say, a telephone central office), and the user node. The user node is typically a remote pedestal, often called a remote digital terminal (RDT).

Figure 11–7 shows a PON topology. The fiber can be forked out to multiple sites with the use of splitters. This approach saves a lot of money by multiplexing many user payloads on fewer fibers than in a conventional point-to-point topology. Of course, since multiple users must

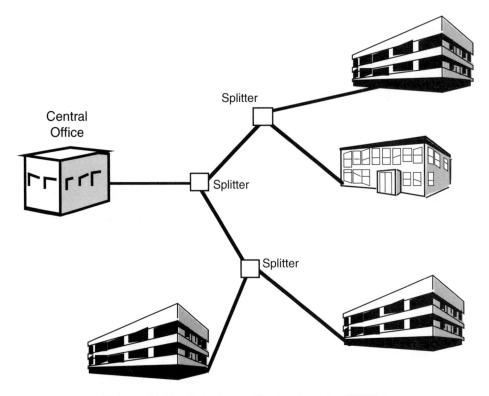

Figure 11–7   Passive optical networks (PONs).

share the fiber, the multiplexing operation must be capable of efficient bandwidth management. The PON uses ATM for this important job, with an increased interest in using Ethernet to perform the same function.

THE "SWEET SPOT"

Some PONs target the "sweet spot" of the local loop technology: the bandwidth between T1 and OC-3 [PESA01]. The term sweet spot is so named because few offerings are available on the local loop that offer services between the T1 rate of 1.544 Mbit/s and the OC-3 rate of 155 Mbit/s in a price range that many consumers can afford. Many network providers think this part of the bandwidth on the local loop is ripe for plunking—

that it offers significant revenue potential. Let's see how by bringing Ethernet into the PON.

OPTICAL ETHERNETS AND ETHERNET PONS

The use of Ethernet and the PON technology in the local loop substantially reduces the cost of providing high-capacity links to the customer. The reason is that expensive components, such as SONET ADM, and ATM switches, can be eliminated, and replaced with less expensive substitutes, as shown in Figure 11–8. At the customer premises, the SONET ADM is replaced with a simple and inexpensive optical network unit. At the Central Office, the SONET ADM and the ATM switch(s) is(are) replaced with an optical line terminal. Of course, this arrangement does not offer the rich functionality of ATM and SONET, but that is precisely the point: Many user interfaces do not need all the powerful attributes of SONET and ATM.

Although Figure 11–8 shows a point-to-point topology, we learned earlier that the PON link can be split into multiple fibers with splitters or combined in a single link with splitters/couplers. Traffic is supported both upstream and downstream with the IEEE 802.3 (modified Ethernet)

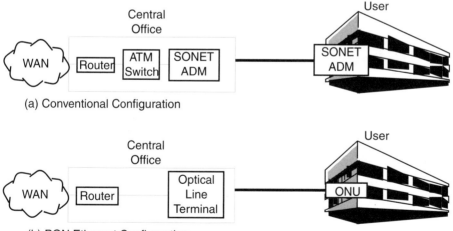

(a) Conventional Configuration

(b) PON Ethernet Configuration

Figure 11–8   Conventional ATM/SONET and Ethernet PON configurations.

frame. As explained in the next section of this chapter, the use of the Ethernet 1,518 byte frame makes better use of the link (in comparison to the ATM 53 byte cell).

Strictly speaking, the technology is not pure (original) Ethernet, in that the traffic upstream from the user to the central office uses dedicated TDM slots, and does not rely on the contention and collision detection aspects of 802.3. An enhanced Ethernet feature called rate limiting allows the network operator to place transmission limits on each port on the link—that is, on each subscriber. Thus, the shared media are managed in a structured manner.

ATM AND SONET

The Internet's major communications links and switches are made up of the ATM and SONET technologies, as shown in Figure 11–9. The figure also shows the layered protocol arrangement for the ATM/SONET operation. For the reader who is unfamiliar with ATM, please refer to the tutorial in the sidebar "ATM and AAL."

ATM and AAL

ATM

- The purpose of ATM is to provide a high-speed, low-delay, multiplexing, and switching network to support any type of user traffic, such as voice, data, or video applications.
- ATM segments and multiplexes user traffic into small, fixed-length units called cells. The cell is 53 octets, with five octets reserved for the cell header. For specific identification, each cell is identified with virtual circuit identifiers that are contained in the cell header. An ATM network uses these identifiers to relay the traffic through high-speed switches from the sending customer premises equipment (CPE) to the receiving CPE.
- ATM provides no error detection operations on the user payload inside the cell (just the header). It provides no retransmisson services, and few operations are performed on the small header. The intention of this approach—small cells with minimal services performed—is to implement a network that is fast enough to support multimegabit transfer rates.
- ATM provides extensive bandwdith management, QOS, and OAM&P services for its virtual circuits.

(continued)

ATM Adaptation Layer (AAL) (continued)

- Since ATM operates with small cells, the ATM adaptation layer (AAL) is responsible (at the sender) for segmenting the user payload into 48-byte units and (at the receiver) reassembling the 48-byte units back into the original payload.
- The five-byte header is the responsibility of the ATM layer and not AAL. Thus, the five-byte header and the 48-byte payload equal the 53-byte cell.

ATM and SONET interwork well together, with SONET providing high-speed bearer links and ATM providing bandwidth management and quality of service (QoS) functions for its virtual circuits. Both are designed to provide extensive OAM&P services, such as continuity testing, bandwidth provisioning, and alarms. SONET provides these functions at the physical layer (layer one) of the layered model; ATM provides them at layer two, the data link layer. However, while many papers, journals, and books describe ATM as operating at layer two, it also performs many layer three functions, such as end-to-end virtual circuits.

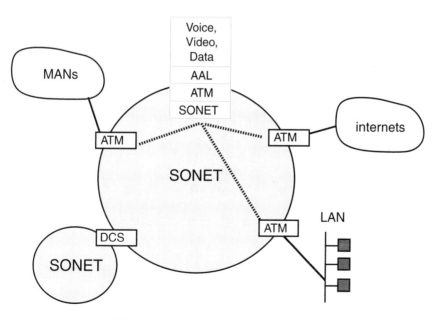

Figure 11–9   ATM and SONET.

In some systems, the SONET and ATM functions reside in the same machine, such as an ATM switch, a Digital Cross Connect (DCS), or a router.

IP AND SONET

The prevalent approach today for moving IP traffic over a wide area network (WAN) is to use the services of ATM and SONET. This practice is called IP over ATM over SONET, since IP is a layer three protocol, operating over ATM and SONET. Figure 11–9 shows this arrangement as well, with the notation of "Data" used to identify the placement of IP (and the associated protocols, such as TCP, and say a layer 7 protocol) in the protocol stack.

For these services to operate correctly, and for different vendors to be able to interwork their products together, many rules are needed. Here are some examples:

- Mapping of IP addresses into ATM virtual circuits
- Mapping of ATM cells into SONET payloads
- Boundary alignments (octet alignments) of IP and ATM octets in the SONET payload envelope
- Correlation (if necessary) of ATM alarms to SONET OAM messages (of which there are many)
- Agreement on specifications for the IP to ATM encapsulation headers

ATM IN THE SONET ENVELOPE

Figure 11–10 shows how ATM cells are mapped into a SONET payload envelope. The payload pointers can be used to locate the beginning of the first cell. Additionally, cell delineation can be achieved by the receiver locking onto the five bytes that satisfy the HEC operations. In this manner, the receiver knows where a cell is positioned in the envelope. The receiver also is able to detect an empty cell.

It is unlikely that cells would be positioned at the first byte of the payload, unless the SONET locked mode operation is in place. If they are, an STS-3c system can carry 44 cells, and bytes 1 – 8 of the 45th cell. The remainder of the 45th cell is placed in the next SONET frame. So, a cell can cross the tributary frame boundary.

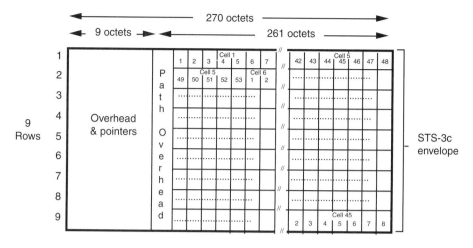

Figure 11–10   ATM over SONET. Note: Example shows first cell aligned exactly in beginning of payload area. May be positioned anywhere in the payload.

IP AND PPP IN THE SONET ENVELOPE

Request for Comments (RFC) 1619 defines the rules for running the Point-to-Point Protocol (PPP) over SONET, as shown in Figure 11–11. Since SONET is a physical point-to-point circuit, PPP over SONET should be a straightforward operation. This section paraphrases RFC 1619 (which is quite terse).

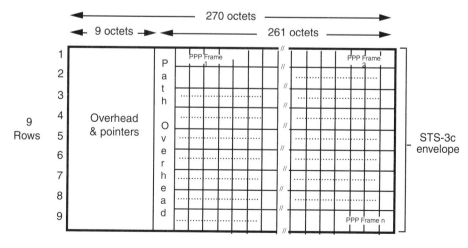

Figure 11–11   IP/PPP over SONET.

There are ambiguities in this RFC, and some implementers have complained about some difficulty in using it as an authoritative guide. One complaint deals with the rules on octet alignment of the PPP payload in the SONET SPE. Listed below are the major rules as outlined in RFC 1619:

- PPP treats the SONET network as octet-oriented synchronous links.
- The PPP octet stream is mapped into the SONET synchronous payload envelope (SPE), with the PPP octet boundaries aligned with the SPE octet boundaries.
- Scrambling is not used.
- The path signal label (C2) is intended to indicate the contents of the SPE. The experimental value of 207 (cf. hex) is used to indicate PPP.
- The multiframe indicator (H4) is currently unused, and must be zero.
- The basic rate for PPP over SONET is that of STS-3c/STM-1 at 155.520 Mbit/s.
- The available information bandwidth is 149.760 Mbit/s, which is the STS-3c/STM-1 SPE with section, line and path overhead removed.

IP Over ATM

In many SONET backbone networks, before IP and PPP are encapsulated into SONET, they are first encapsulated into an ATM cell. Figure 11–12 shows the relationship of running IP over ATM, with emphasis on the CP-AAL5 and the ATM layers. The ATM adaptation layer, type 5 (AAL5) performs its conventional segmentation (and reassembly at the receiver) functions by delineating the traffic into 48-byte units with the addition of an 8-byte trailer as part of the last unit.

The error detection operation is provided by the AAL5 CRC-32 calculation over the PDU, and the padding field is used to fill-in the CPCS SDU to an even increment of 48 bytes.

ATM VS. IP OVER SONET

One of the big issues is the overhead of running IP over ATM versus the overhead of IP directly over SONET, without ATM. Figure 11–13 provides some general information on the differences in the number of bytes needed for these two approaches.

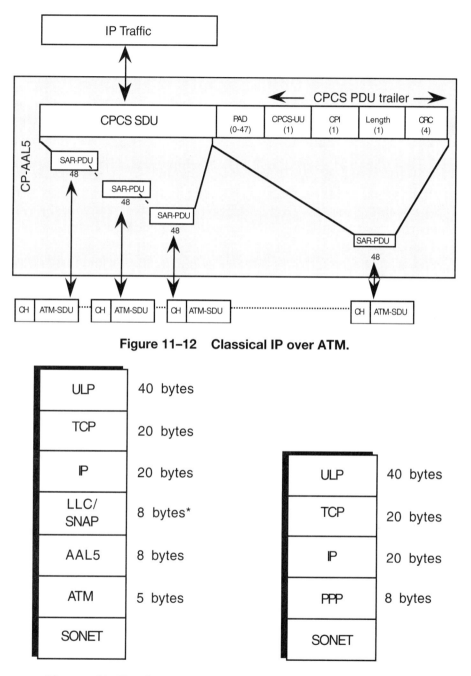

Figure 11–12   Classical IP over ATM.

ULP	40 bytes	
TCP	20 bytes	
IP	20 bytes	
LLC/ SNAP	8 bytes*	
AAL5	8 bytes	
ATM	5 bytes	
SONET		

ULP	40 bytes
TCP	20 bytes
IP	20 bytes
PPP	8 bytes
SONET	

Figure 11–13   Comparison of overhead in ATM and IP protocol stacks. *If PPP is under IP, the SNAP PID can so indicate.

301

The payload is assumed to be 40 bytes. Both protocol stacks have the same overhead at the upper layers since they are both supporting the same upper layer protocols, TCP and IP. The value of 40 bytes is chosen since it is a common size for a packet in the Internet.

The difference lies at the layers below IP. ATM uses the three-byte LLC and the five-byte SNAP (containing the three-byte OUI and the two-byte PID). The IP-only stack does not use these headers.

Please note the "note" in the figure. The ATM stack may not have to carry the full PPP headers and trailers across the network. It can extract the PPP PID field and map it into the SNAP PID field, then reconstruct the PPP headers and trailers at the egress to the network, if needed. This may be feasible since the flags, address, and control fields are present, but never change. Whether this is possible depends on the vendor's design of the ATM node.

Also, note that the total number of bytes passed to ATM is more than a 48-byte payload. Consequently, the traffic must be placed in more than one ATM cell, the details on this operation are shown next.

The "Cell Tax"

Critics of ATM cite the overhead of ATM that results from using a small fixed-length cell, and use the derisive name of "cell tax." The problem occurs when the user payload does not fit neatly into the AAL 48-byte area, and another cell (or multiple cells) must be used. For example, if the payload is, say, 49 bytes (a contrived example to be sure), a second cell is needed to carry the 49th byte. The result is that the second cell contains 52 bytes of overhead or padding (to fill in the 48 bytes), and only one byte of user payload. In other words, for this specific application, the two cells of 106 bytes are carrying 49 bytes of payload. More than half the bandwidth is being consumed by overhead!

Is the ATM Overhead Tolerable?

The answer to the question, "Is the ATM overhead tolerable?" will depend upon who supplies the answer. If the question is answered by a network manager on a private campus, the answer is likely to be yes. This manager is probably not paying hard dollars for bandwidth from a public WAN backbone operator. The attractive features of ATM may make the overhead less of an issue.

The major problem occurs in the situation where a backbone customer is paying for bandwidth and is running the ATM stack. For example, ISPs pay for this overhead when they use a carrier's links. Their incentive is to eliminate ATM and run IP directly over SONET.

Another factor is the overhead of processing AAL, even though AAL5 should not be processed in the backbone network. Interfaces with OC-12 (STS-12c) now have ATM SAR chips. This situation means that a SONET node may process AAL even though there may be no need to do so.

This situation is not "all ATM or nothing." For example, interfaces are now available for OC-48 (STS-48c) for support of direct PPP/HDLC mappings, and as explained in the next section, networks are coming into place that do not run ATM.

EVOLUTION OF THE OPTICAL BROADBAND NETWORK

Today's optical backbone networks are made up of SONET TDM technology, with the access networks operating at OC-3, OC-12, and OC-48, and the long-haul systems operating at OC-48 or OC-192. It is anticipated that WDM will be deployed with IP directly over it in the near future. Figure 11–14 shows a likely migration scenario. An edge router rests be-

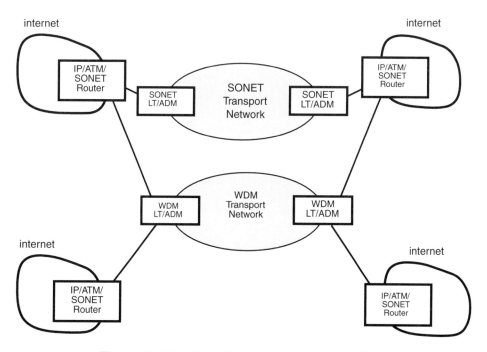

Figure 11–14   Evolution of optical networking.

tween the internets and the optical networks. Based on the destination of the traffic and available technology, the traffic is either sent through the SONET TDM transport network or the WDM transport network.

This approach is attractive because a migration can take place without disruption to the existing transport network.

MIGRATION TO LABEL SWITCHING NETWORKS

For the newcomer to label switching, please refer to the sidebar "Tutorial on Label Switching Networks." As label switching networks continue to grow, there will be opportunities to interwork (and probably combine) label switching routers (LSRs) with WDM routers. As Figure 11–15 shows, native-mode IP networks will continue to exist for many years; in fact, there is

---

Tutorial on Label Switching Networks

- In label switching, instead of using a destination address to make the routing decision, a number (a label) is associated with the packet. The label is placed in a packet header and is used in place of an address (an IP address, usually), and the label is used to direct the traffic to its destination.
- Label switching is much faster in that the label value in an incoming packet header is used to access the forwarding table at the router; that is, the label is used to index the table. This look-up requires only one access to the table, in contrast to a traditional routing table access that might require several thousand look-ups.
- It also can provide scalability. This term refers to the ability or inability of a system, in this case the Internet, to accommodate a growing and large number of Internet users. Thousands of new users (and supporting nodes, such as routers and servers) are signing on to the Internet each day. Imagine the task of a router if it has to keep track of all these users. Label switching offers solutions to this rapid growth and the resulting large networks, by allowing a large number of IP addresses to be associated with one or a few labels.
- Label switching supports the tailoring of services to network customers. This idea is called tailored quality of services (QoS). It means network users do not have to be treated alike. Some can receive different services and different qualities of the same service than others.

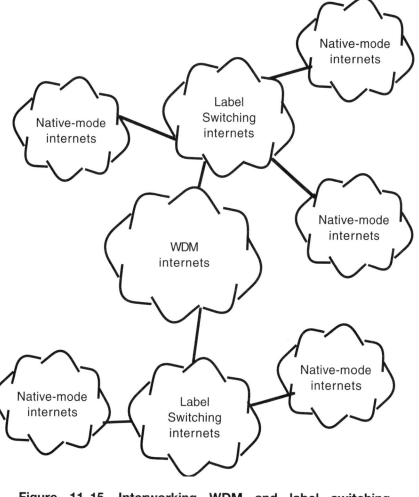

Figure 11–15 Interworking WDM and label switching internets.

little incentive to push label or WDM technology into LANs or conventional point-to-point local loops. To do so would entail changing the software and hardware architecture of user machines, such as PCs, palm units, etc.

So, this part of a network stays the same, and the interfaces from a router back to the user computers are conventional Ethernet, PPP, DSL, V.90, cable modem, and so on.

The router's interfaces out to the network will be Mulitprotocol Label Switching (MPLS), WDM, or most likely a melding of the two. MPLS has emerged as the industry standard for label switching and will become a dominant technology in the next few years.

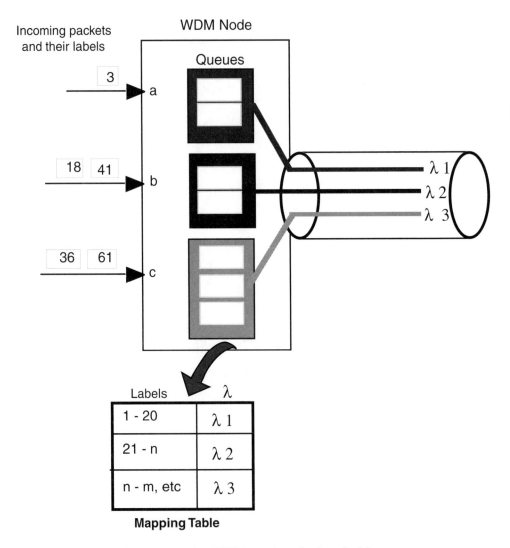

Figure 11–16   MPLS and optical switching.

MAPPING LABELS TO WAVE LENGTHS

The next stage in the optical network evolution is the interworking of MPLS and WDM wavelengths. Figure 11–16 shows this arrangement. The incoming packets arrive at the link interfaces (a, b, and c) at the WDM node. These packets carry an MPLS label, which has been derived from the destination IP address residing in the IP header (and perhaps other fields, such as the destination port number). Through the use of its mapping table, the node places the packets onto an outgoing queue that is associated with a WDM wavelength. The next task is to transmit these packets out of the optical interface. This task entails an electrooptical conversion process, wherein the electrical bits in the buffer are translated to associated optical bits for transmission onto the fiber.

As the traffic is transported through the optical network (not shown in Figure 11–16), the intervening nodes can (a) use the label in the packet to map/switch the packets onto different output links and different wavelengths on these links or (b) ignore the label and optically cross-connect the wavelengths from the input link output link. We call option (a) Label/Lambda switching and (b) Pure Lambda switching. Both options are emerging in this nascent technology.

LABEL SWITCHED PATHS (LSPS)
AND OPTICAL SWITCHED PATHS (OSPS)

In order to take advantage of the speed and efficiency of optical switching, and the traffic engineering aspects of MPLS, it is highly desirable to correlate the MPLS label with the optical channel, specifically a wavelength on the fiber. Figure 11–17 shows how a node (node B) performs the correlation. One entry in node B's LSP cross connect table has been provisioned for label 44. The primary path out of the node is through port (interface) a. The label value of 44 is mapped to label 67 for this port. The traffic associated with label 44 (as well as the label header) is then placed on $\lambda1$ at port a for transmission to the next node. The secondary (backup) route has also been set up, with a mapping of label 44 to label 27, and a cross connect to $\lambda2$ on port b. Similar cross connect tables are configured for all the optical nodes that are part of the LSP (the path from the sender to the final receiver).

The example in Figure 11–17 represents an O/E/O optical/electrical cross-connect (OXC), most likely situated in an edge router to a routing

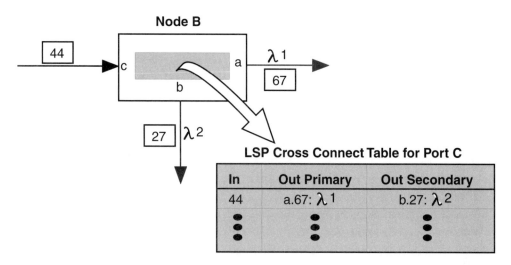

Figure 11–17 Correlating MPLS labels and optical wavelengths: The O/E/O OXC.

domain (the ingress node to a backbone optical network). The optical (O) signals are converted to electrical (E) signals in order to execute hardware and software in the node for making the cross connect and mapping decisions. Obviously, the O/E/O operations must take place at some of the nodes in the network, but it is desirable to avoid the signal conversions. The next example in Figure 11–18 shows how a O/O/O photonic cross connect (PXC) operating in the core (in the backbone) of the optical network would handle this operation.

In this operation, node B is now playing the role of an O/O/O photonic cross connect node, and does not examine the bits on the wavelength. Instead, the wavelengths themselves provide the information to make a cross connect, switching decision. Thus, the optical cross connect table is configured to support an optical switching path (OSP). The OSP is the optical path between two adjacent nodes. The role of node B in Figure 11–18 is likely the role that a non-edge node assumes in the backbone.

In its role as an optical (backbone) switch, node B is not tasked with processing the MPLS label. Rather, it relies on a node at the edge of the network to receive the MPLS packets, examine the label and use a cross connect table to map the packet onto the appropriate wavelength.

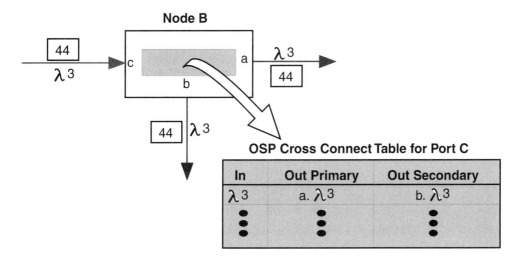

Figure 11–18   The O/O/O PXC optical cross connect.

Of course, it is necessary for the edge node to know which wavelength to use. This configuration operation is set up between the edge nodes and the core (backbone) nodes. First the nodes agree on fiber interfaces and the wavelengths on the fibers that will be used between adjacent nodes. Second, through the use of routing protocols (such as OSPF), all nodes know how to reach each other to deliver traffic to an end user. Third, when an edge node receives a packet, it correlates the IP address in the packet to a label, and simply places the labeled packet onto the fiber and wavelength to reach the next node in the LSP. This node need not look at the MPLS label, because its optical cross connect table reveals how the incoming wavelengths (and of course, the traffic on it) will be cross connected to the output interface to reach the next and (eventually) final node.

PROTOCOL STACK POSSIBILITES

There has been an increased awareness of the benefits of the SONET technology over the past few years. At the same time, it also recognized that the cost and overhead of SONET may not be warranted in some situations.

One that comes to mind is a simple point-to-point link between two buildings on a campus. The rich functionality and expense of SONET may be overkill for this situation. The network manager may not need all the diagnostics and alarms that go hand-in-hand with SONET.

But the issue goes further than the use or nonuse of SONET for certain topologies. As we have examined in this chapter, the issue also involves the use or nonuse of ATM. As noted earlier, some critics of ATM state that ATM has too much overhead and is too expensive for certain applications and topologies.

It is obvious that the deployment of SONET and ATM is not appropriate in many cases. But it should also be understood that a SONET-less implementation will not have the superior provisioning, back-up, and OAM capabilities that are built into SONET. Likewise, an ATM-less implementation will not have ATM's traffic management capabilities. If they are not needed, then don't use them, but recognize the implications of such a scaled-down system and what it means to the network administrator and the customers that use the system.

Figure 11–19 shows several protocol stacks that either exist now or will be deployed in the near future. Our view is that all these implemen-

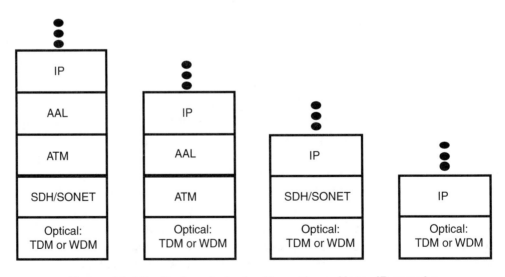

Figure 11–19   Protocol stack alternatives. Note: IP may be running on top of PPP, not shown here.

tations have a place in a communications network, and it is a matter of deciding which protocol stack is appropriate for the specific network requirement.

SUMMARY AND CONCLUSIONS

Optical networks, considered something of a fantasy just a few years ago, are now commonplace. SONET and its ITU-T counterpart, SDH, have been the mainstays of these extrodinary networks. In order to keep these networks backward compatible, and in consonance with prevailing technologies, SONET and SDH were designed principally for synchronous, voice, and TDM payloads, such as DS0, DS1, DS3, E1, and E4 traffic.

IP-based optical networks for asynchronous, data STDM payloads are emerging, and for now, most run IP over ATM. There is considerable interest in looking for substitutes for ATM, and the focus is on running IP directly over SONET.

There is another important aspect to consider. The SONET architecture was designed to accommodate the TDM payloads based on the 64 kbit/s DS0 rate. It is an understatement to say this techology is obsolete. You may wish to take another look at Table 2–4. The row titled "G.711" represents the DS0 signal. Its MOS in this specific study is 4.1. Yet, some of the newer codecs provide quite acceptable MOS ratings, at a fraction of the bandwidth needed to support the DS0 technology. Any revised SONET, or any competitor to SONET, must embrace these more efficient codecs. And this is one reason for the keen interest in VoIP. Among other attributes, commercial VoIP systems use the low bit rate codecs and thus make much better use of the network's precious bandwidth.

To continue the discussion on the evolution of the optical network itself, many vendors and network providers think that IP in WDM networks is the next step, as is MPLS with WDM in the optical backbone. This is the authors' view: MPLS over WDM, using DiffServ and RSVP to replace ATM for bandwidth management and QoS features.

This final scenario is possible, and we think it is likely. Extensive work is underway to define the optical-based network relationships with MPLS, traffic engineering, bandwidth on demand, and QoS features. In addition, the IETF is actively involved in this activity and the IETF's Generalized MPLS extends MPLS from supporting traditional data/packet interfaces and switching to include support of three new classes of interfaces and switching: (a) TDM, (b) lambda switching, and (c) fiber switching [BELL01].

Work Underway

Bandwidth on demand has been provided by network operators for many years. Examples are the switched virtual circuits (SVCs) of X.25, Frame Relay, and ATM. The plain old dial-up service is another example (somewhat limited in its capabilities) of bandwidth on demand.

With the development of optical networks that provide tremendous bandwidth capacity, there is keen interest among customers, vendors, and network providers to deploy network offerings that provide optical bandwidth on demand. But the issue goes further than offering bandwidth on demand. The bandwidth capacity of optical networks is increasing each year by orders of magnitude, and a pressing issue is to develop mechanisms to mangage and control this vital network resource.

The present optical networks are preconfigured to provide bandwidth with proprietary element management systems, and require crafting operations before the bandwidth is made available to the customer. Due to some manual operations involved in this crafting, and due to the fact that end-to-end provisioning often occurs through vendor-specific systems, it is not unusual that a long provisioning time is required before the service is made available to the customer. This situation is occurring when this customer is demanding short provisioning times.

The intent is to migrate to a scheme in which the end user can dynamically request bandwdith from the network, and the network can dynamically find and reserve the required bandwidth for this user. Thereafter, the bandwidth is guaranteed, something like a leased, point-to-point circuit.

Several efforts are underway to define standards for the management of bandwdith in optical networks. One effort is sponsored by the Open Domain Service Interconnect Coaliton [ODSI01], and the other is sponsored by the Optical Interworking Forum [OIF01]. The IETF is taking the lead in the Internet standards area [IETF01a].

These topics are beyond this book, and we refer you to the references cited in the previous paragraph for more information.

A NEW OPTICAL NETWORK MODEL

Other recent efforts that go beyond this book deal with the efforts of the ITU-T to define a new model for optical networks. The ITU-T has also published a layered model for optical networks. We refer you to [G70901] and [G87299], if you wish more information on this subject.

IN CONCLUSION

At this stage of the story of optical networks, we must wait and see what the marketplace decides about the evolution and integration of WDM, DiffServ, MPLS, and lambda switching technologies. But make no mistake, it will happen; it's just a matter of time.

We thank you for sharing our journey into the SONET and T1 worlds. We hope your journery was enlightening and enjoyable.

Appendix A
Transmission Media

This appendix provides an overview of the prevalent communications media, more commonly called links, channels, or trunks. Since most of the newer T1 backbones and SONET deployments use optical fiber, this chapter focuses on this type of medium. This material is written as a basic tutorial; the experienced reader can skip this appendix.

Fiber is a glass transmission medium that interfaces with equipment (multiplexers, channel banks, etc.). It will transport any signal, whether analog or digital. There are three components to a fiber optic system: source, transmission medium (cable), and detector. The source could be an LED or Laser; the transmission medium can be plastic or glass. In telecommunications, the glass used could be multimode step-index, multimode graded-index, or single mode step-index dependent. Third, the detectors could be either PIN or APD.

Specific requirements for the type of transmission facilities depend on the user's application and include but should not be limited to security requirements, the operating environment, transmission throughput, and the availability of transmission and equipment supported. The availability of network connections and the need for high-speed or low-speed capabilities also play an important role in the selection of the communications media. Another important consideration is the possible requirement to integrate voice, video, and data onto the same transmission medium.

PROPERTIES OF LIGHT AND OPTICAL FIBER

Before one can grasp the underlying concepts of fiber optics, several aspects of light should be considered. It is instructive to note that light is part of the electromagnetic spectrum. The light that is visible to the human eye is only a fraction of the entire spectrum range, and light frequencies are several orders of magnitude higher than the highest radio frequencies. Different colors or wavelengths that constitute light are nothing more than different frequencies that propagate at various speeds over the medium.

Fiber optics is the technology of transmitting information over optical wave guides in the form of light. The light energy consists of photons, which is the quantum of radiant energy. The electrical signal to be transmitted is converted at the source into a light signal, which is then modulated and sent to a light-emitting diode or an injection laser diode for transmission through the fiber. At the receiving end, the detector converts the modulated light signal back to its electrical equivalent.

The fiber used in communications is a fine strand of ultra-pure glass weighing on the order of one ounce per kilometer and it is as thin as human hair (50–150 microns in diameter for multimode and 8 microns for single-mode fiber, which are discussed shortly). Plastic fiber also exists, but it is only applied to noncritical short distance needs. With silica optical fiber systems, repeaters (line amplifiers) are required every 20 to 30 miles, which is roughly similar to coaxial repeater's distances in telephone systems. Transmissions over high-quality glass fiber can travel over 100 miles without the need for repeaters or regenerators.

Some of the advantages of fiber optics (compared to copper cable) include superior transmission quality and efficiency, as well as the elimination of crosstalk, static, echo, and delay problems. Fiber also minimizes environmental effects such as weather, water, and freezing. Finally, glass fiber is very small and lightweight. It has a wide bandwidth that allows for the transport of very large payloads of information.

However, fiber does have several disadvantages associated with its use. Since it is comprised of pure glass with a very small diameter, it is fragile and difficult to connect and splice. Also, because glass is not a conductor of electrical current, it cannot carry power to the field regenerators (which are used to strengthen signals on long spans).

Like other media technologies, the fiber optic system has three basic components: the optic fiber or light guide, the transmitter or light source, and the receiver or light detector (see Figure A–1). Most fiber optic links

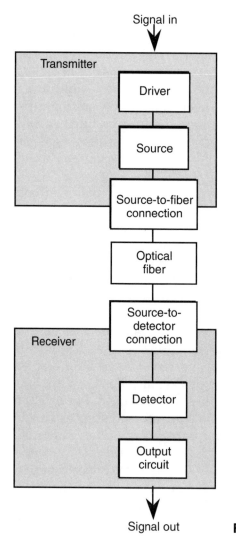

Signal in

Transmitter

Driver

Source

Source-to-fiber
connection

Optical
fiber

Source-to-
detector
connection

Receiver

Detector

Output
circuit

Signal out

Figure A–1   Basic lightwave system.

use infrared light because the components can be made to operate more efficiently in this range than with the visible light range.

Two limiting factors must be considered when designing fiber systems: bandwidth and attenuation. Bandwidth is the difference between the highest and lowest frequency used (previously discussed). Attenuation or loss is the measure of how much light is launched into one end of the fiber compared with how much comes out at the other end. Each component in the system adds some attenuation. The fiber cable attenuation is roughly linear. For example, a five-mile route results in five times as much attenuation as a one-mile route. This loss is the result of absorption, radiation, or scattering of the signal (more will be said on this later). Fiber optic transmissions did not become practical for communications until signal loss due to attenuation was reduced to less than 20 dB/km. Fiber optic systems today exhibit attenuation of less than .5 dB/km.

ELECTROMAGNETIC SPECTRUM

Like radio waves, light is electromagnetic energy utilizing part of the electromagnetic spectrum. Electromagnetic energy is radiant energy that travels through space at about 300,000 km/s (186,000 miles/s), which is conveniently called the speed of light.

This energy is composed of an electromagnetic field whose strength varies sinusoidally. An electromagnetic wave is depicted as a sine wave. Figure A–2 illustrates the electromagnetic spectrum. Two points are noteworthy. First, the frequencies of light are several orders of magnitude higher than the highest radio frequencies. So, fiber optic systems are immune to radio frequency interference (RFI). Second, visible light (light we can see) is only a small part of the entire range of light. As was mentioned earlier, most fiber optic links use infrared light because this technology is relatively inexpensive to implement. The electrical components are cheaper and simpler than the ones used in the visible range because of the lower operating frequency.

Radio waves are also described in terms of frequency, as are kilohertz (kHz) or megahertz (MHz). Wavelength is typically expressed in nanometers (nm, one billionth of a meter).

The shorter the wavelength, the greater the loss (drawing from basic transmission principles). Today, 800 nm is considered shortwave and is used for low bit rates and short distances. It is typically used for hooking computers to mainframes, in automobiles, or in airplanes and space shuttles. The 1300 nm and 1550 nm wavelengths are considered longwaves and are used for long distances and high bit rates, typically telecommunication applications. These wavelengths are also referred to as windows. So, the fiber systems today operate in the 1300–1550 nm window of the electromagnetic spectrum.

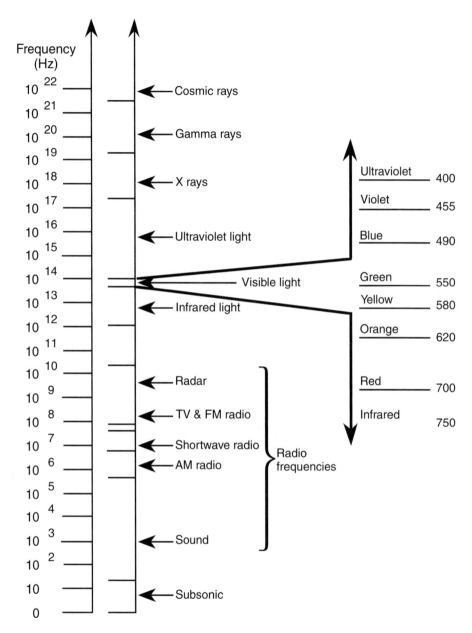

Figure A–2   The electromagnetic spectrum.

PROPERTIES OF LIGHT: REFLECTION AND REFRACTION

What is commonly called "the speed of light" is actually the speed that light travels in a vacuum. Light travels slightly slower in other media (i.e., air or water). When light goes from one medium to another, it changes speed and is bent or refracted, as shown in Figure A–3.

Not only does light travel at different speeds in different media, different wavelengths (colors) travel at different speeds within the same medium. The different speeds of the various wavelengths mean that the colors are refracted differently within the medium. A prism works on this principle.

The white light entering a prism is composed of all colors and the colors are refracted differently because of their different speed of travel through the prism. The light emerging from the other side is divided into the colors of the spectrum. Figure A–3 shows this concept in more detail.

To explain this idea, consider an example of light traveling through two different media: water and air (see Figure A–4). The incident ray is the original ray from a source. The angle of incidence is the angle between the normal (a line drawn perpendicular) to the surface and the incident ray. The Law of Reflection says that angle of incidence, –A, is equal to the angle of reflection, –B. The refracted ray, –C, is in the medium of lower index of refraction. The refracted ray bends further away from the normal than the reflected ray. As –A reaches a specific value (called the critical angle), the refracted ray –C, emerges just grazing the boundary approaching 90 degrees (see Figure A–5).

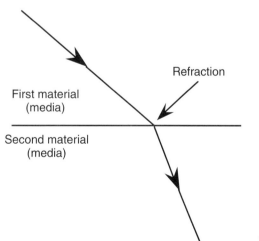

First material
(media)

Refraction

Second material
(media)

Figure A–3   Refraction principle.

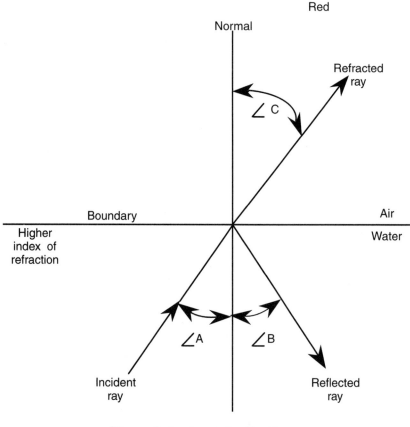

Figure A–4   Law of reflection.

If the –angle of incidence, A, is further increased beyond the critical angle, then the incident ray does not pass into the upper median, but is totally reflected at the boundary surface. This is called total internal reflection (see Figure A–6).

Total Internal Reflection

The optical fiber works on the principle of total internal reflection. Once light begins to reflect down the fiber, it will continue to do so. The fiber is constructed of two layers of glass or plastic, one layer surrounding the other, as shown in Figure A–7. These layers are then enclosed in a protective jacket. The inner layer, the core, has a higher refractive index than the outer layer, the cladding. Light injected into the core and

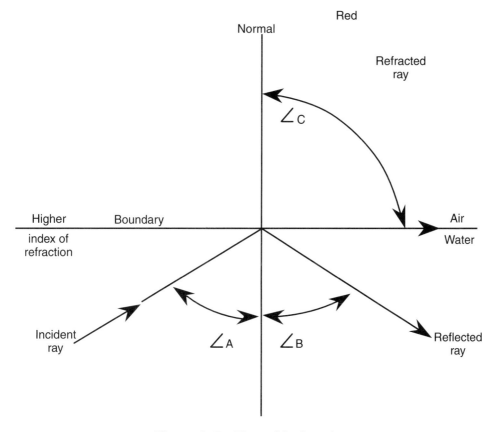

Figure A–5   The critical angle.

striking the core-to-cladding interface at greater than the critical angle will be reflected back into the core, as shown in Figure A–8. Since the angles of incidence and reflection are equal, the light will continue to be reflected down the core. This concept is not unlike a very long and narrow billiards table. A ball shot at an angle into the cushion will bounce off at the same angle and continue bounding from cushion to cushion down the length of the table, always at the same angle. Light striking the interface at less than the critical angle will pass into the cladding and be absorbed and then dissipated by the jacket.

Numerical Aperture

Numerical aperture (NA) is the light gathering ability of the fiber (see Figure A–9). Obviously, it is advantageous for the fiber to accept and

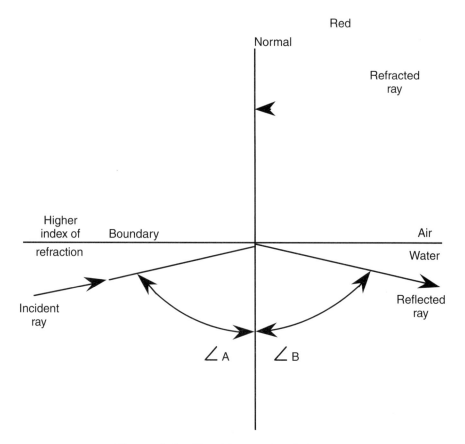

Figure A–6   Total internal reflection.

propagate as much light as possible. Since light will be reflected only if it strikes the cladding at an angle greater than the critical angle, we can form a cone, called the acceptance cone. The acceptance cone defines which light will be reflected and which will not. Light injected at angles within the cone will be reflected; rays entering at steeper angles will not.

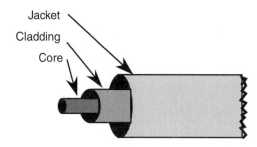

Figure A–7   Structure of optical fiber.

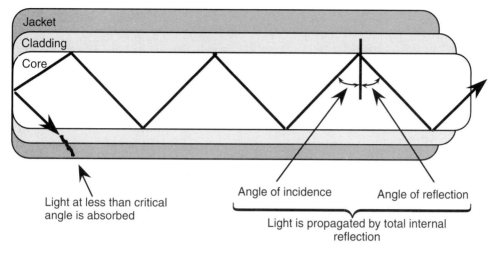

Figure A–8   Total internal reflection.

Therefore, a fiber with a large NA, as in multimode step-index, has a larger acceptance cone than single-mode step-index and will gather light better. However, as discussed earlier, single-mode step-index fiber is the most advantageous for telecommunications to use because of its high bit-rate and cable length.

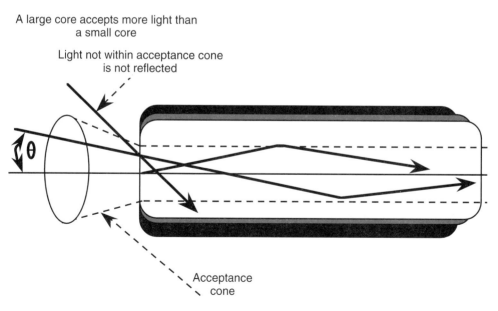

Figure A–9   Numerical aperture.

TYPES OF FIBERS

With this background information in mind, let us examine the various types of fibers available in the marketplace today. The two basic classifications of optical fiber are defined here and explained in more detail in the following sections:

- Multimode: Allows light to take many paths (modes) as it travels through the fiber
- Single-mode: Has a core so small that only one path (mode) is available for light to travel through the fiber

Multimode Step-Index Fibers

The simplest fiber type is the multimode step index fiber (see Figure A–10(a)). This fiber has a core diameter ranging from 125 to 400+ microns (.005 inch to over .016 inch, see Figure A–10(b)), which allows many modes or rays of light propagation. A larger core diameter permits more modes. Since light reflects at a different angle for each mode, some rays will follow longer paths than others. The ray that goes straight down the core without any reflecting will arrive at the other end sooner than other rays. Other rays arrive later, and the more times a ray is reflected, the later it arrives. Thus, light entering the fiber at the same time may arrive at the other end at slightly different times. With this phenomenon we say that the light has "spread out." This spreading of light is called modal dispersion and is discussed in more detail in the section titled "Fiber Losses."

Dispersion, among other factors, makes the multimode step-index fiber the least efficient of the fiber types. It is used for short runs and lower operating frequencies, such as linking a computer mainframe to peripheral equipment. On the other hand, the fiber's large size and simple construction offer advantages. First, because of the large numerical aperture it gathers light well. Second, it is the easiest to install. Third, it is inexpensive in comparison to the other types. The disadvantages are the large dispersion of the signals and the relatively low bandwidth with resultant lower operating speeds.

Multimode Graded-Index Fiber

One way to reduce modal dispersion is to use multimode graded-index fiber. With this fiber, the refractive index is highest at the center of the core

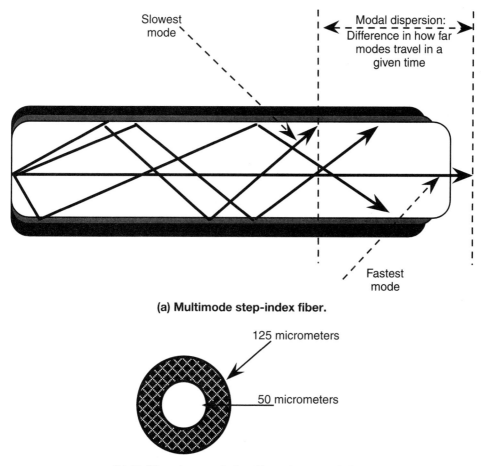

(a) Multimode step-index fiber.

(b) Multimode step-index fiber characteristics.

Figure A–10 Multimode step index fibers.

and gradually tapers off toward the edges. Since light travels faster in a lower index, the light furthest from the center axis travels faster. Because the rays following different paths travel at various speeds, the rays reach the same point at roughly the same time. Modal dispersion is still present, but now it is as low as 2 ns/km. Notice in Figure A–11 that the light is no longer sharply reflected, it is now gently bent.

Multimode graded-index fibers are small, typically 125 microns. The fiber's size still makes it fairly easy to install, and its size and graded index make it efficient. The complexity of the core makes it more expensive than the multimode step-index fibers. Nevertheless, it is very popular.

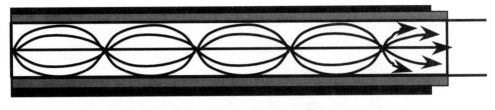

Figure A-11   Multimode graded-index fiber.

So, the multimode graded-index fiber offers an intermediate choice between the other two types (multimode step-index and single-mode step-index) and its advantages and disadvantages lie between these two types.

Multimode graded-index fibers are suited for medium distances and medium operating speeds (typically, it supports bandwidths of up to 150 MHz). It can be found in the telco local loop, local area networks, high rise buildings, college campuses, and medical facilities.

Single-mode Step-index Fibers

Another way to improve modal dispersion is to reduce the core's diameter until the fiber will only propagate one mode efficiently (see Figure A–12). This approach is used in the single-mode step-index fiber,

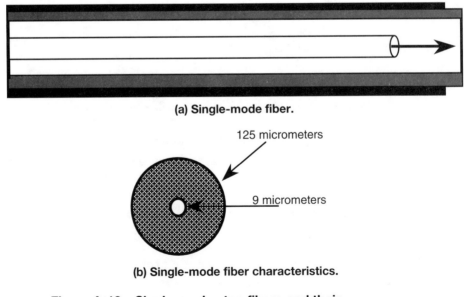

(a) Single-mode fiber.

125 micrometers

9 micrometers

(b) Single-mode fiber characteristics.

Figure A-12   Single-mode step fibers and their characteristics.

which has a core diameter of only 2 to 8 microns (.00008 to .0003 of an inch). These fibers are by far the most efficient, but their small size makes them unattractive for all but the most demanding high-speed, long-distance applications. Their advantages are minimum dispersion, high efficiency, and large bandwidth with high operating speeds. On the negative side, they are expensive, difficult to connect, and (because of their small numerical aperture) require a laser as the light source.

Single-mode step-index fibers are used for long distances (for telecommunications typically, 30 miles without field repeaters) and high operating speeds (e.g., 10 Gbit/s, such as public high-capacity telecommunications networks). Most SONET networks employ single-mode fiber.

SOURCES AND RECEIVERS OF OPTICAL FIBER SIGNALS

At each end of a fiber optic system (link) is a device for converting electrical-to-optical or optical-to-electrical energy. The source is an electro-optic converter. The detector at the other end is an optic-electro converter. The source is either a light-emitting diode (LED) or a laser diode. Both are about the size of a grain of table salt. They are small semiconductor chips that emit light when current is passed through them. The next section points out the general characteristics that play a part in their effectiveness and application.

Light-Emitting Diodes (LEDs)

A semiconductor, constructed so that spontaneous light emission takes place, is called a light-emitting diode. Light is emitted spontaneously when atoms or molecules rid themselves of excess energy without any outside intervention. Ordinary light from the sun or a light bulb is another example of spontaneous emission. As long as voltage is applied, electrons keep flowing through the diode and recombination continues at the junction. The recombination energy is released as a photon of light.

A photon is a quantum of energy. Photons are massless particles, and only massless particles can travel at the speed of light. Each photon has an amount of energy proportional to the frequency of the light wave, and thus is said to be inversely proportional to the wavelength. Each light wave can then be described as a photon energy, a wavelength, or a frequency. The higher the frequency or shorter the wavelength, the more energy carried by a photon.

The compounds used in the LEDs and lasers influence the wavelengths emitted. Here are several examples:

- Gallium phosphide, 560 nm wavelength (green)
- Gallium-arsenide phosphide, 660 nm wavelength (red)
- Gallium-aluminum-arsenide, 820–850 nm (infrared)
- Gallium-indium arsenide phosphate, 1300 and 1550 nm (infrared) long-wavelength devices

In telecommunications, the 1300 nm wavelength is the most popular at this time. The evolution from the 1300 to 1550 nm technology depends, in part, on improved technology for sources.

Some LED materials are not suitable for use in semiconductor lasers. However, all semiconductor laser materials can be operated as LEDs.

Common LEDs emit a visual red or green lightwave, whereas the fiber optic LEDs emit a nonvisible infrared lightwave that minimizes the effects of fiber cable attenuation. Figure A–13 shows two common types of LEDs: the edge-emitting LED and the surface-emitting LED. A main difference between these LEDs is that the edge-emitting LED has greater output power than the surface-emitting diode.

To state matters simply, the decision to use LEDs or lasers revolves around the issues of price and performance. This list compares LEDs to lasers (lasers are examined in the next section). LEDs:

- have lower output power
- have a long life-expectancy
- have slower speeds (transmit data rates of up to 90 Mbit/s through graded-index fiber cable over distances of 29 km [about 12.4 miles])
- are composed of several lightwaves
- use incoherent light
- use wider spectral width
- have no single-mode compatibility
- are easier to use
- are lower in cost

To expand on several of these points, the light generated by an LED is incoherent light because the total amount of light energy released is

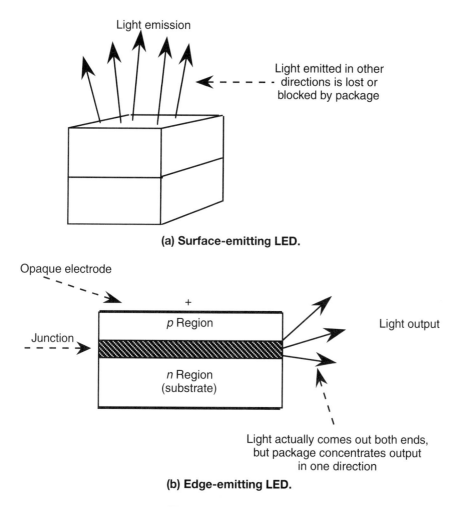

(a) Surface-emitting LED.

(b) Edge-emitting LED.

Figure A–13   LEDs.

completely random in both phase and direction, producing a wide spectrum of light rays (see Figure A–14). The light generated by an LED is composed of several lightwaves, each having a random wavelength and phase relationship. Thus, the combined effect of electromagnetic waves having different wavelengths and phases results in a weaker beam of light. Incoherent lightwaves tend to interfere with each other in the same manner as electrical waves, causing a reduction of the intensity of the light beam. In comparison to lasers, LEDs do not generate well-focused beams the way lasers do.

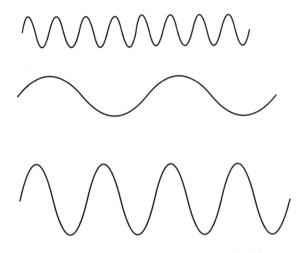

Figure A–14   Incoherent light (LED).

Lasers (Light Amplification by Stimulated Emission of Radiation)

Semiconductor lasers are somewhat like LEDs, but they produce light in a different way that results in higher output powers and more directional beams (see Figure A–15). Lasers provide stimulated emission rather than the simpler spontaneous emission of LEDs. Stimulated emis-

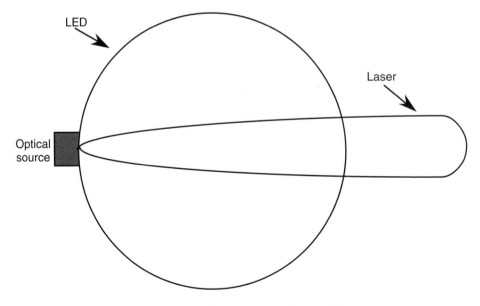

Figure A–15   The beams of LEDs and lasers.

sion occurs when a photon of a specific wavelength stimulates an excited atom to release energy at the same wavelength. The light wave stimulates the excited atom or molecule to oscillate at the light wave frequency. The oscillation amplifies the original light wave. As shown in Figure A–16, stimulated emission is at the same wavelength and in phase (or coherent).

At low drive currents, the laser acts like a LED and emits light spontaneously (low levels of incoherent emission). As the current increases, it reaches the threshold level above which lasing action begins. A laser and LED made of the same material would have the same center wavelength, but the LED would emit a much broader range of wavelengths. This list compares lasers to LEDs. Once again, the tradeoffs of their use are mainly price and performance. Lasers:

- have higher output power
- have shorter life expectancy
- are more sensitive to variations in temperature, requiring more complex transmission controls
- are faster (transmits data at 2.4 Gbit/s over 60 km [37 miles] using single-mode step-index fiber)

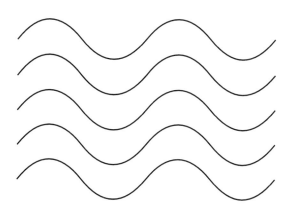

Figure A–16   Coherent light (laser).

- use coherent light
- has single-mode compatibility
- are more difficult to use
- are higher in cost

Detectors

A photodiode is the device that accepts the incoming light, reshapes it, and outputs an amplified digital signal. When all components of a fiber optic system are working properly, the output digital signal will duplicate the original input digital signal.

The detector performs the opposite function of the source function: It converts optical energy to electrical energy. The detector is an opto-electric converter. The most common type is the photodiode, which produces current in response to incident light. The incident light (ray) is the original ray from the source. The two most popular types of semiconductor photodetectors in use today in fiber optics are positive-intrinsic-negative (PIN) diode and avalanche photodiode (APD). The name of the PIN diode comes from the layering of materials. PIN and APD photodiodes are two types of photodetectors that meet the requirements of:

- A large and accessible active area
- Adequate bandwidth or response speed
- High noise separation
- High sensitivity at the operating source wavelength

PIN. PIN photodiodes are not true photodiodes, but fast-acting photoresistors. PINs:

- are relatively inexpensive
- are easy to couple
- have high quantum efficiency
- exhibit excellent response time (in subnanoseconds)
- offer high bandwidth (greater than 20 GHz)

These factors make PINs very popular for use in lightwave communication systems. PIN photodiodes work well for information bandwidth up to 50 MHz over system (link) lengths of up to 50 km.

APD.   An APD provides internal gain, so its responsivity is much higher than that of a pin diode. The APD is also more difficult to install. APDs:

- are relatively expensive
- require a high voltage supply (50–100 V)
- require elaborate bias circuitry
- provide gain (i.e., are more sensitive)
- provide internal amplification of photo current
- are well-suited to applications requiring high receiver sensitivity (receiver sensitivity specifies the weakest optical signal that can be received)

APD responsivity varies with wavelength, so it is specified either at the wavelength of maximum responsivity or at a wavelength of interest. Silicon is the most common material used for detectors in the 800- to 900-nm range. Silicon photodiodes are not suitable for the longer wavelength of 1300 nm and 1550 nm. Materials for long wavelengths are principally geranmium (Ge) and indium gallium arsenide (InGaAs).

Optical Equipment Units—Transmitter

The basic transmitter contains a driver and a source (refer to Figure A–1). The input to the driver is the signal from the equipment being served. The output from the driver is the current required to operate the source. Digital circuits use simple high and low pulses to represent binary 1s and 0s of data. Each bit must occur with its "bit period," which is defined by the clock.

Receiver

The basic receiver contains the detector, amplifier, and output section (again, refer to Figure A–1). The receiver is the principal component around which the design or selection of a fiber optic system revolves, because the receiver has to make up for the attenuation or loss in the light signals. The output section can perform the following functions:

- Pulse reshaping and retiming
- Separation of the clock and data

- Gain control to maintain constant amplification levels in response to variations in received optical power and variations in the receiver operation from temperature or voltage changes

Transceivers

A transceiver is a transmitter and receiver packaged together for bidirectional communication. The advantage of a combined card is that only one common card is installed instead of two. Also, if protection switching (back-up communications) is used, two cards are used instead of four which saves space in the shelf. This approach translates to smaller packaging and saves on the number of spare cards. The disadvantage is that if either the transmit or receive section of the card malfunctions, then the whole card must be replaced.

Repeaters

If the distance is so great that the signal will be too highly attenuated (weak or distorted) before it reaches the receiver, a repeater is used. The repeater accepts the signal, amplifies it, reshapes it, and then sends it on its way by feeding the rebuilt signal back to a transmitter.

One of the disadvantages of analog systems is that they use nonregenerative repeaters that amplify the signal as well as any noise or distortion that entered with the signal. Analog signals cannot be easily reshaped, because the repeater does not know what the original signal looked like.

The advantage of digital transmission is that it uses regenerative repeaters that reshape and retime the original signal without any accumulated noise or distortion accumulating.

FIBER CABLE STRUCTURE

Protecting the Fiber

In the real world, the optical fiber as previously described has little application. To use the fiber technology effectively, the comparatively fragile fibers must be protected from physical damage by incorporating the fiber(s) into a cable that provides external protection from various environmental concerns listed below:

- Dirt
- Moisture

- Sunlight
- Abrasion
- Crushing
- Temperature variations

Jackets

The external cable that is used for fiber protection is called a jacket. It can be made from the following materials: polyethylene, polyurethane, or polyvinyl chloride (PVC; see top Figure A–17(a)).

Fiber optic cables must not require pampering or special treatment, so the goal is to make them rugged enough to withstand the same environment withstood by coaxial cables or twisted-wire cables.

During installation, the fiber could be stepped on, run over by vehicles, or subjected to large stress loads while being pulled through a conduit. Once in place, the fiber may be exposed to extremely low or high temperatures and other environmental hazards. Therefore, the fiber cable must be able to survive this abuse, be easy to repair, be space-efficient, and still be economically competitive with conventional cable.

Numerous designs have been developed to meet varied requirements. No single cable configuration is best for all applications. However, practically all of the designs include the following (see Figure A–17):

- Coatings to protect individual fibers
- Filler or buffer material
- An external protective jacket
- Strength-bearing materials

Some cables will also include:

- Armor to protect against crushing or rodent damage
- Copper wires for carrying electrical power

Fiber Cable Structure

Optical fiber cable is comprised of one or more optical fibers and strength members contained within a protective sheathing (see Figure A–17[a] and [b]). Increasing demands are being placed on the mechanical cable design to meet the installation and environment requirements of end users such as telephone companies and CATV distributors. Although glass fiber has a tensile strength greater than steel, it cannot withstand

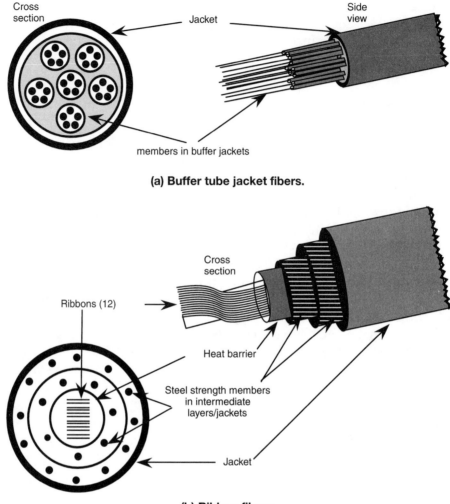

(a) **Buffer tube jacket fibers.**

(b) **Ribbon fibers.**

Figure A–17   Fiber cable structure.

elongations greater than about 2%. Compression of the fiber should also be avoided if reliable performance is to be maintained. The cable must then serve as a reinforcement structure to limit the loading on the fiber and to protect it from the environment. However, the cable design itself may introduce losses whenever a structural element of the cable comes into contact with the fiber. Some cable designs contain the fiber inside protective tubing before being integrated with the cable strength members while others place the fiber between two grooved tapes.

There are many variations in fiber available for placement in fiber optic cable. The end use and environment (mentioned earlier) must be considered when selecting either the fiber alone or cabled fiber.

Strength Member

The strength or tension member (also known as the load-bearing member) minimizes any stretching force applied to the fibers during or after installation (again see Figure A–17). If the fiber cables are made from steel or fiberglass epoxy, they are considered to be a central member. Central members allow cable flexing, prevent buckling, provide temperature stability, and facilitate stranding. If the fiber cables are made of Kevlar aramid yarn (as in cable that is susceptible to lightning damage), then it is considered to be a strength member. Strength members are the primary tensile load-bearing member, but they are susceptible to lightning damage. Polyurethane or other filler materials are used to help cushion the fibers and reduce any stress placed upon them.

The fibers may be placed in plastic tubes, or buffers, before being incorporated into the cable. Two methods are presently used for supporting the fibers within a cable: loose-fit and tight-fit. For most applications, the loose-fit is considered to be the best. However, tight-fit cables outlast loose-fit cables by 60:1 when run over repeatedly by vehicles. Therefore, in cable design, there is no "best" type for all applications.

Number of Fibers in a Cable

Fibers are used in pairs, generally to allow simultaneous communications between two points (known as duplex operations). While one or two fibers may make up a cable, fiber optic cables commonly include up to 24 individual fibers.

FIBER LOSSES

Many factors contribute to the loss of power on a fiber optic link. The most common factors include:

- Spectral attenuation
- Absorption and scattering
- Modal dispersion
- Spectral dispersion

- Fiber numerical aperture
- Connecting and splicing errors
- Cleaving errors
- Coupling losses
- Bending losses

Each factor will cause some loss. The main concern is when total loss occurs. This is determined by the measurement of how much power is emitted by the source compared to how much is received by the detector. Total loss is referred to as loss budget analysis.

Bending losses were described in the section on cable installation and numerical aperture was described in the section on cable construction. The other factors are described in more detail in this section. Also included in this section is a list of terms and their definitions.

Spectral Attenuation

An important consideration in the performance of optical fiber is spectral attenuation. As discussed earlier in this chapter, some wavelengths travel through the fiber better than others. As illustrated in Figure A–18, an 820-nm wave travels well through the fiber, while a 950-nm

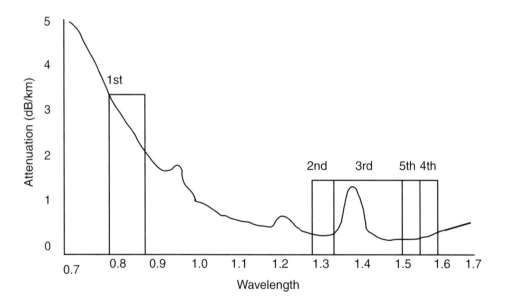

Figure A–18   Attenuation performance of silica-based optical fiber.

wave is sharply attenuated. This difference in propagation efficiency is partly the result of the dopants or impurities added to the molten glass to create the proper refractive index in the fiber. Attenuation in a fiber is specified at a certain wavelength: 10 dB/km at 820 nm. The loss figure will change, perhaps drastically, as the wavelength changes: 10 dB/km at 820 nm could be 40 dB/km at 950 nm.

Absorption and Scattering

Figure A–19 shows the result of two loss mechanisms: absorption and scattering. Chemical impurities can absorb light, thereby converting the light energy to heat. Structural defects or stress patterns in the fiber can scatter or redirect the light so that it escapes the core and is lost. Or, due to other considerations, the fiber may be constructed such that absorption or scattering probability is inherent in the system.

Radiation-Hardened Fiber

Some fibers have been designed specifically to survive exposure to nuclear radiation, which can cause temporary or permanent darkening of conventional fibers. This special application is true of some step-index multimode fibers, which will have different transmission characteristics.

Modal Dispersion

As we learned earlier, light reflects at a different angle for each mode (ray). Some rays will traverse longer paths than others. The ray that goes straight down the core of the media without reflection will arrive at the other end sooner than others generated at the same time. The

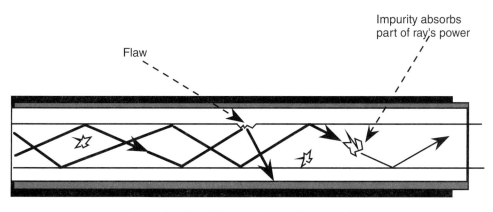

Figure A–19 Absorption and scattering.

more times a ray is reflected, the later it will arrive. Thus, light entering the fiber at the same time may arrive at the other end at slightly different times. The end effect is that the light has "spread out." This spreading of light is called modal dispersion and may result in the misinterpretation of the signal at the receiver.

Spectral Dispersion

Spectral dispersion (also called material dispersion) occurs when different wavelengths travel at different speeds through a medium. As Figure A–20 shows, the signal is spread out just as it is by modal dispersion. To limit the spreading, spectral purity of the source is desirable. An LED source, for example, has a spectral range about 17 times as wide as a lasers' source. Because of this greater range, LED light has greater spectral dispersion.

List of Terms

Before we examine the balance of this section, an explanation of some terms will be helpful.

Coherent light is a single frequency of light that has characteristics similar to a radiated radio wave frequency. The single light frequency travels in intense, nearly perfect parallel rays without appreciable diver-

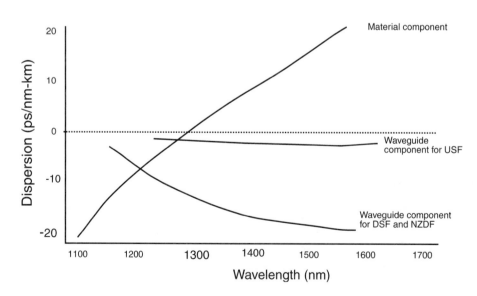

Figure A–20   Dispersion components.

gence. Coherent light communications are communications using amplitude or pulse-frequency modulation of a laser beam.

The term incoherent denotes the lack of a fixed phase relationship between two waves. If two incoherent waves are superposed, interference effects cannot last longer than the individual coherent times of the waves.

Noncoherent radiation is radiation in which the waves are out-of-phase with respect to space and/or time.

Incoherent light from an LED requires an optical fiber that is clad with a reflective coating to hold the light waves inside the fiber. With coherent light (all rays are similar frequency and polarization), a simple unclad optical fiber might be used. Coherent light can be developed by a laser (lightwave amplification by stimulated emission of radiation).

References

[ALCA01] Go to www.alcatel.com.

[ALEG99] The WaveStar™ Bandwidth Manager: The Key Building Block in the Next Generation Transport Network, Bell Labs Technical Journal, Volume 4, Number 1, January-March, 1999.

[ASCO94] Ascom Timplex, (August, 1994). "Technical Document SG1380C," *Customer Support/Educational Services,* 16255 Bay Vista, Clearwater, Florida 34620.

[BELL82] Bell Laboratories, (June, 1982). *Transmission Systems for Communications,* Bell Laboratories, Holmdel, New Jersey.

[BELL89a]. (September, 1989). "Synchronous Optical Network (SONET) Transport Systems: Common Generic Criteria," TR-TSY-000253, Issue 1.

[BELL90b] Bellcore, (1990). *Telecommunications Transmission Engineering,* Volume 2, Facilities, 3rd Edition.

[BELL94a] Bellcore, (1994). "BOC Notes on the LEC Networks, 1994," SR-TSV-002275, Issue 2.

[BELL01] Bellato, Alberto, et al, GMPLS Signalling Extensions for G.709 Optical Transport Networks Control, *draft-fontana-ccamp-gmpls-g709-00.txt*

[BLAI88] Blair, C. (September, 1988). "SLIPs: Definitions, Causes, and Effects in T1 Networks," *A Tau-tron Application Note,* Issue 1.

[BNR90] Bell Northern Research, (1990). "Fiberworld, An Overview," *Telesis,* Volume 17, Number one/two, Bell Northern Research, Ottawa, Ontario Canada.

[CHRA99]. Chraplyvy, Andrew R., High Capacity Lightwave Transmission Experiments, Bell Labs Technical Journal, January-March, 1999.

[DENN95] Denniston, F. J., and Runge, P. K., (October, 1995). "The Glass Necklace," *IEEE Spectrum.*

[FUJI01] SONET Transport FLASH-192 Product Description. Fujitsu document number FLASH192/PD/4.0/11.99/CM

[GUDG01] Gudgel, John. "New Carrier Market Opportunity: Back-haul from International Cable Systems," Lightwave, July, 2001.

[G70901] Interface for the Optical Transport Network, ITU-T Recommendation G.709, February, 2001.

[G.87299] Architecture of Optical Transport Networks, ITU-T Recommendation G.872, February, 1999.

[HEWL92] Hewlett Packard, Inc., (1992). "Introduction to SONET Networks and Tests," An internal document published by Hewlett Packard, Inc.

[HILL91] (1991). "SONET, An Overview," A paper prepared by Hill Associates, Inc., Winooski, VT, 05404.

[IETF01a] The best way to obtain up-to-date information on the working goups and their papers on optical networks is to go to *www.ietf.org*, click on working papers (or working groups), or key in a search for (a) optical and then (b) MPLS. These two subjects are closely associated with each other.

[JACK99] Jackman, Neil, A. et al., "Optical Cross Connects for Optical Networking," Bell Labs Technical Journal , January–March, 1999.

[JOHN99]. Johnson, Steven R. and Nichols, Virginia L., Advanced Optical Networking—Lucent's MONET Network Elements, Bell Labs Technical Journal, January–March, 1999.

[KRAU94] Karuse, T. D., (January 31, 1994). "Network Survivability: One Size Doesn't Fit All," Telephony.

[LEE93] Lee, B. G., Kang, M., and Jonghee, L. (1993). *Broadband Telecommunications Technology,* Artech House.

[NORT01] Nortel Networks Document Number 56020.39/01001, Issue 1. Nortel Networks, 5404 Windward Parkway, Aplharetta, GA 30004-3895.

[NORT95] Nortel, (1995). *Nortel Learning Institute,* Document # PS 8890.

[ODSI01] Go to *www.odsi-coalition.com* for more information on the activities of the ODSI and for the specifications and souce code for ODSI's work on optical bandwidth on demand.

[OIF01] *www.oiforum.com* provides information on the OIF's work on an optical network user-network interface (UNI).

[PESA01] Pesavento, Gerry, and Kelsey, Mark. "Ethernet in the First Mile," Lightwave, June 15, 2001.

[REID95] Reid, A. B. D., Mulvey, M., (July, 1995). "Analytical Methods for Timing Aspects of the Transport of CBR Services Over ATM," *BT Technical Journal,* Vol. 13, No. 3.

In addition to the references cited here and in Chapter 1, part of this book is based on national and international standards published by ANSI, Bellcore, and the ITU-T. (Addresses for these organizations are listed at the end of this section.). AT&T and Nortel furnished us with a wide variety of material and we are grateful to these companies for their contributions.

Appendix A was developed largely from GTE courses and workbooks, that were created by Sharleen, as well as the excellent *Technician's Guide to Fiber Optics* by Donald J. Sterling, Jr. (Delmar Publications Inc., Albany, NY). Many illustrations were courtesy of AMP Incorporated.

For the reader who needs more details on SONET, we recommend the following references published by ANSI and Bellcore (some of which are cited in Chapter 1).

TECHNICAL ADVISERIES AND TECHNICAL REFERENCES

TR-TSY-000009, "Asynchronous Digital Multiplex Requirements and Objectives," Issue 1, Bell Communications Research, May, 1986.

TR-TSY-000047, "Functional Criteria for Alarm Monitoring of Digital Transmission Facilities and Associated Equipment," Bell Communications Research, January 1985.

TR-TSY-000191, "Alarm Indication Requirements," Issue 1, Bell Communications Research, June 1985.

TR-TSY-000440, "Transport Systems Generic Requirements (TSGR)," Issue 1, Bell Communications Research, September 1989. Includes:

> Volume 1, "Common Requirements and Digital Loop Carrier Systems"
> TR-TSY 000499, "Common Requirements"
> TR-TSY-000057, "Digital Loop Carrier Systems"
> Volume 2, "Integrated Digital Loop Carrier System"
> TR-TSY 000303, "Integrated Digital Loop Carrier System" (including Feature Set B and Feature Set C)
> Volume 3, TR-TSY-000925 "ISDN Transport, Interface and Related Requirements"
> TR-TSY 000393, "ISDN Basic Access Digital Subscriber Lines"
> TR-TSY 000397, "ISDN Basic Access Transport System"
> TA-TSY 000398, "Universal Digital Channel (UDC)"
> TA-TSY 000754, "ISDN Primary Rate Access Transport System"
> Volume 4, "Digital Fiber Optic Systems and Digital Radio Systems"
> TA-TSY 000038, "Digital Fiber Optic Systems"
> TA-TSY 000752, "Microwave Digital Radio Systems"
> Volume 5, TR-TSY-000919 "SONET Transport Criteria"
> TR-TSY 000253, "SONET Transport Systems: Common Criteria"
> TR-TSY 000496, "SONET Add-Drop Multiplex Equipment"
> TR-TSY 000233, "Wideband and Broadband Digital Cross-Connect"
> TR-TSY 000782, "SONET Digital Switch Trunk Interface"
> TA-TSY 000917, "Regenerator Generic Criteria"

TA-TSY-000435, "DS1 Automatic Facility Protection Switching (AFPS) Feature for Digital Terminal Systems Requirements and Objectives," Bellcore, Issue 1, February 1987

TA-NPL-000436, "Digital Synchronization Network Plan," Bellcore, Issue 1, November 1986

TR-TSY-000010, "Synchronous DS3 Add-Drop Multiplex (ADM 3/X) Requirements and Objectives," Issue 1, Bellcore, February 1988

TR-NPL-000054, "High Capacity Digital Service (1.544 Mbit/s) Interface Generic Requirements for End Users," Issue 1, Bellcore, April 1989.

TR-TSY-000194, "Extended Superframe Format Interface Specifications," Issue 1, Bellcore, December 1987

TR-NPL-000320, "Fundamental Generic Requirements for Metallic Digital Signal Cross-Connect Systems DSX-1,-1C, -2, -3," Issue 1, Bellcore April 1988

TR-NPL-000424, "Generic Requirements for Manual Digital Signal Cross-Connect Frames DSX-3," Issue 1, Bellcore, July 1988

TR-TSY-000499, Transport Systems Generic Requirements (TSGR): Common Requirements (A Module of TSGR, TR-TSY-000440)," Issue 3, Bellcore, December 1989

PUB 62411, "High Capacity Digital Service Channel Interface Specifications," September 1983, plus Addendum, October 1984

SR-ISD-000307, "NC/NCI Code Dictionary—Industry Support Interface," Issue 1, Bellcore, March 1988

ANSI T1.107–1988. ANSI, "Digital Hierarchy—Formats Specifications"

ANSI T1.102–1989. American National Standard for Telecommunications, "Digital Hierarchy—Electrical Interfaces"

ANSI T1.103–1987. American National Standard for Telecommunications, "Interface for Specification for Synchronous DS3 Format"

ANSI T1.403–1989. American National Standard for Telecommunications, "Carrier-to-Customer Installation—DS1 Metallic Interface Specifications"

ANSI T1.404–1989. American National Standard for Telecommunications, "Carrier-to-Customer Installation—DS3 Metallic Interface Specifications"

ANSI T1.201–1987. American National Standard for Telecommunications, "Information exchange—Structure of location entities for the North American Telecommunications Systems"

ANSI T1.214–1990, American National Standard for Telecommunications, "Telecommunications—Operations, administration, maintenance, and provisioning (OAM&P)—Generic network model for interfaces between operations systems and network elements"

ANSI T1.214a-1992, American National Standard for Telecommunications, "Telecommunications—Operations, administration, maintenance, and provisioning (OAM&P)—Generic network model for interfaces between operations systems and network elements (Managed object class definitions for performance monitoring)"

ANSI T1.215–1990, American National Standard for Telecommunications, "Telecommunications—Operations, administration, maintenance, and provisioning (OAM&P)—Fault management messages for interfaces between operations systems and network elements"

ANSI T1.229–1992, American National Standard for Telecommunications, "Telecommunications—Operations, administration, maintenance, and provisioning (OAM&P)—Performance management functional area services for interfaces between operations systems and network elements"

ANSI T1.231, "Layer-1 in-service digital transmission performance monitoring

CCITT X.732, ISO/IEC DIS 10164–13:1992, "Open systems interconnection—Systems management, Part 13: Summarization function" (ANSI)

T1 Technical Report No. 12, "A technical report on a methodology for specifying telecommunications management network interfaces"

"Coding requirements for telecommunications products," Telecommunications Industry Forum (TCIF); February 10, 1989 (ECSA)

ISO DIS 10164, "Systems management, Part 1—Object Management function" (ANSI)

ISO DIS 10164, "Systems management, Part 2—State Management function" (ANSI)

ISO DIS 10165, "Structure of management information, Part 1—Information model" (ANSI)

ISO DIS 10165, "Structure of management information, Part 2—Definition of management information " (ANSI)

ISO DIS 10165, "Structure of management information, Part 4—Guidelines for the definition of managed objects" (ANSI)

ANSI: American National Standards Institute, 11 West 42nd Street, New York, 10036 2122

Bellcore: Bellcore Customer Service, 60 New England Avenue, DSC 1B-252, Piscataway, NJ 08854–4196 (Tel: 201–699–5800)

ECSA: Exchange Carriers Standards Association, 5430 Grosvenor Lane, Bethesda MD 20814

Acronyms

B3ZS: Binary-3-zero substitution

B6ZS: Binary-6-zero substitution

B8ZS: Binary-8-zero substitution

A/D: Add-drop

A/D: Analog-to-digital

AAL: ATM adaptation layer

ACSE: Association control service element

ADM: Add-drop multiplexer

ADPCM: Adaptive differential PCM

AIS: Alarm indication signal

AMI: Alternate mark inversion

ANSI: American National Standards Institute

APD: Avalanche photodiode

APS: Automatic protection switching

ASE: Application services element

ATM: Asynchronous transfer mode

BC: Block check

BER: Bit error rate

BERT: Bit error rate test

BI: Bipolar code

B-ICI: Broadband inter-carrier interface

B-ISDN Broadband-ISDN

BIP-8 Bit interleave parity

BITS: Building integrated timing supply

BLSR: Bi-directional line switched ring

BNR: Bell Northern Research (BNR, now known as Nortel)

BOC: Bell Operating Company

BOM: Beginning of message

BPV: Bipolar violation

BSRF: Basic synchronization reference frequency

CAD: Computer-aided design

CAM: Computer-aided manufacturing

CBR: Constant bit rate

CCC: Clear channel capability

CELP: Code-excited linear predictive coding

CEPT1: Consortium of European Poste and Telegraph 1

CES: Circuit emulation service

CH: Cell header

CIP: Common part indicator

CIT: Craft interface terminal

CIU: Craft interface unit

CMIP: Common management information protocol

CMISE: Common management information service element

CO: Central office

CODEC: COder-DECoder

COFA: Change of frame alignment

COM: Continuation of message

COT: Central office terminal

CP: Common part

CPCS: Common part convergence sublayer

CPE: Central premises equipment

CPE: Customer premises equipment

CPI: Common part ID

CPUCS-UU Common part convergence sublayer

CRC: Cyclic redundancy check

CRC6: Cyclic redundancy check 6

CRS: Cell relay service

CS: Convergence sublayer

CSU: Channel service unit

CVSD: Continuously variable slope delta modulation

DACS: Digital access and cross-connect system

DARPA: Defense Advanced Project Research Agency

dc: Direct current

DCC: Data communications channel

DCS: Digital cross-connect system

DDD: Direct distance dialing

DDS: Digital Data Service

DE-4E: DE-4 enhanced

DL: Data link

DLC: Data link control

DLC: Digital loop carrier

DM: Delta modulation

DPCM: Differential pulse code modulation

DRI: Dual ring interworking architecture

DS1: Digital signal at the first level

DS: Digital signal

DSn: Digital signal level n

DSU: Data service unit

DSU: Digital service unit

DSX: Digital signal cross-connect (also called a digital cross-connect)

DTMF: Dual tone multi-frequency

E&M: Ear and mouth

E/O: Electrical/optical

ECSA: Exchange Carriers Standards Association

EEC-1: Electrical carrier-1

EFS: Error free second

EOM: End of message

ES: Errored second

ESF: Extended superframe

ESI: External synchronization interface

F bit: Framing bit

FD: Framing detector

FDDI: Fiber distributed data interface

FDM: Frequency division multiplexing

FEBE: Far end block error

FERF: Far end receive failure

FLAG: Fiber-optic link around the globe

FPS/FE: Framing pulse synchronization-framing extended

FRS: Frame relay service

FT1: Fractional T1

FX: Foreign exchange

Ge: Geranmium

GPS: Global positioning system

HDLC: High Level Data Link Control

HDTV: High definition television

HEC: Header error control

I field: Information field

ICI: Intercarrier interface

I/O: Input/output

IDLC: Integrated digital loop carrier

IISP: Interim interswitch signaling protocol

InGaAs: Indium gallium arsenide

IP: Internet protocol

ISDN: Integrated Service Digital Network

ISO: International Standards Organization

ISUP: ISDN user part

IT: Information type

ITU-T: International Telecommunication Union-Telecommunication Standardization Sector

IXC: Interchange carrier

kHz: kilohertz

LAN: Local area network

LAPD: Link Access Procedure, D

LBRV: Low bit-rate voice

LED: Light-emitting diode

LI: Length indicator

LIU: Line interface units

LOF: Loss of frame

LOP: Loss of pointer

LORAN: Long range navigational (system)

LOS: Loss of signal

LPC: Linear predictive coding

LSB: Least significant bit

LTE: Line terminating equipment

MAN: Metropolitan area network

MAPDU: Management application data unit

MDF: Main distribution frame

MHz Megahertz

MIB: Management information base

MID: Message identification

MSB: Most significant bit

MTP 3: Message transfer part 3

MXRVO: Multiple transmit/receive virtual overhead

NA: Numerical aperture

NE: Network element

NI: Network interface

nm: Nanometers

NNI: Network-to-network interface

NNI: Network-node interface

NTP: Network time protocol

OA: Optical amplifiers (using EDF)

OAM&P: Operations, administration, maintenance, and provisioning

OAM: Operations, administration and maintenance

OC-192: Optical carrier rate-192

OC-1: Optical carrier-1

OC-3: Optical carrier-3

OC-48: Optical carrier rate-48

OC-n: Optical carrier-n

OC: Optical carrier

OCU: Office channel unit

ODU: Optical demultiplexing unit

OLIU: Optical line interface unit

OMU: Optical multiplexing unit

OS: Operating system

OSI: Open Systems Interconnection

OSS: Operating system support

PAD: Padding

PAM: Pulse amplitude modulation

PC: Personal computer

PCI: Protocol control information

PCM: Pulse code modulation

PDM: Pulse duration modulation

PDU: Protocol data unit

PIN: Positive-intrinsic-negative (diode)

PLL: Phase-locked loop

POH: Path overhead

POP: Points of presence

POT: Point of termination

PPM: Pulse position modulation

ppm: Parts per million

PPS: Path protection switching

PRS: Primary reference source

PSTN: Public switched telephone network

PTE: Path terminating equipment

PTM : Pulse time modulation

PVC: Permanent virtual circuit

PVC: Polyvinyl chloride

PWM: Pulse width modulation

QRSSS: Quasi random signal source

RAI: Remote alarm indication

RAM: Random access memory

RBOC Regional Bell Operating Company

RFI: Radio frequency interference

ROSE: Remote Operations Service Element

RT: Remote terminal

S/D: Signal-to-distortion (ratio)

SAAL: Signaling ATM adaptation layer

SAR: Segmentation and reassembly

SDH: Synchronous Digital Hierarchy

SDV: Switched digital video

SDU: Service data unit

sec: Microsecond

SF: Superframe

SHR: Self-healing ring

SMASE: Systems management application service element

SMDS: Switched multi-megabit data service

SN: Sequence number

SNI: Subscriber-to-network interface

SNMP: Simple Network Management Protocol

SNP: Sequence number protection, SNP

SONET: Synchronous Optical Network

SPE: Synchronous payload envelope

SRTS: Synchronous residual time stamp

SS7: Signaling system #7

SSCS: Service specific convergence sublayer

SSM: Single segment message

ST: Segment type

STDM: Statistical time division multiplexer

STE: Section terminating equipment

STS1E: Synchronous transport signal-1 electrical

STS: Synchronous transport signal

STSX-1: STS cross-connect level 1

SVC: Switched virtual call

SYSCTL: System controller card

TA: Terminal adapter

TBOS: Telemetry byte-oriented serial

TCP/IP: Transmission Control Protocol/Internet Protocol

TDM: Time division multiplexer

TL-1: Transaction language 1

TSI: Time slot interchange

TT: Tributary tester, TT

UDP: User Datagram Protocol

UI: Unit interval

UN: Unipolar (code)

UNI: User-to-network interface

USHR: Unidirectional self-healing ring

UU: User-to-user

VBR: Variable bit rate

VC: Virtual channel

VC: Virtual container

VCI: Virtual channel identifier

VDR: Voice digitization rate

VF: Voice frequency

VP: Virtual path

VPI: Virtual path identifier

VPN: Virtual private network

VT: Virtual tributary

VT-G: Virtual tributary group

WAN: Wide area network

ZCS: Zero code suppression

ZBTSI: Zero-byte Time Slot Interchange

Index

Page numbers ending in "f" refer to figures. Page numbers ending in "t" refer to tables.